Rhythms of Resistance

HISTORIES OF MUSICAL OPPOSITION AND
AFFIRMATION FROM AROUND THE WORLD,
VOLUME 1   FIRST EDITION

David McMurray

CENGAGE
Learning™

Australia • Brazil • Japan • Korea • Mexico • Singapore • Spain • United Kingdom • United States

CENGAGE
Learning™

Rhythms of Resistance: Histories of Musical Opposition and Affirmation from around the World, Volume 1
First Edition
David McMurray

V.P Product Development: Dreis Van Landuyt

Custom Editor: Tom Tucker

Development Editor: Brian Coovert

Custom Production Editor: Julie Niesen

Marketing Manager: Rob Bloom

Permissions Specialist: Todd Osborne

Manufacturing Manager: Donna M. Brown

Production Coordinator: Teresa Magee

Cover Design: Swanson Design Studio

Cover Image: Getty Images and David
   McMurray

Compositor: Integra

For product information and technology assistance, contact us at
Cengage Learning Customer & Sales Support, 1-800-354-9706
For permission to use material from this text or product,
submit all requests online at **cengage.com/permissions**
Further permissions questions can be emailed to
permissionrequest@cengage.com

Library of Congress Control Number: 2008933475

ISBN-13: 978-1-426-63533-5
ISBN-10: 1-426-63533-8

Cengage Learning
5191 Natorp Blvd.
Mason, OH 45040
USA

Cengage Learning is a leading provider of customized learning solutions with office locations around the globe, including Singapore, the United Kingdom, Australia, Mexico, Brazil, and Japan. Locate your local office at:
international.cengage.com/region

Cengage Learning products are represented in Canada by Nelson Education, Ltd.

Visit our corporate website at **cengage.com**

Printed in the United States of America
1 2 3 4 5 6 7 11 10 09 08

CONTENTS

PREFACE AND ACKNOWLEDGEMENTS

The text that follows is divided into chapters covering case studies of the historical and cultural context within which popular music is produced and consumed—with special attention being paid to the political functions the music performs. Following each case study is a section composed of notes to video lectures covering the same topics as the chapters. The actual video lectures can be accessed by going to the Blackboard site for the class at Oregon State University titled, ANTH210: Comparative Cultures.

The first part of Chapter 5 was co-authored by Joan Gross and Ted Swedenburg, who graciously gave their permission to have it reprinted here. It originally appeared in *Diaspora* 3 (1): 3-39, Spring, 1994. The last section appeared in McMurray & Gross (2004). Chapter 6 is reprinted here from my book, *In and Out of Morocco: Smuggling and Migration in a Frontier Boomtown*. Minneapolis: University of Minnesota Press. 2001.

INTRODUCTION[1]

This text and accompanying videos compare the ways music operates politically in several cultures around the world. Our focus will be on how music functions as social commentary, as a vehicle of protest and struggle, as well as how it creates a foundation for oppositional cultures. Equally importantly, we will be investigating the ways music acts to provide people, including all of us, with an identity and a way of being in the world, a way of making sense of it.

In other words, this text investigates how people use music and incorporate music into their lives in order to present themselves in certain ways. Music creates a sense of collective identity, or to put it another way, in the words of music critic Simon Frith (1996:275), music works to provide "people with different identities, to place them in different social groups," to "allow alternative modes of social interaction," and to create a sense of communal values and shared communal experience with which they can identify.

THE STUDY OF MUSIC: THE ETHNOMUSICOLOGICAL APPROACH

What is music? If you browse through the textbooks used in university ethnomusicology and world music classes, you will find a fair amount of agreement. Bakan (2007), for instance, considers music to be the purposeful organization of sound into musical forms. His emphasis is on the necessity of human intention. As he puts it, "only when a human being uses a given sound for musical purposes, or perceives or describes that sound in musical terms, does the sound actually enter into the domain of 'music'" (Bakan 2007:4). This definition is seconded by Titon (2002) who defines music (following Blackling [1973]) as "sound that is humanly patterned or organized" (Titon 2002:7). Nettl et al. (2004), while not disagreeing with what has been said about music, places greater emphasis on the way music functions in societies. Many societies do not share our Western notions of what constitutes music, but they all use music for something; they all sing something which is contrasted with other kinds of sounds.

THE STUDY OF MUSIC: THE NONLYRICAL FEATURES APPROACH

Besides questions of what is music and how does it function in different contexts, there is also the interesting question of how we analyze it. In this book we will be relying mainly on the socio-historical context and the lyrical message conveyed in a song to construct our understanding of its political importance. However, there is another equally important side to music: its nonlyrical features. Robert Walser's book (1993), *Running with the Devil: Power, Gender, and Madness in Heavy Metal Music*, is an excellent example of how to analyze nonlyrical features. In the book Walser outlines the ten main nonlyrical features that identify heavy metal as a genre and help create a certain sense of power and freedom for the listener of heavy metal. I think it is worth the trouble to list and briefly describe each of them because they provide an excellent model for the way popular music can be analyzed nonlyrically regardless of the genre.

The first item on Walser's list of nonlyrical features is timbre, that is, the quality of the sound or the characteristic of the sound that distinguishes how the genre is perceived. In this case the timbre refers to guitar distortion, the most important aural sign of heavy metal. Second is vocal distortion. It is typical in heavy metal music for the vocal chords to be strained to the breaking point. Third is "sustain", or the ability of electronic amplification equipment to pick up a sound and continuously loop it. This ability to sustain a sound is another marker of a heavy metal song. Walser's fourth nonlyrical feature is heavy metal's use of power chords, which is the name for the very high-volume, rapid-tempo playing of only two notes in a chord, which produces a series of related tones. These tones usually occur below the notes of the chord, another signature of a heavy metal sound. Walser's fifth is volume, which is a universally recognized nonlyrical feature essential to heavy metal music. Sixth, he lists vocal timbre. Heavy metal vocals are usually a combination of sustain, distortion, and heavy vibrato. The lead singer often punctuates his (heavy metal is very male-dominated, though there are a few female performers and a female fan base) songs with vocal screams or guttural sounds that signify heightened emotional intensity. Number seven is mode, the musical term for the set of notes used in a song that are related to each other by means of special combinations of chords that are thought to go together in a scale. These chord relationships are called modes. They tend to evoke certain emotions in the audience. For instance, a song that uses chords related to each other in what we call in the West a "minor" mode evokes sadness or mystery or foreboding. On the other hand, major chord modes seem to signify brighter, more assertive emotional states. Heavy metal tends to favor the use of certain modes over others in the creation of its signature sound. Number eight in his list is rhythm. The typical 4/4 beat of heavy metal evokes in the audience a sense of unity, of moving as one to the music. It is thus a powerful way of signifying energy and getting bodies up moving together. Number nine is melody. It is less important in heavy metal music than in pop music. Heavy metal melodies tend to hold notes and often involve syncopation, that is, missed beats or adds between beats, which gives the sense of resistance to the pull of the dominance of the melody. Another melodic feature involves vocal flourishes, like high leaps from one note to another, which give the listener a sense of excess and striving on the part of the singer and thus the song. The tenth and last nonlyrical feature Walser lists is the guitar solo. The guitar solo marks out heavy metal music in that the technical difficulty of the solo signifies virtuosity on the part of the lead guitarist, and for the listener represents, according to Walser, liberation, empowerment, and resistance (Walser 1993: 40-54).

THE STUDY OF MUSIC: THE PERFORMANCE CONTEXTS APPROACH

Another approach to the study of music is through analysis of its performance contexts. The earliest and perhaps most famous investigators of the context were the early ethnomusicologists and folklorists represented most famously by Alan Lomax (1993). He and his father collected thousands of field recordings from across Europe and America for the American Folklife Center at the Library of Congress. Lomax is perhaps most famous for his concentration on southern folk music, especially recordings and interviews with Lead Belly, Jelly Roll Morton and Muddy Waters. A more con- temporary example comes from the collection by Andy Bennett (2004), which includes in-depth analyzes of a variety of performance contexts, from the jazz scene in Kansas City, to Chicago blues, to London Salsa, to Karaoke usage, rave scenes, and even Brittany Spears mania. Going even further into just one scene, the work of Wendy Fonarow (2006) on indie pop music in Britain sets a new standard of ethnographic excellence. She breaks down the club space of performance into three sections, or audience zones, depending on the kind of fan found in that space. In addition she discusses the behaviors and attitudes of the British musicians, club employees, fans, and music industry bigwigs.

THE STUDY OF MUSIC: THE SUBCULTURE APPROACH

Ethnographic work into the world of musical production and consumption has been led by British investigators over the last thirty years, particularly while developing the study of subcultures. A subculture defines itself over and against mainstream culture and other subcultures by adopting a whole series of stylistic and symbolic practices that mark them as distinct, practices that may include insider jargon, tattoos and other forms of body adornment, a certain outfit or uniform, and of course allegiance to certain genres of music. The pioneers of this kind of research were grouped around Stuart Hall, the director of the Centre for Contemporary Cultural Studies at the University of Birmingham from 1969 to 1979 (it closed in 2002). The most famous works of the group include Hall and Jefferson (1975), Hebdige (1979) and Willis (1978). They all assert in different ways that oppressed, disenfranchised, and marginalized, youth groups will consume music as a form of rebellion against the powers-that-be. For them, the consumption of music represents an act of ritualized resistance against mainstream cultural conformity which, in the process of consumption, also creates a sense of solidarity within the group. These two notions of music as both capable of creating community as well as expressing opposition are the foundations for our approach to the study of music.

POLITICS OF MUSIC

Politically speaking, for most people around the world (who of course are not thinking of music in expressly political terms), music defines them in political ways by defining spaces they reside in, it distinguishes who they are from others they are not; it expresses their deepest values and provides them with a sense of their life's worth, of where they've come from and of where they're heading. Music gives many of us a way of being heard. We identify with it as a way to locate ourselves within the cultural matrix that surrounds us.

This goes double for ordinary people around the globe who suffer from colonialism and racism, from the oppressions of poverty and severe economic crises, from material deprivation and cultural oppression. Music allows them to stand and be counted, it nurtures and sustains a sense of belonging to an oppositional subculture rooted in rejection of unequal power relations.

A particularly poignant example of the struggle to make oneself heard is illustrated in Andrew Jones' (1992) story of the rise of rock in China and its practitioners' attempts to "cut like a knife" through the hypocritical, propagandist musical control of the State; providing, instead, an authentic countervailing voice. As interesting and important and Jones' work is, it is but one chapter in the historically unfolding narrative of the development of popular music in China. More recent authors have pointed out that forms of state influence and interference in post-Tiananmen Square Chinese music production take more subtle forms. On top of having to deal with various, insidious forms of control, musicians must be able to earn enough to afford the food, housing, instruments, and practice time and space necessary to develop their music, all aspects of everyday life that the State has a lot of control over. Quite possibly, the vision of an earlier, rebellious rock "moment" in China, while real enough, has been exaggerated out of proportion by the Western press (Efird 2001). By contrast, in more recent times, Chinese popular rock musicians have avoided overt anti-governmental lyrics and instead expressed anti-foreigner sentiments. This trend has been brought on as much by the bands' needs to avoid confrontation with the authorities as by their bitter experiences with rapacious foreign record companies (Huang 2001).

The example of Chinese rock alerts us to several lessons we would do well to remember in our study of the politics of popular music: First, popular culture is never static, so cultural politics is always the study of ever changing meanings and constantly evolving historical developments. Second, the politics of popular music is a complex subject and so the meanings and importance we attach to it do not exhaust its possibilities. What we think about a subject is conditioned by the influences of many external factors and most likely will change over time and space. Take, as an example, the heritage of blues music in the contemporary United States (which will come back up in the concluding chapter). Today, especially White Americans tend to revere the blues as the quintessential expression of a people's suffering, as the original folk/ protest music. Yet in its own time in the beginning decades of the twentieth century it was part of a mix of musical genres listened to by southern African Americans. It was an important part of the hip, cool music consumed by its audience, but it did not dominate; it was not naive folk music; it was not a cry in the wilderness. It was really only transformed into that, that is, what we think of today as "The Blues," during its revival in the 1950s when British musicians reintroduced it to a new generation of white American fans. This peculiar gulf between the original reception of the blues in Black America, and its later revitalization in white America is a fascinating cautionary tale told in compelling fashion by the author and musician, Elijah Wald (2004).

Brian Ward (1998) and Craig Warner (1998), taking a more recognizable tack, postulate that African American popular music provides a kind of soundtrack for recent historical struggles. Ward suggests that the long history of postwar rhythm and blues (including black r&b of the 1950s to black pop and soul in the 1960s through 1970s disco) parallels the historical movements sweeping Black America. For instance, the original struggle in the south against the rise of rock 'n roll was a musical mirror image of the struggle against desegregation. Likewise, Black America's production and consumption of soul and funk music were integrally tied to the rise of the civil rights and black power movements. The music of all of these genres, according to the author, "acted as a bulwark against the psychological ravages of racism, frustration, often poverty, and sometimes despair in the black community" (Ward 1998: 451). Warner echoes Ward's position by identifying one of the dominant themes running from the blues to hip hop, what he calls the "gospel impulse," which is a belief expressed through music that "life's burdens can be transformed into hope, salvation, [and] the promise of redemption" (Warner 1998: 28).

Membership in oppositional subcultural movements has proven to be an option attractive to white American youth raised in the midst of post World War II affluence. In fact the twin rise of a politicized rock music and the white, male counter-culture of the 1960s that formed its audience is usually held up as the quintessential example of the ways music operates to create a sense of communal belonging while at the same time being created to express that community's political aims (Bennett's [2001] chapter 2 explores this history). Unfortunately, the blindness of the movements' members to the equally important women, Native American, and Chicano liberation movements also marks the period (Echols 2002).

Equally interesting—and more controversial—has been the development since the 1980s of musical mega-events (Band Aid, Live Aid, Farm Aid, "We Are the World," etc.) in which popular music broadcast around the world has created a virtual community in the name of raising awareness of and dollars for one progressive cause after another. Garofalo (1992) raises questions about the political efficacy of mass music and mass events, and tends to answer them in the affirmative. Mega-events, if nothing else, he argues, at least open up new spaces where political change could take place. They are moments in time when live music and political events seem to shape the terrain.

Rounding out this brief excursion into writings about the ways music and politics are intertwined is the story of hip-hop. Chang's (2005) incredible history makes a strong case for viewing the rise of hip-hop music as the direct result of essentially political decisions made by the earliest deejays about how to cope with the destruction of the Bronx. Thanks especially to the work of DJ Kool Herc and Africa Bambaataa, the rival gangs became rival hip-hop crews, territorial boundaries gave way to massive outdoor parties open to all, aggression recently aimed at fellow Bronx dwellers got rechanneled into new dance competitions, and all of this took place as the city fathers consciously engineered the borough's destruction. From the early 1970s until the hip-hop scene moved elsewhere in the early 1980s, the popular music and lifestyles of one of America's most burned out, torn up, despised and avoided cities set the tone for cutting edge popular cultural styles for the whole country.

As an aside: Just as music empowers some and creates a positive sense of solidarity, so too does it work to oppress others. This dark side of music becomes clearest during times of war. From Joshua's use of trumpets to bring down the walls on the inhabitants of Jericho to the ways music accompanied the inflicting of pain in the wars in the former Yugoslavia in the 1990s, music has often been used to oppress the enemy (Cloonan and Johnson 2002).

Yet in spite of the potential for music to cause harm, it goes without saying that the majority of the time we spend listening to music we do so for the sheer pleasure of the experience. Music just moves us. It is not functioning necessarily at these moments as anything more than a way to give shape to our emotional desires, to take us out of the here and now, and to provide us with a pleasure seldom achieved except when listening to music. But that being said, there are also important political functions of music that operate in parallel with its pleasure and that turn us and the music into social forces. We will see two aspects of the politics of music cropping up time and again in the case studies that follow, so let me lay them out more clearly.

1. An important dimension of the political function of popular music is as social protest and social criticism, as a kind of resistance, usually via the oppositional character of the lyrics (though not always), which recognize and condemn injustice and inequality, and provide a morally outraged attack on them. Music operates to provide inhabitants struggling for survival with a way to fight against forces that would deny them a future as legitimate citizens of their own land and nation.

2. A no less important role of music is as an affirmation of our individual and collective humanity and thus as a foundation of our identity. One of the most effective ways of fighting against demoralization and social disintegration is by using musical forms to express and create attachments to particular spaces and places associated with freedom from oppression and alienation. Music creates in us the recognition that we are not in this alone. Music restores in us a lost sense of community. Music represents a uniquely powerful cultural force in that it can be grasped and internalized in so many different ways (performing it, listening to it alone or with others, and perhaps most importantly, dancing to it, feeling it through our bodies). In responding to a song we are drawn into intensely emotional alliances with others who follow the music. We unite with them on the basis of the ways the music "grounds" us, to borrow a Rastafarian notion. The music constructs for us a sense of ourselves, a way to present ourselves to the world, a way to experience collective identity by means of the shared absorption of a pleasurable—often emotionally profound—experience.

Parenthetically, some have argued that the search for pleasure can also at times be a kind of political act. I am thinking particularly of the way African American society has been at the forefront of the defiant practice of seeking out a space and a place clear of attempts to control minds and, particularly, bodies. It was and is a tradition of "lawbreaking," which involved sneaking away and setting up a pleasure zone where all were free to express themselves as they saw fit. That tradition or practice or state of mind, call it what you will, is what has customarily been called "funk." I am not referring to the musical genre by the same name, though the music shares in some of the same associations; for instance, being erotically charged, off color, loose, crude, grotesque, and so forth.

"Funk," in its older usage, is the name for the sensual violence involved in the seeking out of spaces clear of authority where dancing and drinking and pleasure of all kinds can be enjoyed free of any controlling system like the church or elders or other forms of control that white society has at its beck and call. Manthia Diawara (1993), who first drew attention to the phenomenon, calls this the search for the Black Good Life society. Diawara points to the scene in the movie, Rage in Harlem, where Screamin' Jay Hawkins plays "I've Got a Spell on You" at the Undertakers' Ball as one cinematic example of the Funk society in operation. The home brew-based, impromptu, country bars illustrated in the film The Color Purple might be another. The dancing scene in the Black Baltimore record shop in the movie/musical Hairspray would be a third. Diawara calls this tradition an escape into freedom to seek pleasure. That freedom to be free of social and moral controls has been a source of creativity for Black people in America for centuries. Whites as well as Blacks have derived much creative energy from this Black funk tradition. Prince or George Clinton are perhaps the best known contemporary examples of the culture of funk, with its privileging of the grotesque, the carnivalesque, of violence and sexuality. Black funk culture is uncompromising in it resistance to any imposition of morality on the part of the church or government or civil authorities. Instead, funk is about the search for pleasure via the search for cultural freedom, which is one of the freedoms African Americans have struggled to make available to everyone, Diawara argues. We all benefit from the struggle to enjoy the mind and body as we all see fit.

WESTERN AS OPPOSED TO AFRICAN MUSIC

A few aspects of music may be universal. Its sacred, religious potential might be one; its powerful emotional appeal (to the point of inducing ecstatic states) may be another, related aspect; its hybrid origins may be a third, that is to say that all music, somewhat like all languages, evolved out of combinations of other musical forms and styles. There exists no pure, authentic, original music which gave birth to all the rest.

Yet music is also culturally specific. Perhaps less so today than ever before, thanks to the monopoly on global marketing enjoyed by a handful of music multinationals; nonetheless, music differs substantially from culture to culture. This is due to both structural as well as socio-historical specificities undergirding cultural differences.

Let's look first at some of the structural differences. As an example, John Chernoff, a renowned Western specialist of African music, provides a useful summary of the main differences in the organizing principles of Western as opposed to African music. As Chernoff (1979, chapter 2) puts it, Western music revolves around "the harmonic potential of tones," which are organized into exact intervals with the rhythm being the time between each step. Harmony occurs when the tones are played simultaneously while melody occurs when the tones are played successively and "harmony and melody are what count most" in Western music. Rhythm plays a secondary role and is less complex than harmony and melody. We divide the music into standard units which are so easily recognized that we can usually tap our foot or clap our hands to mark the even pace of the rhythmic beat as it ties the different notes (tones) together in a progression. "What is most noticeable about the rhythm" in Western music "is that it serves to link the different notes to each other. We say, for instance, that a piece of music has a certain rhythm, and as we count out the beats, we will notice certain things." Chernoff continues, "First, most of the instruments play their notes at the same time, and second, if we have a sequence of notes that runs into a phrase or a melody, the whole thing will start when we count 'One.'" The fact that everyone starts from the same place is significant in Western music because it allows dozens of musicians to be led by one conductor counting off the beats from the same starting point. So typical is the fact that "the rhythm is counted and stressed on the main beat" that "we have the special word 'syncopation' to refer to a shifting of the 'normal' accents to produce an uneven or irregular rhythm."

In Africa, on the other hand, harmony and melody take a back seat to rhythm. In fact the complexity of rhythm is the hallmark of African music. It is hard to say what, exactly, is the "rhythm" of a song because, as Chernoff emphasizes, every African song has at least two rhythms running through it (this type of music is called "polymetric"). "There seems [to the Western ear] to be no unifying or main beat." African music can make us "uncomfortable because if the basic meter is not evident, we cannot understand how two or more people can play together or, even more uncomfortably, how anyone can play at all." Chernoff points out that African musicians do not all count from the same starting point, but enter into the music in relation to other instruments (these staggered, or independent entrances are called "apart-playing"). Sometimes the various drums carrying the rhythms play in combination with each other (though not in the same meter), but other times they may actually play what are called cross-rhythms, or conflicting patterns and accents. African music creates changing and evolving relationships between multiple rhythms in ways similar to Western harmony, but not Western rhythm, that is, "the basic organization of the rhythms is the essential composition." A main beat tends not to materialize to guide the process until the end of a phrase or series of phrases. As a consequence, Western listeners often feel lost. Ironically, one African musician told Chernoff that he felt lost and could not hear his part if he didn't have another drum playing a cross-rhythm to keep him on track. He needed another rhythm to respond to, to provide him with a kind of musical conversation.

This is not to say that patterns don't matter in African music. They just take the form of certain rhythms establishing an alteration with each other and then repeating that alteration periodically. One of the most common African forms of this is the famous "call-and-response" technique involving the swinging back and forth between a solo and chorus or from solo to instrumental reply. The response is the chorus which is a rhythmic phrase repeated regularly in a patterned answer to the lead. The lead is where the improvisation takes place, only to be followed again by the repetitive chorus.

SOCIO-HISTORICAL SPECIFICITIES OF MUSICAL FORMS

Those, in a reductive nutshell, are some of the structural differences between Western and African music. But I mentioned earlier that structural-level differences account for only one aspect of the cultural specificity of music. There also exist socio-historical differences which make popular expressive cultural forms such as music unique to a place or a people. I call them "socio-historical" because I am referring on one hand to the kinds of social settings or social contexts in which music takes place or which music creates, which are often quite different from one place to another. The absolute centrality of the dance hall and its formative influence on the evolution of contemporary Jamaican music would be one example. The music played by the marching teams in the Bahia, Brazil, *Carnival* would be another.

Just as important are the indissoluble links between the music of a given people and place and the history or heritage associated with them. The centuries of slavery that define Brazilian history have left an incalculable impact on the musics of that nation, not just in terms of the African origins of much of the music and dance and religions of the country, but also in terms of the way racial differences have operated to distinguish a 'white' elite from an African majority and how music has reacted to that accumulated legacy of centuries of oppression in the process of its development. Hawai'i presents another fascinating example of the way music has flowed through its history and today stands as perhaps the most important symbol of resistance to the marginalization of native Hawaiians.

I have decided to concentrate in the case studies in this manual on the socio-historical aspects that give cultures a certain specificity. I will attempt to highlight whenever relevant the two political functions of music I identified earlier, viz., its importance as a medium of social protest and criticism; as an overt form of resistance and opposition vital to the struggle for cultural survival of people around the world. Secondly, I will emphasize its role as one of the pillars in the foundations of our individual and collective identities. I want to illustrate wherever possible the ways music constructs certain meanings for us and draws us into alliances. Finally, I want to provide the socio-historical context for several musical subcultures from around the world so that we might fruitfully compare and learn from the ways music establishes community based on a shared sense of how people interpret their collective heritage, and then how they transform that heritage into a powerful social force for change.

The music of every society is open to investigation from a number of different angles. Our angle will be to attempt to gain some understanding of the historical and cultural conditions that gave rise to certain genres of music. We will be investigating the cultural past and present of various groups of people by using their musical creativity as our guiding light, as the thread that leads us in our search for some understanding of how we—as well as other people—live in the world. Music is dynamic, fluid, constantly undergoing change, and so it is well situated to act as a vehicle for the study of human history and culture.

In sum, there are three things to keep in mind while reading this text.

1. Music serves many purposes. We are concentrating on two political aspects or purposes of music in this text.

2. Music involves creative activity that is concretely situated in a particular cultural and historical context. Music and its particular context shed light on each other; the one helps us to understand the other.

3. Popular music is part of everyone's cultural heritage and can be analyzed seriously. The anthropological study of music can tell us interesting things about our own culture as well as the culture of others. We are usually unaware of the context within which music that is not our own is situated. Moreover, we are often quite chauvinist about "our" music. So it is useful to break down the biases and prejudices against "foreign" or "strange" musical traditions in order to develop an understanding of some of those differences and ultimately to increase our pleasure in the extraordinary vitality of music circulating around us and around the world.

VIDEOS ACCOMPANYING

Remember, the actual video lectures can be accessed at the following url: http://oregonstate.edu/media/classes/index.php?className=anth210

Scroll down under the "Classes on Demand" heading and select "ANTH210: Comparative Cultures."

Video 1

The first video introduces the course for students taking it in a classroom setting at Oregon State University. It does not refer directly to this text.

Video 2

This video dovetails with Chapter 1, "Introduction." The first overhead stated that there are three parts to the answer to the question:

What Is Music?

Music is the art of sound in time; it is an ordered pattern of sounds.

Music is the use of sound and silence to get things done (including create emotional states).

What music expresses & how it is organized are culturally specific and culturally determined.

The next overhead listed some of the many functions of music. Can you fill in the examples below with the songs used to illustrate the different categories? (Remember, some of the categories were not illustrated with songs.)

1. Political (form of protest, basis of identity)

2. Social (tells the news, a myth, a story or legend)

3. Cover up or blots out other unwanted sounds

4. Create an emotional state (lullaby, love song)

5. Sell products (advertisements, bar music, store musak)

6. Make money (paid performances, busking)

7. Religious functions (praise, prayer, funeral, marriage, etc.)

8. Martial functions (sports, hunting, warfare, national anthems)

In the next overhead we listed some features of African music. We said, first, to remember that there is no one "African Music," but many forms. We then went on to characterize African music(s). What did we say were its three features?

African music is polyrhythmic

African music is communal

African music is interactive

On the last overhead we listed two features of Western music. Can you remember the songs we used to illustrate the two?

Emphasis on harmony (Sweet Honey in the Rock used as an example)

Intensity of dynamics (a James Bond theme song used as an example)

Video 3

This video set out to provide numerous American musical illustrations of the two forms of political music being discussed throughout the course.

The first song played was used to illustrate how a mainstream pop song can carry a political message, often times about star-crossed lovers who are fighting against economic or racial or parental oppression. We used the song "Girl You'll be a Woman Soon" to make this point.

The next song discussed dated back to the 1930s and was by Woody Guthrie. His mournful ballad was used to illustrate the working man protest songs of the era. The song was called The Ludlow Massacre.

The next song was another Depression Era tune protesting the plight of farmers at the time. The song was covered by the talented guitarist, Ry Cooder. It's title was "Taxes on the Farmer Feeds Us All."

The next song, Strange Fruit, was a famous 1930s era protest against the lynching of African Americans. The singer was the famous blues singer, Billie Holiday.

The next song, We Shall Overcome, we said belonged in the top 20 all-time protest songs, if measured by its importance to the Civil Rights Movement in the 1960s.

The next set of songs came from the contemporary period. We said that rap, in particular, was a very effective form of protest music, particularly when it came to cop killings of African Americans. The songs we mentioned which illustrated this were:

Ice-T and his song called Cop Killer

NWA and their song called F . . . K. the Police

Pearl Jam and their single called W.M.A.

Bruce Springsteen and his song called American Skin

Public Enemy and their song called 41/19

We then turned to protest music produced by Native American groups. The first song made a cross-racial comparison between being a Native American and being African American. The song by Robby Bee and the Boyz from the Rez was called "Ebony Warrior."

The next example we played was off the soundtrack to the movie, Smoke Signals. It was a humorous protest song that used traditional Indian musical style to poke satirical fun at the Hollywood cowboy icon, John Wayne. The song, by the Eagle Bear Singers, was called "John Wayne's Teeth."

We then shifted to discuss the second kind of political function of music, that is, the use of music to create attachments to particular places and spaces; to create a sense of being a member of a community.

In talking about how music makes us feel that we belong to a group, we first mentioned the examples of Christian musical genres important to the creation of a sense of community for Christians. Black American Christians have historically used gospel music to do this. Young white and black Christians have also developed Christian forms of most every kind of popular music out there today.

The song that we actually played to illustrate the way music helps create a sense of community was Stand By Your Man by Tammy Wynette. We said it spoke to poor, rural, southern white women who could identify with its message of perseverance, loyalty, love and forgiveness.

We said there was another kind of white community solidarity formed through music and used The Drop Kick Murphys as an example of the music of white ethnic solidarity. The group pays their respects to their musical heritage without turning it into an exclusive, racially motivated form of solidarity. The song we played was called "Skinhead on the MBTA."

We next turned our attention to the politics surrounding the music produced in the wake of the September 11, 2001, terrorist attacks. We said that in terms of overt political statements, the majority appeared to come from the country music genre and that, though there was a good deal of diversity, the majority seemed to take up a right-wing, wrap-me-in-the-flag perspective.

We used an example from the work of Charlie Daniels first. We then played Lee Greenwood's all-purpose patriotic song, Proud to Be an American. We also included Toby Keith's tough guy, "boot in your ass" response.

We then said that country music also produced one of the most thoughtful and emotionally insightful songs in the form of Alan Jackson's Where Were You. Jackson, we said, resisted the temptation to push our patriotic buttons; instead, he viewed the tragedy as a time to rethink what's important to each of us. He also pushed a message of peace and love, which stood in stark contrast to the macho posturing of some of the other country stars.

Patriotic posturing was not limited to the country music genre. Rock musician Neil Young's commercially crass "Let's Roll" also pandered to desires for revenge.

In contrast to the country works of Daniels, Greenwood and Keith we also mentioned the work of Steve Earle. He wrote a very unique song about the American boy, John Walker Lindh, who fought with the Taliban in Afghanistan. Conservative newspapers and talk show hosts had ripped

Earle for being sympathetic to America's enemies. We suggested that the song, which is part of Earle's "Jerusalem" album, is "sympathetic" only in that he tried to get inside the head of Lindh and to understand why he chose the path that he did. The song was called, John Walker's Blues.

But more influential were the several tuneful meditations on 9/11 put out by Bruce Springsteen on his CD called "The Rising." The song titled Worlds Apart included Qawwali music, probably from Pakistan. The whole song was rather reminiscent of a Sufi poem and may have been meant to invoke images of Afghanistan. In any case the other songs like Into the Fire were attempts to recount what happened on 9/11 only through the eyes of a fireman's wife, without any overt political posturing or messages attached, except one of sympathy for those who lost loved ones.

We concluded by suggesting that in the end, what music does best in times of trouble is give expression to our shock and grief. We then ended the session by playing an example of this in the form of a video excerpt from the "America: A Tribute to Heroes" concert which took place soon after 9/11. The excerpt consisted of Neil Young covering an old, anti-war song of John Lennon's called Imagine.

NOTES

1. I am an expert in anthropology but a rank amateur when it comes to musical analysis. The authors cited in the bibliography have taught me a great deal about the subject; still, the text is dependent on a more socio-historical framework than a musicological one.

The Politics of Music in Afro-Brazilian Culture

Brazilian Snapshot

The state of Brazil covers enough territory to make it the fifth largest nation in the world, bigger than Europe. Its population is around 170 million, about 80% living in the many big cities along the Atlantic seaboard. The interior is composed of a vast central plateau and rain forest drained by several mighty rivers, the biggest of which is the famous Amazon River (Morris 2006). Catholicism remains the dominant religion in Brazil, but Protestantism and other African-inspired religions (like Candomblé) were recognized at the end of the nineteenth century when Brazil became a republic. Today, the non Catholic religions are gaining membership at a very rapid rate. The number of Brazilians claiming to be Evangelical Protestants reached 15% in 2000 while the number claiming to be Catholic dipped to 74%. A healthy 10% of the Congress are evangelicals and the presidential candidates now court the Evangelical vote during national elections (Benson 2007). Poverty in contemporary Brazil is also gaining ground, so is child labor, so is malnutrition amongst poor children. Wealth is also very present in Brazil, but it is concentrated in the hands of the upper class, both in the cities and in the countryside (Poverty Net. 2007). In fact Brazil ranks as the fourth worst country in the world in terms of wealth distribution: Brazil's richest 20% receive 30 times more than the poorest 20% (Infoplease. 2007).

The "Discovery" of Brazil

The Portuguese explorer Pedro Álvares Cabral stepped onto Brazilian soil in the spring of 1500. He had intended to make his way East to India but had swung wide around West Africa and ended up across the Atlantic Ocean in the New World. It was easy to make such a mistake in those days. Open sea navigation was still difficult because only latitude could be measured, not longitude. Besides, little of the terrain away from the coasts had been mapped; little was understood about the geography of most of the world. (In fact the Portuguese even thought that human skin would burn under the ferocious sun at the equator. And if that did not finish you off, they believed, the sea monsters roaming the open oceans surely would.) Furthermore, wind and ocean currents and geographical proximity almost guaranteed that Spanish and Portuguese sailors would be the first Europeans to land in the New World regardless of their navigational skills.

Let us stop a minute here to ask, "Why were the Americas conquered by Europeans and not by Africans or Asians?"[1] The most common sense answer would probably be something like, "The Europeans were more ambitious," or "The Europeans had a certain genius for getting things done," or "The Europeans enjoyed a harsher climate that made them more industrious," or "The Europeans were less burdened with powerful kings and emperors who confiscated their wealth, thus they could be more entrepreneurial." Something of that sort usually comes to mind. Well, as the old Cole Porter song says, "It ain't necessarily so." Let me explain:

At the time of Cabral's discovery of Brazil, that is, at the end of the fifteenth and beginning of the sixteenth century, people all around the world were setting out on similar ocean voyages: East Africans were sailing back and forth to the Arabian Peninsula and Southeast Asia, Indians were sailing to and from Africa, Arabs were sailing to India and China, and the Chinese were sailing to Africa—not to mention the many Pacific Islanders who routinely sailed hundreds of miles over the open ocean in their outrigger canoes.[2] As one expert on the subject put it, "Maritime technology differed from region to region but no one region could be considered to have superiority in any sense implying evolutionary advantage, and novel ideas and techniques were being spread in all directions by rapid criss-cross diffusion" (Blaut 1993:181).

The Portuguese (and the Spanish) actually lagged behind much of the rest of the world at the time. They were on the very fringes of most trading networks and had been fighting internally for centuries against the Moors. To try and make up for the lag they had both decided to relink themselves with the gold producing regions of West Africa. They revitalized old sea routes to do this. They eventually continued on down the coast of Africa and (with the help of African and Indian sailors) pioneered a route to India.

As I mentioned above, the countries of the Iberian Peninsula, that is, Portugal and Spain, had several advantages over the rest of the world when it came to discovering the Americas. They were much closer than any except the West Africans, and they had wind and ocean currents working for them. Those advantages were increased considerably by the use of the Canaries and other islands of the Atlantic (Madeira, and the Azores) as jumping off points for voyages. The West Africans, who could have given them a run for their money, were mainly oriented inland at this time, busy trading north and east across the African continent, and so they were not involved in maritime commerce except along their coast. The North Africans, the other possible rivals, were suffering from an economic slump at the time and were also under assault from the Turks and the Spanish. Furthermore, most of their trade moved along the overland trans-Saharan routes that linked them with West Africa. The East Africans who were maritime traders had to contend with sailing against the prevailing winds in order to move from the Indian into the Atlantic Oceans. Besides, their nearest port was almost 3,000 miles farther away from the New World so little progress was made along that ocean route in an east-west direction.

It must be stressed, by way of conclusion to this little digression, that it was thanks to the gold brought back from the New World that Europe became the dominant power in the world. Between 1561 and 1580 approximately 85% of the entire world's production of silver came from the Americas. The influx of gold and silver may have been so high that the money supply of the whole Old World doubled as a result of the early conquests. AND ALL OF THAT SUPPLY PASSED THROUGH THE HANDS OF EUROPEAN MERCHANTS AND EUROPEAN PORT CITIES. IT FLOWED INTO EUROPE, THROUGH EUROPE AND FROM EUROPE TO ASIA AND AFRICA so that the Europeans who controlled it were the ones who could offer better prices for all goods—labor as well as land—in all markets, than anyone else had ever been able to offer at any time in history (Blaut 1993:189).

Our adventurer, Cabral, sailed away from Brazil almost empty handed. He thought he had merely discovered a new island in the Atlantic on the route to India. His purpose in setting sail was to continue the journey in search of the wealth of the Orient, that land where pepper, cloves, mace, cinnamon, and ginger were traded literally for their weight in gold. He had hoped to make himself rich on the spice trade, just as Vasco da Gama had done the year before when he returned to Lisbon from the East with a cargo that returned to his investors a profit of 6000%![3]

Explorers who followed in Cabral's wake never found much in the way of gold, silver, or spices, but they did begin a lucrative trade in brazilwood, a wood located in the narrow coastal woodland belt which produced a prized red dye. Within a little more than a decade of his discovery, Cabral's "island" was known officially on maps as "Brazil," after the wood of the same name. Small Portuguese trading posts developed along the coast for the purpose of trading with the local Indians for the wood they cut. By the end of the 1500s, over 100 ships a year made the passage from Brazil to Lisbon loaded with precious brazilwood.[4]

The trade in brazilwood created problems for Portugal because it attracted competition, particularly from the Dutch and the French. The scores of bays and inlets all along the more than 3,000 miles of Brazilian coastline were difficult for the Portuguese navy to monitor. The Portuguese king, Joaò III (1521-1555) decided to try a new way of insuring Portugal's claim on the land: he ordered that Brazil be colonized. Men, seeds, and domesticated animals were dutifully dispatched and the first Portuguese settlements in the New World were established along the coast in 1532 and 1533 near the present day cities of Santos and São Paolo.

Brazil's luxurious, narrow coastal belt gives way quickly below the Amazon to the Brazilian highlands. Much of the coast is actually hemmed in by a steep, almost mountainous escarpment. Above the Amazon to the north of the country lie the gently rising Guiana highlands and the drier, northeastern steppe region known as the Sertão. To the west all the way up to the Andes Mountains of eastern Peru stretches the Amazon basin, the largest rainforest in the world. The Amazon River and its 200 tributaries drain, with the help of the Plata River system to the south, a basin practically the size of Europe. In some places within the basin over 200 inches of rain fall every year, enough to make the Amazon 14 times larger than the Mississippi. The river is over 100 feet deep for most of its course and in many places you cannot see across it. Small ocean going vessels are able to navigate 2,300 miles upriver to the Peruvian city of Iquitos. The mighty river pushes so much water with so much force that its muddy complexion is still visible in the ocean 250 miles off the coast of Brazil!

INDIANS IN BRAZIL

No one knows for sure, but somewhere between 2 and 4 million Indians inhabited the lush coast and the Amazon Basin as Portuguese colonization got underway. Almost from the beginning, Jesuit missionaries moved among the Indians trying to convert them to Christianity. Interestingly enough, the Jesuits often used music to do so.[5] They forbade the performance of Indian music but encouraged Indians to learn and perform Christian hymns. They also gathered the Indians together into village settlements known as *aldeias*, where they taught them various European trades as well as how to read and write.

For the early Portuguese settlers, the Indian laborers living in the *aldeias* were the only source of women. So very quickly on the Portuguese men took advantage of their relative power and wealth to turn Indian women into their concubines, mistresses, or wives and thus began populating the new colony with their mixed offspring (known as *Mamelucos*).

Indians provided the Portuguese colonizers with more than just sex in the first decades of colonization. Burns (1993:39-40) mentions that the Indians showed the newcomers how to hunt and fish, how to build light canoes, how to prepare manioc (which rapidly became the staple food of the Portuguese in Brazil), how to build more open houses suitable to the Tropics, how to sleep in cooler, safer, and more comfortable hammocks (a word, like "manioc," which came from an Indian language) and even how to use tobacco (another Indian word that passed into European languages).

However, the Brazilian Indians were most important to the early Portuguese in their role as the only source of labor available in the colony. Despite the protestations of their Jesuit protectors, the Indians were quickly enslaved to work the colonizers' fields and to wait on the colonizers' tables.

The Jesuits battled back at court in Lisbon to keep the converted Indians from being enslaved, but the colonial forces proved to be too strong for them.

Conditions for the Indians grew much worse as they began experiencing extremely high death rates because of the introduction of new diseases and through over work. Many of those who did not die or did not intermarry with the Portuguese slipped away into the interior of the country out of reach of the new settlements. Sad to say that a similar process is ongoing today as the few intact Indian groups continue to struggle to survive the deadly encroachment of outside interests, whether they be settlers, gold miners, big ranchers, or giant corporate multinationals after their natural resources.

AFRICANS IN BRAZIL

The Portuguese colony in Brazil really came into its own in the 1540s with the development of sugar plantations. The new plantations supplanted older Mediterranean sugar cane growing regions by drawing on what Blaut (1993:191-192) calls the twin advantages of colonialism: empty land and cheap labor. He mentions that by 1600 Brazil was exporting 30,000 tons of sugar a year worth 2,000,000 British pounds—greater than the sum yearly total of all British exports! Wealth was being accumulated so quickly in Brazil in the sixteenth century that the sugar plantations were able to double their capacity every two years. On top of that, sugar production costs accounted for only one-fifth of the income generated, and that included the cost of slaves.

Brazil by that time was importing tens of thousands of African slaves a year to work on the expanding sugar plantations. Lisbon had always been a leader in the trading of slaves, with West African slaves having been imported into Portugal as early as 1433. The black slaves, unlike the local Indians, proved much more resistant, naturally, to imported Old World diseases for which they already had developed immunities, so they were better able to survive the atrocious working conditions in the sugar mills and cane fields, so much so that a triangular trade route developed which moved European goods to Africa, African slaves to Brazil, and Brazilian sugar to Europe. During the next three centuries over 3.5 million African slaves survived the Atlantic crossing to take up captive residence in Brazil (Burns 1993:43). After the 1690s Africans were also used to work in the mines of Minas Geras Province and then eventually in the coffee plantations established around São Paolo and Rio de Janeiro.

The black slaves came from various locations along the western coast of Africa. Angola, another Portuguese colony, supplied most of the slaves bound for Brazil during the seventeenth century. Slaves came mainly from the so-called "Gold Coast" during the years 1700-1770, and from Nigeria and Benin (formerly Dahomey) during 1770-1850.[6]

More African slaves were shipped to Brazil than to anywhere else in the Americas. The dependence on slaves in the colony of Brazil grew so great over time that Salvador, by the early nineteenth century, was thought by visiting foreigners to be a black city. None of the regions of Brazil had less than 27% slaves in its population, and the whole colony, counting slaves and freedmen, was almost half black by the first decade of the 1900s. Brazil finally abolished slavery in 1888, making it the last slave holding country in the New World to do so (Fryer 2000:6-7).

BRAZIL'S AFRICAN CULTURAL HERITAGE

Nowadays the African contribution is seen as a prominent and essential strand that can be traced throughout Brazilian popular music and dance and is in fact central to them. The African element has not merely enriched the whole of Brazilian popular music: it has decisively shaped it (Fryer 2000:8).

Brazilian music, like its North American counterpart, grew out of a host of influences, so it would be unhelpful to privilege one source to the exclusion of another. However, as the quote above suggests, the African influence in Brazilian popular music has certainly been foundational. The Brazilian ethnomusicologist, Oneyda Alvarenga, listed 13 elements of Brazilian music which he thought originated in Africa. Roberts (1972:72-74) lists them as follows:[7]

1. the frequency of six-note scales with a flatted seventh-note (a feature of the "blues scale" of the U.S.);

2. the common use of certain rhythmic phrases;[8]

3. call-and-response singing involving a single solo line (often improvised) followed by a short, unvarying chorus;

4. breaking up of the neat melodic framework that European music tends to use;

5. the *umbrigada*, or belly-bounce, in dancing;

6. using a large number of musical instruments, including various drums known collectively as *atabaque*;

7. the great importance of drums generally in Brazilian dances and their frequent function as organizers of the choreography;

8. dramatic dances;

9. a certain rather nasal tone of singing;

10. importance of wind instruments (may be of both African and Portuguese influence);

11. popularity of bowed string instruments (fiddle especially, though, again, this could be of both West African and Portuguese origin);

12. vocal (not instrumental) harmonies based on parallel thirds: when group singing is not in unison or near-unison (an African form called "heterophony") it most frequently uses parallel thirds with one voice singing more or less the same tune a third below the other;

13. use of frequently syncopated and more complex rhythmic approach (than Portuguese music) with displaced accentuations and cross-rhythms against the percussion.

We will be coming back to many of these African attributes of Brazilian music throughout our study of Brazil. What I want to concentrate on here is three important forms of music that developed in Brazil from African origins.

The first form of music accompanies the African-Brazilian religious rituals which are referred to collectively as *candomblé*. Many of the songs and instruments associated with *candomblé* come directly from West Africa, particularly Nigeria. The songs are usually sung in Brazil in the African languages of Yoruba or Fon. As Fryer (2000:9) says of *candomblé*, "Originally this was a music of resistance, whose primary function in the teeth of persecution was to keep Africa and African deities alive in the minds and hearts of captive Africans."

The second kind of African-origin music accompanies the dance/martial art form known as *capoeira*. This particular form, most common in Bahia, is derived directly from Angola. Some of the words used in the *capoeira* songs come from the various languages of that region of Central Africa. The songs of the dance are played on an instrument called a *berimbau*. "This too was at first a music of resistance, which helped young African slaves in Brazil prepare for rebellion by clandestinely learning and practicing fighting skills" (Fryer 2000:9).[9]

The third variety of Afro-Brazilian music we will discuss in this section evolved eventually into Brazil's most famous dance and music: the samba. The dance developed from the Kongo-Angola region and was first known as the *batuque*. You know it more today as the music of Brazil's

Carnival. Each year samba clubs, or schools, located in the *favelas* (ghetto-like slums) around Rio de Janeiro compete with each other to see who can put on the most elaborate street procession. Hundreds of dancers wearing extravagant costumes gyrate their hips to the intense percussive rhythms that form the basis of the music. The idea of celebrating before the advent of Lent originated, of course, with the Portuguese. But the music associated with it sprang from black Brazil and continues today to provide an important form of identification with and celebration of that African/slave cultural heritage.

Candomblé

The various African peoples who made up the slave population of Brazil brought with them to the New World their various African religions. In Brazil, the African deities are known as *orixás*, from a Yoruba word. During the centuries of slavery the slaves hid their original religions behind a mask of Catholicism. The slaves thus practiced what is known as a syncretic religion, that is, they took elements from both traditions and blended them into their own. As an example, around Bahia, the Yoruba god of iron and war, Ogun, is also understood to be St. Anthony. They are one and the same. Likewise, around Rio the Yoruba god of hunters, Oxóssi, is also personified in the form of St. Sebastian. Different saints and gods mingle in different combinations throughout the country and even throughout the New World (Haiti and Cuba have a similar system). This syncretic practice allowed the slaves to appear to be Christians to their white overseers and priests, all the while keeping alive their original faith in African gods.[10]

The African belief systems still thriving today in Brazil do not form the equivalent of a church. There is no overarching hierarchy, nor are there prescribed beliefs or rituals or ceremonies that all must follow in *candomblé*. Instead, there are a multitude of decentralized branches. Usually the believers belong to a house of worship with its own ways of doing things which differs slightly from neighborhood to neighborhood, town to town, and region to region. Parenthetically, it is interesting to note that African-based faith seems to be growing in Brazil. Witness the fact that in Salvador, Bahia, in 1942 there were 67 *terreiros* (houses of worship) in the city, each with approximately 300 members. In the early 1980s, according to Fryer (2000:13), there were over 900 such houses! Schreiner (1993:82) claims that three-quarters of Bahia's population attend *candomblé* services and only pretend to be Catholic if they have jobs in white-dominated sectors of society. That is why, even though Brazil is predominantly Catholic, a large share of its population attends some form of *candomblé* ceremonies.[11]

Each of the Yoruba gods has his or her own special day of the week, special foods, particular symbols (animals, plants, etc.), and, most importantly, special songs. Each of the followers of *candomblé* develops a special relationship with one of the gods/saints during their initiation into the faith and that *orixá* then becomes them or enters into them during trances.

And that is where the music enters in. No matter which god is involved, as Fryer (2000:18) puts it, they all are summoned by music without which worship cannot take place.

A series (usually three) of hollow-log type drums provide the foundation for the music, accompanied normally by rattles and clapperless bells. One master drummer controls the performance, though he is in constant exchange with the dancing devotees. He is the one who signals, not only the pace of the dance, but also the entrance of the various deities. "Cutting across the established beat with the rhythm of a particular *orixá*, he is able to trigger in the dancer's brain the learned response that expresses itself in the state of 'possession.' From that moment on, the dancer *is* the *orixá*, and behaves accordingly" (Fryer 2000:20).

Blacks in Brazil, though a majority, live on the margins of society. They do the grunt work, that is, the hardest work for the least pay—when they can find it. They live in the most squalid housing with the worst schools. They suffer from the highest disease and infant mortality rates. They are the ones associated in the media with crime and violence. Not surprisingly, their *candomblé* religious practices also come under fire. False preachers distort the religion for their own financial gain by promising to induce trances in exchange for money. The tourist agencies try to capitalize on *candomblé* by turning its sessions into commercialized, folkloric spectacles tourists must pay to witness. The Brazilian ruling elite supports this move by encouraging a kind of condescension towards all things African, viewing them as the romantically quaint relics of a by-gone past which the whole nation enjoys—at a distance, of course, and denuded of any critical edge.

Yet in spite of these attempts to disrupt and discredit Afro-Brazilian culture, it thrives as an important element in the struggle, not just for survival, but for the right to the dignity of having an identity of one's own. *Candomblé* plays an important role in the maintenance of an autonomous cultural space for black Brazil, a space that is free to be an expression of the unique African/slave history that is the celebrated heritage of the majority of Brazilians.

The vital importance of Afro-Brazilian culture extends even into the political realm. Maria José Espírito Santo França (1999:54), a practicing *candomblé* priestess (with a Ph.D.), claims that *candomblé* acts as a nucleus for the struggle to spread democracy throughout Brazil and to resist the further degradation of the quality of life for the slum dwellers. It is through local, neighborhood associations such as the *candomblé* houses of worship that the poor come together to fight for their rights as full citizens. At the heart of the matter, she says, is the struggle over self-determination and the right to completely free expression for those most isolated and alienated from dominant Brazilian society.[12] Put another way, Candomblé provides a kind of cultural resistance against the sense of futility experienced by Brazilians of the lower classes. It gives them hope and provides them with a sense of community and social order in an otherwise heartless world (Morris 2006: 230).

Capoeira

Secular activities also play a role in keeping alive the links with Brazil's African heritage. *Capoeira* is a famous example of such a dynamic link to that past. As mentioned earlier, *capoeira* is a kind of martial arts dance. Black Brazilians reportedly used it to fend off the police during the latter part of the nineteenth and first part of the twentieth century. But it originally developed as a form of training among slaves to help them escape and defend themselves. This was not a hypothetical need during the slavery era in Brazil. Tens of thousands of slaves, either through mass insurrection or by individual cunning, escaped to freedom and formed free communities known as *quilombos*. The biggest of these was the famous collection of some nine fortified communities that formed the territory known as Palmares, in the state of Pernambuco in the northeast. At its peak Palmares counted over 20,000 inhabitants, most of them black but with a small addition of Indians and even some whites. The threat to the slave plantation economy posed by these runaway communities was so great that the Brazilian colonial government attacked them whenever possible. Palmares had to withstand military assaults almost every year. Still it lasted as an independent state throughout the whole of the seventeenth century, thanks to the fighting skill and will of its ex-slave inhabitants (Fryer 2000:68-71; Burns 1993:47).

After the abolition of slavery in the 1880s *capoeira* developed from being mainly a martial art to being equally a dance performance and an athletic game. It also became more highly specialized by developing a master and apprentice style of transmission. Today it is open to people from all walks of life, men and women, and even to foreigners, many of whom have traveled to Brazil to learn the form or worked with Brazilian *capoeira* masters abroad.

Regardless of its transformation through time, music has remained absolutely central to *capoeira*. The main instrument is now the berimbau, which is a long stick made into a bow by a single wire string. Attached at the bottom is a gourd that acts as the resonator. The string is plucked with a coin by one hand and then struck with a small stick by the other. The gourd rests against the body of the musician and can be pushed and pulled against the body to alter its resonance.

As with *candomblé*, so, too, in *capoeira* the musician and the dancers/competitors work together. One keen observer described it this way:

The music guides and is guided by the play; it begins and ends the competition; it slows the game when players are in danger of losing their tempers; it speeds the game up if it lags; it pokes fun at a poorly executed move or a spoilsport; it lauds virtuosic or amusing play. To regard *capoeira* as merely a martial art ... is to miss the main point of the game: the creation and solidification of community, which is initiated and strengthened by music performance (Fryer 2000:38).

The onlookers at a *capoeira* competition also sing short verses to accompany the action. A long and interesting quote on the subject from an American student of *capoeira*, J. Lowell Lewis follows below. He learned under *Mestre* (master) Nô, who in this scene is in the process of fighting one of his ex-students named Braulio who had now become a master in his own right. The excerpt is particularly revealing about the centrality of music to the *capoeira* competition:

Even though the masters had paused several times to find their wind, they were demonstrating extreme endurance given the intensity of their struggle and the difficulty of their moves ... Experts and casual observers alike were fascinated with the variety of attacks and defenses, the beautiful yet deadly moves these two could improvise, and everyone wanted to see the resolution ... [T]he audience had thrown quite a bit of paper money into the ring. If the players chose to, they could begin a variation of the game by competing to pick up the money, thereby claiming it for themselves. So far ... they had been ignoring the money ...

I myself was a fledgling player, a student of the older master for some months ...

Without warning, Braulio did a cartwheel into the center ... and picked up the pile of money with his mouth ... The crowd exploded with laughter and approval ...

After some negotiations, Braulio was convinced to return the money to the center of the ring and the game was restarted ... As they crouched there, *Mestre* Nô suddenly leaped backwards into a double backflip, lowering himself on the second revolution to pick up the money in *his* mouth. He came to rest on his haunches, mouth stuffed with bills, looking like the cat who ate the canary. This time it was Braulito's turn to look sheepish as the crowd laughed approvingly. Excited and moved by this inspired trickery, without stopping to consider the consequences, I burst into song:

ô me dá o meu dinheiro	oh give me my money,
ô me dá o meu dinheiro	oh give me my money,
valentão	tough guy,
ô me dá o meu dinheiro	oh give me my money,
valentão	tough guy,
porque no meu dinheiro	because on my money
ninguén ponhe a mão	nobody puts a hand

As I started singing, many of the players looked up to see who it was, especially since I obviously had a foreign accent. Although it is accepted for anyone to join in on a chorus in *capoeira* singing, even audience members who are not participating in the physical contest, usually only masters or respected senior players initiate songs, since the soloist must carry the song, giving a clear indication of pitch and rhythm. Therefore as I was ending the verse I became quite nervous as I realized what I had done. Would anyone respond to my call, or would they all keep silent, a snub to the pretentious foreign novice who dared to interfere in the creation of this exceptional game?

It was with relief and thankfulness, then, that I heard a full chorus come in on the refrain:

ô me dá o meu dinheiro	oh give me my money,
ô me dá o meu dinheiro	oh give me my money,
valentão	tough guy

I didn't try to continue the song for more than a few repetitions, since I realized that I only knew that one solo verse, but as I sang I understood that the reason the chorus had responded enthusiastically was that I had done the most important thing right. I had chosen an appropriate song to capture that moment in the game, to highlight the action and allow the audience and players a chance to express their delight in the quality of play.[13]

The *capoeira* of today need no longer be practiced in secrecy. That was not the case 100 years ago. Back then the drummers would quickly alter their rhythms and play a drum pattern used to warn of the approach of a white man or overseer if they were spotted in the neighborhood of the competition. Even as late as 1920 the *capoeria* musicians and performers had to be ready to flee if the mounted police appeared (Fryer 2000:38-39). Today the sport is not just tolerated but celebrated as part of Brazil's heritage—more importantly, as part of Brazil's African heritage. That is of interest to us because it demonstrates the way this musical martial art has evolved from its possible origins as defense training for African-Brazilians threatened by the oppressive inequalities of slavery and servitude, into a symbol of that collective past that is now "worn" proudly. The music and the matches of *capoeira* form a part of the Afro-Brazilian identity of the people of Bahia. They cultivate it on one level as a way of reaffirming their proud ties to those communities of the past that organized the art form as a way of subverting the oppressive power relations of their day. To practice it today, to promote it within the context of contemporary Brazilian society is, then, at one level to make cultural connections with a form of expression developed centuries ago. Yet on another level, to be involved with *capoeira* means to be involved potentially in keeping alive an oppositional culture; it means reproducing practices of resistance and potent symbols of the refusal to tolerate injustice on the part of practitioners in the past and the present.

SAMBA

"For me, samba has always been a form of protest music, from its very beginnings until today. It comments upon and criticizes situations." So Vinicius de Moraes, the author of *Black Orpheus*, is quoted as saying during the 1970s (Schreiner 1993:154). This statement is hard to justify on the face of it for the samba has evolved, over its almost a century of existence, into many different forms: from love songs to patriotic ballads to the "cool," light jazz of the bossa nova—not what one thinks of, exactly, as protest music.[14] But we will see in what follows if we can discover what Vinicius may have been thinking when he made that claim.

The end of slavery in the 1880s and the end of the coffee boom in the 1890s sent thousands of provincial black Brazilians into the city of Rio de Janeiro. The samba developed in the early twentieth century as part of the expressive culture of the residents of the new black shantytowns (*favelas*) springing up on the hill (*morro*) to the north of the main part of town.

Samba has always been understood to be a descendant of the *batuque*, a circle dance once performed by slaves which was known for its strong percussive rhythms and its use of the *umbigada*, a dance move where the male and female dancers literally bumped bellies. With the migration into Rio, the dance also became associated with *Carnival*, that is, the Latin Catholic celebration that marks the beginning of Lent.

In the early part of the twentieth century, *Carnival* in Rio took place at three distinct levels: the poor held their celebration in one part of town and danced and paraded to the sounds of what would become the samba, the middle class paraded in another part of town, while wealthy white society developed its own separate festival marked by lavish and expensive costumes and processions which were accompanied by *Carnival* march music imported from Portugal.

The earliest actual mention of a song being called a "samba" did not occur until 1916 when the musician known as "Donga" (Ernesto dos Santos) and his lyricist Mauro de Almeida registered the song titled, "Pelo Telefone" (On the Telephone). They had been gathering for several years with other black, mulatto, and poor white musicians from the poorer sections of Rio. They used to meet, interestingly enough, in the back rooms of the house of a famous *candomblé* priestess (*mãe-de-santo*) named Tia Ciata who had emigrated from Bahia. She allowed her back rooms to be used for musicians' parties; so as a consequence, they became the meeting grounds for the first generation of true samba musicians, including, besides Dongo, the composer Sinhô and the musician Pixinguinha and his band, as well as a collection of musicians who had emigrated from Bahia. The lyrics to the first samba seem rather tame and innocuous. However, it has been suggested that the telephone reference is an allusion to the old practice of someone on the inside calling up brothels and bars and house parties to warn of impending police raids. If that is the case, then the song becomes much more interesting as an artifact of the time period in Rio when massive urban renovation and police harassment kept the poor black population of the city always on their guard.[15] In fact until 1930, the samba and other forms of Afro-Brazilian performance, such as the *candomblé* had to go underground because they were more or less banned in Rio as "uncivilized" and as a threat to public order. Here are the lyrics to "Pelo Telefone"

> The master of the follies
> Had me advised on the telephone
> Not to quarrel with pleasure
> If I wanted to have fun
> Ai, Ai, Ai

Leave your worries behind you, my boy
Ai, Ai, Ai
Be sad if you succeed and you'll see.
I hope you get a thrashing
So you'll never try again
To take a woman away from another
After you've performed your tricks.
Look, the turtledove,
Kind sir, kind sir,
It is outright embarrassed.
The little bird
Kind sir, kind sir,
Has yet to dance a samba,
Kind sir, kind sir,
Because this samba,
Kind sir, kind sir,
Gives you goose bumps
Kind sir, kind sir,
And makes you weak at the knees
Kind sir, kind sir,
But it's great fun.
(Schreiner 1993:105):

Throughout the decades of the 1920s, 30s and 40s samba lyrics dealt with one of two things: women and love affairs or with the figure of the urban hustler, known in Portuguese as the *malandro* (Shaw 1999:7). This particular character proved to be popular for various reasons. The one which interests us most is the way he combined a mocking attitude towards conventional morality with a swaggering, confident, public presentation of self. Slave-based societies around the world have historically produced such characters at different times who embody a heroically defiant stance towards dominant white society. They flaunt elite society's norms while succeeding in life and love on the basis of their cunning. They also, and this is crucial, make a practice of struggling against any and every form of exploitation practiced by "the man" against "their people," that is, any form of class and racial exploitation which victimizes poor blacks.

Brazil during the 1930s and 40s was a difficult place for black Brazilians. Many of the good jobs were being taken by the thousands of white European immigrants flooding into the country. The ruling elite and much of white society stereotyped black Brazilians—particularly males—as belonging to the criminal underworld.

In the second half of the 1930s Brazil came to be ruled over by a quasi-fascist dictator named Vargas who used modern mass communications and propaganda techniques to instill discipline and patriotism in the people. His regime censored songs as well as other forms of popular culture that were not to their liking. They also promoted songs which praised the nation or which shed a positive light on the government's initiatives.

Songs about the *malandro* did neither. Being a street-wise hustler, such a character preached against the virtues of work while praising forms of petty vice. He always made a practice of maligning manual labor. He passed his time, instead, being the best dressed, smoothest talking con man in the crowd. Two-toned shoes, white linen suit, silk shirt, and tilted straw hat formed his costume of choice and represented his disdain for the middle class values of modesty and hard work. A 1931 samba written by Noel Rosa called "Mulato bamba" neatly summarizes the character of the *malandro*. The reference to the dry cleaner's is to suggest how concerned he is with his personal wardrobe. The lyrics and translation appear in Shaw (1999:7):

Mulato bamba, 1931, Noel Rosa

Este mulato forte	This strong mulatto
É do Salgueiro	Is from Salgueiro
Passear no tintureiro	Hanging around in the dry cleaner's
Era seu esporte	Was his favorite sport
Já nasceu com sorte	He was born lucky
E desde pirralho	And since he was a kid
Vive à custa do baralho	He's lived from a pack of cards
Nunca viu trabalho	He's never seen a day's work

The samba that celebrated the *malandro* figure was just one direction the music took during its first decades of existence. The government succeeded in the 1930s in fostering the development of a counter variety, of a tamer form of samba that competed with the more risqué and subversive version. This came about by establishing official government control over *Carnival*. Samba music lost its exclusive association with the stereotypical black Brazilian underworld. White society under the Vargas regime began to embrace samba as the music of Brazilian society in its entirety. Its associations with Afro-Brazilian culture became its selling points. It was exotic and sensuous and raucous and celebratory, but now in a way that was understood to be nation-affirming. These traits were rapidly becoming associated with the establishment's image of Brazil itself. As one commentator on the Brazilian scene put it: "Samba, like other Afro-Brazilian cultural forms, such as *feijoada* (Brazil's national dish) and *candomblé*, was to become a national symbol, produced and consumed by a cross-section of Brazilian society and projected abroad as a reflection of Brazil's mythical racial democracy" (Eduardo Diatahy B. de Menezes, quoted in Shaw 1999:11).

Interestingly, the incentives and censorship of the Vargas regime caused many samba composers to toe the official line and produce what the government wanted to hear. It also caused many others to become more subtle, to use irony and ambiguity to subvert the surface message of their lyrics. As an example, the cleverer composers during the early 1940s brought into being a new national character, known as the *otário* (mug or sucker). For all intents and purposes he was a hard working, upstanding citizen of the nation. He tried to do what he was supposed to, but kept tripping over his innocence, ignorance and stupidity. He came across as an impoverished stooge of the system, not even aware when fortune smiled on him. The following samba illustrates this well. The *otário* character, Bastião, works hard and is honest but is kept from advancing by his lack of education. He also, ironically enough, seems to be unable to get to his beloved work on time:

Bastião, by Wilson Baptista and Brasinha (Shaw 1999:13)

Bastião	Bastião
Valente na picareta	Brave with a pickaxe
É um covarde	Is a coward
Quando pega na caneta	When he picks up a pen
Que tempo enorme ele consome	He takes an enormous amount of time
Quendo tem que assinar o nome	When he has to sign his name
Bastião	Bastião
Foi criado na claçada	Was brought up on the street
Não viu cartilha	He never learned to spell
Nem tabuada	Or to do math
Bastião	Bastião
Sempre toma o bonde errado	Always catches the wrong trolley
Não sabe ler	He can't read
Nem bilhete premiado	Not even a winning (lottery) ticket

The split that developed in the samba during these decades continues even today. The lighter, more commercially successful samba, such as the *samba-cançao*, evolved during the late 1940s and 50s first, into a vehicle for the rise to international stardom of Carmen Miranda, and then into the jazz-influenced, melodious, bossa nova (new style). Miranda, who began her working career as a hat maker (and always made her trademark flamboyant costumes herself), rose to become the highest paid performer in the U.S. by 1951. Hollywood got its money's worth, however. She was forced to do the Bahia-bandana-banana routine in movie after movie and then in early television. They wouldn't let her branch out and they weren't interested in a more nuanced portrayal of Brazil or its music. Treated as something of a kitsch icon today, her popularity and reputation were such that at her death in 1955, over a half million people turned out in Rio de Janeiro to mourn the passing of this samba star (Shaw 1999:114-117).

On the other hand, the more traditional Afro-Brazilian samba of the shantytowns, the *samba-de-morro*, became the official processional music of the *Carnival*. The celebration itself evolved during the 1960s into the massive, international spectacle that we know today. The music's lyrics have been shortened in today's sambas while the percussive, rhythmic force has been increased considerably as the ranks of various rival samba school drum corps, singers and dancers have swelled into the hundreds.

MUSICAL DEVELOPMENTS IN BRAZIL SINCE THE SAMBA

Brazilians would get righteously indignant at the thought of their musical heritage being divided simply into "samba" and "post-samba" periods. And rightfully so. For the samba, though still popular and important, ended its dominance of everyday popular music in the 1950s. Lots has happened in

Brazil since then. As I mentioned above, at that time, middle class, jazz-influenced musicians such as Antonio Carlos (Tom) Jobim. João Gilberto, the writer Vinícius de Moraes, the guitarist Baden Powell de Aquino, Luiz Bonfá and a few others fashioned a music built around "dissonant harmonies, polyrhythmic patterns, percussive acoustic instrumentation, and a 'cool', almost colorless voicing of conversational lyrics" (Treece 1997:7). The bossa nova style was the result.

Though popular throughout Brazil, it took the release of the award-winning film, *Black Orpheus* in 1959 (with songs by many of the aforementioned musicians) to really get the music launched internationally. Today bossa nova is connected in the U.S., most unfortunately, with cocktail lounges or even dentist offices. It was not always the case. Stan Getz and many other North American and European jazz musicians recognized the quiet, gentle, seductive attraction of the bossa nova and began incorporating it into their club dates and recordings in the early 1960s. Getz, Gilberto, Jobim and Gilberto's wife, Astrud, teamed up in 1964 to record the English-Portuguese duet version of "Girl from Ipanema" (written in 1962 by Moraes and Jobim) which marked the high point for bossa nova. The album went to Number Two on the pop charts—and this just as the Beatles were making history with their dominance of the Top Ten (McGowan 1991:71).

The release of "Girl from Ipanema" coincided, unhappily, with the beginning of a 20-year long military dictatorship in Brazil. Some musicians and intellectuals critical of the regime accused bossa nova of being in bed with the dictatorship. The escapist, romantic, 'sun, sea and sand' orientation of the music made people complacent, the critics charged. Bossa nova filled the minds of its listeners with romantically inconsequential thoughts.

Things are never as simple as they first appear. The case against bossa nova proves it. Without rehearsing all of the details here, let me just say that bossa nova arrived in reaction to Hollywood-dominated/Carmen Miranda images of Brazilian samba in the late 1940s. Thus it deserves to be credited with having restored a more autonomous, more Brazilian music to the nation. Bossa nova musicians established a level of professionalism and control over their music which set a standard that even the new regime could not change, so the defenders argue. Thus the music made it possible for at least some musicians to escape both exile and internal drudgery by offering them an alternative as relatively free, professional performers. On another level, bossa nova also came to stand for a kind of harmonization of the self and nature, a sort of integration between the music and the self and the eternal rhythms of the landscape in what was a quite progressive ecological model for the time. The music continuously reproduces a lyrical and melodic image of a community at peace, bound by love and harmony. Witness the fact that Tom Jobim spent all of his life battling to defend the last areas of original forests along the Brazilian coast. This was not by accident. His commitment, it could be argued, flowed in part out of his bossa nova, 'sun, sea and sand' music (Treece 1997:7-11).

MÚSICA POPULAR BRASILEIRA (MPB)

The bossa nova era proved to be short-lived. By the mid-1960s a large number of strident young musicians appeared to take over the country's music scene by storm. They specialized in mixing typically Brazilian compelling melodies and rich harmonies. Some of them devised defiantly aggressive message lyrics while others strove to create more poetic, intelligent, or uniquely beautiful songs. Of course they were also shaped by the oppressiveness of the military dictatorship. As trade unionist and opposition politicians were silenced, students, journalists, and musicians became the voice of conscience in Brazil (McGowen 1991:77-78).

As early as 1964, Bahia had solidified its position as the breeding ground for these new MPB stars. Such famous performers as Gal Costa, Gilberto Gil, Tom Zé, and Caetano Veloso all hailed from around the northeast. They spearheaded the new cultural charge against the dictators during the mid-1960s. The regime responded by promoting apolitical rock groups to draw attention away from their MPB critics, and by using prison or exile as punishments when that didn't work.

Many in the MPB movement fought back musically by instigating a return to Brazil's roots. They would resist against the electrified rock music of the regime with a revalorization of acoustic instruments and the Afro-Brazilian cultural origins of the people.

Baden Powell, an Afro-Brazilian bossa nova guitarist raised in the *favelas* of Rio de Janeiro, embodied this fresh movement. His name became synonymous with the new Afro-samba style which subordinated melody, lyrics, and harmony to the rhythms of *candomblé* and *capoeira* (Treece 1997:20). The idea behind the new style was to create a new sense of communal identity around older religious and regional forms of community. Since the peasants of the rural ranches and the poor of the urban *favelas* were the ones who suffered most under the dictatorship, their musical traditions would be adopted and celebrated in musical acts of defiant resistance. Equally important was the idea of uniting Brazilians by creating a popular musical identity out of a blend of traditions, rhythms and styles.

Since so many performers hailed from the northeast, not surprisingly, many of the newly discovered country and folk sounds came from there. The Bahian regionalist musicians collectively put out an album in 1968 called *Tropicália ou Panis et Circensis*, and from that the movement became known as Tropicália. Their music, as Treece (1997:26) describes it, was a chaotic blend of "rural and urban, local and international, traditional and modern sources, such as electrified rock, bossa nova and rural folksong." They shocked national audiences gathered live or in front of televisions to watch them perform during the national song competitions that had become a fixture of Brazil in the 1960s. Gilberto Gil provoked outrage by mounting the stage at the 1968 national song festival wearing African clothing. Caetano Veloso followed by shocking the assembled crowd with his "libertarian rock" musical number, "É Proibido Proibir" (Forbidden to Forbid) (Treece 1997:26). He appeared backed by a rock band known as Os Mutantes who were wearing plastic clothes. He never managed to finish the song.

Gilberto Gil, Caetano Veloso and others did manage to irritate the military regime. The generals had intensified their oppressive authority during 1968 in any case and so it was not surprising when both were arrested without being charged in 1969. They then fled to England soon after where they lived until returning to Brazil in 1972.

The Tropicália movement died with the 1960s, though both Gil and Veloso carried on during the 1970s. Gil went in the direction of rediscovering his Afro-Brazilian roots by first becoming interested in one of the Bahian *Carnival* afoxé dance troupes, Filhos de Gandhi. He then made a pilgrimage to Africa where he met with Fela Kuti and other musicians. His 1977 album *Refavela* included an homage to the *candomblé* god Xangô, as well as music for his adopted *Carnival* marching troupe (McGowan 1991:90-91). In the 1980s he became a firm backer of the re-Africanization movement in Bahia (which we will take up in a moment).

The end of the military regime in the middle 1980s coincided with the rise in urban Rio and São Paolo of rap groups. Rio de Janeiro went in the direction of a more relaxed hip hop/funk style while São Paulo adopted more hardcore rap. One rap group in particular, Os Racionais MC's, became nationally popular. They patterned themselves after Ice T and took their inspiration from his CD, *Home Invasion*. The use of foreign ideas and images to both express a confident, powerful persona while also crying out against local abuses proved to be an easy translation to make because the *favelas* of São Paulo shared many of the characteristics of American ghettoes. The group's hit song came in 1994 with "Fin de semana no parque" (a weekend in the park) from the album of the same name. The song lashed out defiantly at white Brazil while also chronicling fights with the police and the generally miserable conditions of the city's black poor (Magaldi 1999:314).

The popularity of the aggressive rap of São Paulo has disturbed many leftist intellectuals and activists in Brazil who are made uncomfortable by the adoption of "foreign" music, clothing styles, etc., as defiant badges of local identity. This says less about the local youth's interest in being associated with such symbols of economic and political power and more about the still very paternalistic nature of racial politics in Brazil. The educated and the elders apparently still feel the need to speak for the little people and are made uneasy when they don't seem to listen or don't seem to need guidance anymore (Magaldi 1999:314).

The same wholesale adoption of (mainly) American musical styles exemplified by São Paulo rap was repeated in the 1990s with the development of Brazilian hard rock. This new breed of rockers, whether reggae inclined or into thrash metal, reject being identified as overtly political. Their identification is first and foremost with the youth of the nation. And like Brazilian rappers, they see no problem in adopting foreign styles into their own codes. So much is this the case with rockers that the majority of those with hit singles are now singing in English.[16] At least one of these groups, Sepultura, has achieved international exposure as an example of "Brazilian rock." Sepultura grew more and more politicized with each album during the early 1990s. One in particular stands out. Called *Chaos A.D.*, it contains songs dedicated to Brazilian Indians ("Kaiowas"), against the police murder of prisoners in a São Paulo prison ("Manifest"), against biotech abuses ("Biotech is Godzilla"), against war ("Territory"), and so forth. A sampling of the words from "Biotech is Godzilla" are fairly representative of the group's political stance: Rio Summit, '92/Street people kidnapped/ Hid from view/"To save the earth" (Sepultura, *Chaos A. D.* Roadrunner. RR 8859-2. 1994).

SAMBA IN BAHIA

One final but very significant contemporary development needs to be mentioned. We have not said anything so far about the *Carnival* practices in other Brazilian regions that have developed through the decades. The procession in Rio has come to be almost synonymous with *Carnival* in the minds of foreigners. That isn't the case in Brazil. São Paolo has its own smaller *Carnival* and so does Salvador, Bahia, where in recent years the festivities have been significantly "re-Africanized" with the coming to dominance of *axé* music.

Axé takes its name from the Yoruba word "*Àse*" which means "generative power," and refers to the ability to get things done, to bring something into existence. It is associated with certain *candomblé* ceremonies as well as with the general Yoruba philosophy of the force possessed by all forms of life (Drewal 1999:152). In common parlance over the last two decades it has become synonymous with the re-Africanization movement in Bahia, particularly with the rise of the new Afro-Brazilian music made popular by the *Carnival* parade groups from the black quarters of the city of Salvador.[17]

In the late nineteenth century and beginning decades of the twentieth century the charge that something in Brazil was too "Africanized" was a criticism. Between 1905 and 1914 Afro-Brazilian costumes and dances, such as the *batuques* mentioned earlier, were actually banned. Black Brazilians in Salvador responded defiantly in the next decade by creating marching groups based on African associations. These were called *afoxés* and were, according to Fryer (2000:24), "semi-religious Carnival groups composed of *candomblé* devotees wearing white tunics of West African style and singing songs in Yoruba."

In the 1970s the so-called "re-Africanization" movement kicked into high gear in Bahia and the *afoxés* parading groups were reborn. The city of Salvador was a natural center for such a cultural rebirth, claims the leader of one of the bloco-afro/*afoxés*, João Jorge Santos of the group Olodum. The city's population is over 70% black or mixed blood yet its city council is 91% white. In the city and country at large black males earn only 41% of the salary white males earn, so racial and economic tensions have been simmering for some time.[18]

The first groups came right out of the poor black districts of Salvador and reenergized black youth with their playing style. They reportedly captured the imagination of the whole town. They revived the importance of the drum as the centerpiece of the music while adding smaller, bongo-type drums called timbales that were borrowed from the Cuban and Puerto Rican music scenes. The Bahian *Carnival* music is today much more frenetic and forceful than in the past, thanks to the new emphasis on drums, which, not coincidentally, are a symbol in and of themselves of pride in

Africa. Africa is understood to be the motherland of dancing and drumming and learning to play them and to dance well are acts of respect for those African rhythmic roots.

The new *afoxés* also improvise on traditional *candomblé* rhythms for the marches, mixing them in with the basic samba beats—and sometimes with the rhythms of merengue, reggae, and salsa as well (the music which results bears the name "*axé* music" which, for many, is synonymous with an Afro-reggae hybrid music). This revalorization of the heritage of *candomblé* during the Catholic Lenten festival of *Carnival* is another way in which Afro-Brazilians in Salvador reaffirm their attachment to their African origins, as opposed to—or just as often, in hybrid combination with—the dominant colonial European heritage of Brazil. They have seized on this most important of Brazilian festivals to rework it to give it a distinctive black "feel" and to reinvent it as a celebration of the resistance and resilience of African traditions in the New World.[19]

VIDEOS ACCOMPANYING

Remember, the actual video lectures can be accessed at the following url:http://oregonstate.edu/media/classes/index.php?className=anth210

Scroll down under the "Classes on Demand" heading and select "ANTH210: Comparative Cultures."

Video 4

This video is based on a documentary film about Afro-Brazilian culture. The first section we saw concerned the samba. This section claims that there are two kinds of samba. One is the favela (shantytown) samba, based among the urban poor of Rio de Janeiro. This music is based on the everyday emotions, concerns, and life of the poor. The other kind, we called the Carnival samba, is the co-opted form organized and run by mafia-like organizations working more or less for the elite and the government.

The first overhead we saw summarized this division. We stated that:

"Carnival Samba" is characterized by four things:

1. Cooptation of samba by carnival festivities

2. Schools controlled by mafia and government

3. Schools control carnival

4. Schools promote costumes; marching; elite control; mindless but costly entertainment (bread and circuses)

We then went back to the movie to illustrate the extent to which the poor favelas are the real home and source of inspiration for Afro-Brazilian culture. The samba singer being highlighted discussed the extent to which class divisions poison and divide Brazilian society. The black Brazilians are overwhelmingly located among the ranks of the unemployed and the working class. The middle class works mainly for the government which, until recently, was a military dictatorship. Regardless of class background, all Brazilians are united by their love of music.

The second overhead we saw identified the characteristics of the second type of samba, called: "Favela Samba"

1. lyrics reflect shantytown (favela) life and concerns

2. Sambas more likely to protest oppression, class and racial inequalities

3. Afro-Brazilian culture based around favela samba acts as an affirmation of black Brazilian culture & a basis of identity and group solidarity

The next film clip took us back to the rural samba origins in the villages of the north and east of the country. The villagers from these areas were the ones who migrated to the cities and formed the favela slum dwellers who developed the samba. The clip shows an old African dance that probably formed the basis of the modern samba.

The next overhead listed the characteristics of African music which we had talked about earlier and which characterized the circle dance of the Brazilian village.

Village Circle Dance demonstrates how much African music is:

1. Communal

2. Rhythmic

3. Participatory

4. improvisational

(focus on candomblé)

The film clip demonstrated the extraordinary extent to which originally African gods are still believed in by Brazilians of all classes and colors. This is particularly true in the case of the god of the sea, Yemanja. The next segment of the film showed an initiation rite of a girl into an congregation of candomblé practitioners. Interestingly enough, the priest in charge of the ceremony spoke in an African language during it all. The film suggested that candomblé drumming forms the foundation of all black Brazilian music, and that candomblé communities form a very important bond and source of identity for its members.

The first overhead in this segment listed characteristics of candomblé

1. appeals to mainly black Brazilians

2. incorporates African and Western beliefs

3. priests chant in an African language (Yoruba)

4. believers are bound together by rituals

5. believers adopt special god who possesses them, watches over them

6. music is viatl to rituals; provides solidarity and sense of belonging

(focus on capoeira)

The film clip used in this segment illustrated the beauty and complexity of the form of martial arts dance called "capoeira." The dance was developed during slavery times to disguise slave conditioning and martial arts activities which, naturally, would have been seen as a threat to the slaveholding plantation society that dominated Brazil. The African-derived instrument, called the berimbau, was central to the performance.

The overhead in this session listed the following traits of capoeira:

1. way of disguising slave preparations for physical resistance

2. they trained under the guise of dancing

3. berimbau instrument used to accompany the dances

(focus on Salvador, Bahia, capital of the northeast and capital of black Brazil)

The movie segment used in this section is mainly an interview with one of Salvador's most famous musicians, Gilberto Gil, who, since the 1960s, has been at the forefront of the celebration of Brazil's African heritage.

The last overhead lists some of the important aspects of Salvador to the music of Brazil. Salvador, Bahia:

1. capital of Black Brazil

2. home of Afro-Brazilian cultural revival

3. protest music common

4. Music plays an important role in everyday life

Video 5

This video returns to the beginning of the Chapter Two text to take up the question of why and how Europe "discovered" the New World.

The first overhead lists the following:

The "Discovery" of Brazil

Question: If Spain and Portugal were not ahead of other nations, why did the Europeans conquer the New World and not the Africans of Asians?

Standard European Answer:

Europeans were better navigators; more industrious; more curious; smarter

Better Answer:

Asia was too far away, Europe was closer; wind and sea currents aided Europeans; European fishermen provided information; West Africans traded inland; North Africans were under assault

We then turned and looked, one by one, at the reasons behind the European victory in the race to win mastery of the high seas. We saw that during the 15th century, the Chinese, under Admiral Cheng-Ho, were actually more nautically adventurous than their European counterparts. Another thing we said was important to remember was that Europeans were not more technologically savvy than other peoples. In reality, no one region or society had superior navigational technology at the time, as witnessed to by the astrolab displayed in the overhead, which is reprinted below:

Mariner's Astrolabe

Used to determine latitude of a ship at sea by measuring the noon altitude of the sun or the meridian altitude of a known star. In the northern hemisphere the North (Polar) Star sits roughly at the North Pole so the degrees it is above the horizon marks the degrees above the equator of the observer's position.

Wind Currents

We then showed an overhead which illustrated the wind currents which hindered European discoverers from heading around Africa (moving north to south) but facilitated the movement (from east to west) the Old to the New World. The two biggest obstacles to European movement south were the relatively calm windless belt known as the Doldrums, and then farther south the S.E. Tradewinds which moved up along the African coast and made circumnavigation very difficult. To avoid those winds, Cabral, the European discoverer of Brazil, had pushed way out in the Atlantic. He went so far that he mistakenly bumped into the New World.

Northern Direction of West African Trade around 1500

This overhead demonstrated one of the important reasons why the West African populations did not compete for mastery of the Atlantic at the time; namely, all of their trade contacts were overland to the north and east. Ocean-based trade was of minor concern to them.

The Ottoman Empire

This overhead suggested that the other potential competitors to the Portuguese and the Spanish, the North Africans, were at the time under growing threat from the expanding Ottoman Empire, as well as under threat from the Spanish. So they did not participate in the race to map the oceans.

Reasons African Musical Roots Are so Strong in Brazilian Music

1. Demographic impact of slave population

2. Late date of slave abolition

3. Catholic religious syncretism

4. Importance of quilombos

5. Resistance of slaves to masters' culture

6. Expansive, creative energy of African musical cultures

We then saw a series of overheads illustrating each of these points.

1. The map of slave destinations illustrated the point that the movement of slaves to Brazil was much greater than to any other New World destination. Around 3,646,000 slaves were imported directly from Africa into Brazil (compared to 399,000 imported directly into the USA). Why were the slaves needed? Sugar production!

   The illustration and discussion of the vital importance of the sugar cane plantation economy to Brazil (and the world) and its dependence on African slaves (as opposed to Native Indian slaves who were killed off by Old World diseases which the African slaves were already immune to).

   We then showed an illustration related to the growth and development of the Brazilian coffee industry.

   A map of Brazil showed where most of the slaves arrived; namely, Recife, Salvador, and Rio de Janeiro (by the end of the 19th century, the population of Brazil was about half black, that is, directly from Africa or of African descent).

2. The Brazilians were the last people to abolish slavery in the New World (1888) so Africans were being imported throughout the 19th century, thus African cultural influences were still fresh right through the 19th century.

3. Catholic religious **syncretism**: the mixing of various belief systems; creating something new out of the elements of several other belief systems. (We mentioned the way Rome conquered Greece and then created many of its own gods from Greek models borrowed into Roman beliefs. We also showed an overhead that illustrated the way the Greek zodiac was formed by borrowings from the earlier Babylonian civilization which also had a zodiac.)
   We then saw some pictures of the way, in Brazil, that African beliefs were mixed with Catholicism (Yemanja being present at an alter along with the Madonna and Child, for example). Or we mentioned that many of the African gods and Christian saints were inter-twined into one spiritual persona.

4. We then showed an illustration of the Brazilian film about the quilombos, or runaway slave communities, in Brazil. Zumbi, the last leader of the most famous quilombo, called Palmares, was really a leader of a whole state populated by runaway slaves. His legend has grown with time to the extent that he is now a hero for many black Brazilians because he successfully resisted bondage and oppression. We mentioned that the quilombos attracted Indian and white people as well as slaves. They were all seeking freedom and dignity. Within a few decades the colonies of runaways were dominated by native born descendants of slaves. The armies under the command of the white European elites eventually destroyed the last quilombo in 1690, almost a hundred years after they were first established. But the spirit of Zumbi lives on, almost reaching immortal status today among the poor.

5. The general resistance to the master's culture was discussed using the three examples we've already been studying, namely, samba, candomblé, and capoeira. We discussed how they have used these, particularly candomblé, as sources and means of organizing for the struggle to

achieve economic and political rights on the part of poor, black Brazilians. The neighborhood communities developed around candomblé meeting houses provide a foundation of black Brazilian identity. The music, particularly of candomblé and capoeira, provides a way of keeping alive an oppositional culture. The musical performances maintain ties to the ancestral African roots. To be involved in these performance practices helps keep alive potent alternative, oppositional symbols and thus a sense of belonging to an oppositional culture and community. The final example we used was a picture of a samba malandro figure, a kind of urban wolf who embodies a kind of heroic defiance of elite society and its norms, which the malandro flaunts. Just as importantly, the malandro figure stands up against the establishment, against forms of victimization of the poor.

6. Finally, we discussed the expansive, creative energy of African musical culture wherever it's found and in whatever form. We suggested that African-inspired music in the New World may have formed the most important musical influences of the 20th century. It has been found to resonate around the world in part because of its importance as a cultural symbol of defiance and affirmation which taps into people's desire to be free of economic and political oppression.

Video 6

Jennifer Krause interview. She teaches Brazilian guitar and percussion.

She began by telling us the story of the most recorded song in history, "The Girl from Ipanema," which is a song by Tom Jobim, the famous bossa nova composer.

She then suggested some possible explanations for the origins of music, particularly its origin as part of work routines or any repetitive task. Of course we also have in the form of our voice, an impressive instrument always with us.

She then discussed with us the samba. She said that it had African origins, began as a dance based on belly bouncing. She mentioned that there are many variations on the samba: the "singing samba," (Samba cancao) and the "samba batucada" (percussive samba) are two examples. In general, the samba is based on a 2/2 beat, but these beats are broken down into more intricate parts.

She next showed us how the various samba instruments operate and then played us an example of a carnival samba troupe (100 people!) playing a samba. It was a call and response-based tune. The whistle was also pointed out as the way changes are signaled to the whole group.

Jennifer played "The Girl from Ipanema" to give us a sense of what bossa nova was about. We then played a song called "Felicidade" which combined samba and bossa nova music within it. We could then easily hear the shift from the more percussive samba to the quieter bossa nova.

In the next section we talked about the list of African influences on Brazilian music listed in the chapter 2 reading. The overhead showed the following:

African influences on Brazilian music

1. the frequency of six-note scales with a flatted seventh-note (a feature of the "blues scale" of the U.S.) Jennifer mentioned that this could have come down from North America (the blues) via African-American music spreading throughout the world as easily as having come directly from Africa.

2. the common use of certain rhythmic phrases[1] Jennifer mentioned that you can see identical percussive patterns in African and Brazilian music.

3. Call-and-response singing involving a single solo line (often improvised) followed by a short, unvarying chorus

4. breaking up of the neat melodic framework that European music uses Jennifer thought that the polyrhythms of African and Brazilian music do resist being neatly written in the European-style of writing down music. It's not that it breaks the European framework, it just developed independently of it.

5. The *umbrigada*, or belly-bounce, in dancing
   Both African and Brazilian belly movements are central to many dances.

6. using a large number of musical instruments, including various drums known collectively as *atabaque*
   Yes, both African and Brazilian ensembles use lots of drums and other percussive noise makers

7. the great importance of drums generally in Brazilian dances and their frequent function as organizers of the choreography
   Jennifer thought this was probably the case, as many dancers basic steps are based on the drum rhythms being played. The drums keep the time and act as unofficial directors

8. dramatic dances
   (we skipped it)

9. a certain rather nasal tone of singing
   Nasal tones exist in Portuguese, the language of Brazil. Jennifer wasn't familiar with any African languages, but it is the case that nasal tones resonate it the nasal passages and are important as vocal additions to the music.

10. importance of wind instruments (may be of both African and Portuguese influence)
    Jennifer was unfamiliar with this aspect.

11. popularity of bowed string instruments (fiddle especially, though, again, this could be of both West African and Portuguese origin)
    Jennifer was also unfamiliar with the role of early bowed string instruments

12. vocal (not instrumental) harmonies based on parallel thirds: when group singing is not in unison or near-unison (an African form called "heterophony") it most frequently uses parallel thirds with one voice singing more or less the same tune a third below the other
    (skipped during interview)

13. use of frequently syncopated and more complex rhythmic approach (than Portuguese music) with displaced accentuations and cross-rhythms against the percussion
    Jennifer thought that this applied. But then she disagreed with calling them "displaced." They are just accents. Only in reference to what a Euro-American musician might call them could they be fairly labeled "displaced." Jennifer then demonstrated the difference by playing intermittent beats between the 1 and the 2 in first, the way a North American would do it, and then playing it the way a Brazilian would do it.

We then went back and summarized using the following overheads:

Possible Origins of Music

1. Developed out of work rhythms

2. Developed as a form of communication?

Differences between Samba & Bossa Nova
Bossa nova:

1. Has a slower tempo (usually)

2. Places greater emphasis on lyrical content

3. Uses more complex melodies

4. Centered more around the guitar

NOTES

1. Notes from Blaut (1993). What follows is excerpted from pages 181-184.
2. Blaut (1993:181) mentions that, "Two non-European examples are well known: Cheng Ho's voyages to India and Africa between 1417 and 1433, and an Indian voyage around the Cape of Good Hope and apparently some 2,000 miles westward into the Atlantic circa 1420." In Gavin Menzies' (2002) study of the great Chinese voyages of the early 15th century, he claims that an enormous Chinese armada actually circumnavigated the globe. All evidence was destroyed by the ascendance to power of the "land-loving" Mandarins over the "nautical-minded" eunuchs, the two powers nearest the emperor at the time that were battling to determine the future direction of Chinese foreign policy.
3. See the entertaining account of the spice trade in *The Scents of Eden* by Charles Corn (1998). On page xxiv, Corn suggests that the spice trade did as much if not more than New World bullion to make Europe into a world power.
4. This and what follows is taken mainly from Burns (1993).
5. This is the claim of Schreiner (1993:9).
6. The sources for slaves refer only to Salvador, Bahia. Apparently records concerning the slave trade for other parts of Brazil were destroyed during the latter half of the nineteenth century. See Fryer (2000:5).

    Curtin, in *Why People Move: Migration in African History* (1995:14-15), mentions that western Africa may have become the dominant source of slaves for the European slave trade for two reasons (besides proximity to the New World). First, there was a tradition in Western Africa that people defeated in battle were customarily enslaved by the victors. Thus an internal slave trade existed in the region already. Second, population density in western Africa was light so there was little pressure on the land. In fact, land had no value as a productive commodity. What mattered was the labor to work the land. So slaves were the most available source of revenue, a more important investment than land. As Curtin (1995:15) puts it,

    > In the traditions of Medieval Europe, land was key to productive capability, and ownership of land often included the control over a labor force to work it. In contemporaneous Africa, land was owned, but it was owned corporatively by kinship groups or by the state. It was not always plentiful, but it was readily available at a low price or no price to those who could make use of it—that is, to those who owned the labor to work it. In Europe, then, land ownership tended to imply easy control over labor, while in Africa ownership of labor tended to make for easy control over land.

7. I have taken them verbatim from Roberts (1972), who is something like the Grand Ol' Man of studies of African influence on New World music.
8. See Roberts (1972:73) for the notation to the phrase in question.
9. Abbey Newport, who was a student at OSU during the 1999-2000 academic year; who grew up in Salvador, Bahia; who gave many good suggestions for improving this chapter; and whose mother is Brazilian (whew!) said that she had been told a different origin story for *capoeira*. She had heard that the slaves caught fighting were punished by the overseers so when one approached, they transformed their fighting into dancing to disguise their activities.
10. The three sections included here follow closely the discussion provided in Fryer (2000). Other sources will be noted as they are included.
11. This is the claim made in McGowen and Pessanha (1991:23). Abbey Newport added the observation that today in Salvador membership in a *candomblé* circle is no longer much if any impediment to one's social standing. Many of those in bohemian/intellectual/entertainment circles attend services on occasion (Gilberto Gil, for instance) and many of those are whites. All things African are quite in vogue right now and so the stigma once attached has diminished considerably, she reports.
12. See Espírito Santo França's article, "Candomblé and Community" in the interesting collection of radical activists' work, *Black Brazil: Culture, Identity, and Social Mobilization*, edited by Crook and Johnson (1999:53-58).
13. Fryer (2000:31-32) takes this long quote from Lewis (1992:xxiii, 1, 13).

14. Or as another example, the strong macho current running through a good number of samba lyrics would seem to militate against any easy association of samba with protest. See the in-depth analysis of the all-male preserve of samba lyrics in Shaw (1999).

15. Shaw (1999:5-6) says that between 1904 and 1906 over 600 buildings were torn down to make way for a grand avenue running right through what had once been a poor inner city section of the town. The destruction was meant to "civilize" Rio. It marked the definitive move of all poor blacks to the *favelas* on the outskirts of the city. This kind of urban apartheid proved quite successful: by the end of the 1940s the whole of Rio de Janeiro was 27% black while its *favelas* were 95% black. (The following discussion of the *malandro* is taken from Shaw's [1999] book.)

16. Abbey Newport claims that groups like Sepultura really appeal only to the white middle class youth market in Brazil because they are the only ones who understand the English lyrics.

17. Drewal (1999:152-153) states that *axé* as a concept has been fetishized these last few years to the point where it is used to sell cosmetics as well as to "sell" the city of Salvador which welcomes tourists to its Carnival with billboards plastered with the "greetings and blessings of AXÉ."

18. The group Olodum has a web site (www.e-net.com.br/olodum) with a series of Jorges Santo's writings as well as articles about their music and social programs

19. This final section on the re-Africanization of the Bahia Carnival is derived from Fryer (2000:23-26).

THE ROOTS OF JAMAICAN RASTA AND REGGAE

Jamaica is a islan',
but is not I lan'[1]
(Joe Ruglass)

Every time I hear the crack of the whip
My blood runs cold.
I remember on the slave ship
How they brutalize my very soul.[2]
(Bob Marley)

If you look through any library stacks for books on Jamaica written before independence in 1962, you will find a majority of them highlight the island's natural beauty, human diversity, or engaging folklore. Look on the internet today, for that matter, and you will see that most web sites promote the touristic image of Jamaica: the island as haven for cruise ships and newlyweds come to sample the north shore's sun and fun.

Oddly enough, this is not the image of Jamaica most of us are familiar with. We know Jamaica through its music, particularly reggae, and that music is shot full of references, not to palm trees and coral reefs, but to the horrors of slavery or the promise of an African salvation. That music speaks of Rasta and ganja and oppression. Bob Marley, the recognized superstar of Jamaican music, sings of Jamaica as Babylon or else as the concrete jungle.

This is not the image of Jamaica that the Chamber of Commerce wants to publicize. Nonetheless, this is what reggae has given us. It has exposed the underside of life in this Caribbean "paradise." In the process it has also altered the way music is played in the world, both in terms of the unmistakable reggae style, with its accent on the second and fourth beats, as well as in its commitment to music as a form of protest, as a kind of resistance, as a call to the righteous to "get up, stand up for your rights!" as the song goes.

To begin to understand what contemporary Jamaican music is all about, we must first go back and try to comprehend the enormous impact slavery and colonialism have had on black Jamaican lives. That heritage more than any other has shaped the experiences of which reggae now sings. The legacy of racial and class oppression saturates Jamaican consciousness; so too do the struggles against it, of which the music forms a vital part.

JAMAICAN ORIGINS

The original Arawak Indian inhabitants of Jamaica disappeared within 50 years of Columbus' siting of the island in 1494. More accurately, they were exterminated by the Spanish invaders who brought disease and destruction in their wake. Those Indians who had not been murdered or had not died of some imported illness were enslaved and then worked to death building Spanish settlements, growing Spanish food, and working in Spanish mines (Abrahams 1957:8).

Jamaica became known during its second century of existence as a pirates' cove, especially the wild north coast and in the bay behind the new British fort at Port Royal, built when the British seized the island from the Spanish in 1655. The contest between the two emerging world powers was at base economic. However, the British had been defeated by the Spanish in the Caribbean on several occasions (St. Kitts in 1629, Tortuga in 1637, Santa Cruz in 1650), so the chroniclers used the excuse of inhumane treatment of British captives to justify seizing Jamaica (Gardner 1909:29).

Jamaica sits conveniently just west of the windward passage between Haiti and Cuba in such as way that from the island's location, high seas marauders could harass the trade moving between Europe and Central America, as well as between North and South America. Most of the harassment was carried out by pirates working loosely for the British against rival Spanish shipping. The pirates were given what was known as a commission by the British, which meant their plundering of Spanish ships was technically legal. Once armed with the commission, they were known as "privateers" instead of "pirates," and they would bring the ships they had stolen into Port Royal to be sold to the highest bidder.

Interestingly, the long-term economic vitality of Jamaica proved to be tied up with piracy, for it was thanks to the loot stolen by the pirates that the island was able to develop tobacco, cotton, and sugar plantations. The capital needed to buy the land and expensive equipment came from wealthy British merchants. They bought the pirated gold and silver cheap, sent it back to England to be sold at a much higher price, and then used the proceeds to buy the land, slaves, and machinery needed to run plantations. In fact, several of the most successful British pirates, such as the famous Henry Morgan, actually plowed their profits back into the island and became Jamaican plantation owners (Pawson and Buisseret 1975:31).

The sugar plantations needed masses of laborers to grow and harvest the cane as well as to operate the crushing mills, the boiling houses, curing houses, and distilleries (Campbell 1987:16). With the killing off of the local Arawak Indians, the labor needs of the island's new elite quickly outstripped local supply, so they turned to the importation of West and Central African slaves. Hundreds of thousands of Africans came to Jamaica in bondage over the next three centuries.

Horace Campbell, in his fascinating work on the political significance of Rastafari in Jamaica, *Rasta and Resistance*, makes the important point that Jamaican resistance to exploitation and injustice began during the slave crossings from Africa to the Caribbean, known as the Middle Passage. The slaves, who were kept below deck stacked against each other like sardines, once they were allowed up on the decks, would often attack the crew or even throw themselves overboard to avoid enslavement. So rebellious were many of the slaves that it took normally from one to three years of constant punishment to "season" a slave and make him docile enough to work in the fields. Again, many refused, to such an extent that between one-quarter and one-third of all slaves died during the "seasoning" process (Campbell 1987:14-15). Women, too, played a key role in early slave resistance by refusing to bring the next generation of slaves into this world. They did what they could in order to make sure the their children would not go through what they had experienced. As a consequence, the slave labor supply needed constant replenishment with new slaves from Africa because the already enslaved population refused to reproduce itself.

The Jamaican society brought into existence by the plantation economy was a highly stratified one. White planters and white colonial administrators sat atop the social pyramid, field slaves formed its foundation. In between were located the mixed race offspring of the planters and female slaves. These middle strata, called "the coloreds," that is, the mulatto groups, were usually freemen who filled the ranks of the professions and other low-level managerial and administrative functions in society. Below them were the free Blacks who had the status of the coloreds but were more socially despised for being Black (Chevannes 1994:3). On the plantations themselves there were divisions between the overseers, slave foremen, the slave skilled craftsmen, and house slaves on the upper rungs of society, and as already mentioned, the field slaves on the very lowest rungs of the social ladder.

The field slave worked 18 hours a day. On top of that he had to spend the time necessary to grow most of his own food on a small plot of land allocated to his family. The plantation was not required to feed him (Campbell 1987:17).

Besides the killing pace of the field work and the often times lethal levels of punishment meted out for the slightest rule infractions, slaves also had to live with extreme levels of psychological degradation. In the early days of slavery, poor white indentured servants lived lives not unlike African slaves and often worked in the fields beside them. However, by the middle of the eighteenth century, blackness was becoming associated in the European mind with inferiority and such ideas of racial superiority and inferiority were coalescing into an ideology that justified slavery as the "natural" state of human affairs. White Europeans, whether rich or poor, came to believe that they were meant to rule over Africans and that Africans were created to serve whites.

The extreme social divisions that developed around the plantation economy proved to be crucial to the development of Rastafarianism. As Campbell points out:

> The existence of a repressive culture which harmonized the economic exploitation
> of Black people with the idea of white supremacy prevented the constitution of a
> Jamaican national consciousness, hence the Black man's consciousness as an
> African constituted the centerpoint of his identity. It is this identification with
> Africa which laid the foundations for the doctrine of Rastafari—an ideology which
> combined the resistance against oppression with an underlying love for the
> freedom and emancipation of Africa and African peoples. (Campbell 1987:19)

The African population in Jamaica could not look upon the plantation owners as their fellow Jamaicans any more than the owners could look upon the slaves as their fellow islanders. As the quoted poem that opens this chapter makes clear, slaves back then and Rastas today are alienated from their own country. They long to reunite with the original homeland, with Zion, that is, with Africa. That is why the idea of repatriation back to Africa has historically been so central to Rastafarianism. This is also, of course, why the images and texts from the Bible that comment on the exile of the Jews have resonated so powerfully within Rasta and Reggae circles. They too long to escape from the modern Babylon and return to their Zion, as the lyrics from the much-covered Melodians 1970 rock-steady ballad makes clear:

> By the rivers of Babylon
> Where we lay down
> And there we wept
> When we remembered Zion

One small step on the road of return to Zion was taken by some of the very earliest slaves brought in bondage to Jamaica. During the takeover of the island by the British in 1655, many of these first slaves managed to escape into the central highlands of the island. They became known as the Maroons. They established free communities which gave sanctuary to runaway slaves. They also carried out night raids on the plantations and helped lead several slave revolts. A full blown rebellion developed into what became known as the Maroon War between 1729-1739. It was led by a Maroon commander, Cudjoe, who managed to carry out so many guerilla-style raids and so successfully coordinated the actions of many of the remote Maroon communities that the British sued for peace in 1739. The terms of the treaty gave the Maroons self-government over their towns, the right to fish and hunt unmolested, the right to own their own lands, and the right to be free of British harassment and attempts to enslave them. In exchange, the Maroons had to stop harboring runaway slaves (Campbell 1987:20-21).

Those still under slavery developed their own more subtle means of resisting white domination. One of the most interesting forms of cultural resistance was the development of folk heroes in slave oral literature. The king of all such characters in Jamaica evolved from the West African Ashanti spider/trickster figure who came to be known as Anansi (or Anancy). The slaves could identify with him because he played the fool in front of his superiors in order to outwit them. His exploits were legendary, even involving battles with nonexistent tigers and lions. He escaped from every trap imaginable and never missed the chance to put his adversaries in their place. Just as importantly, Anansi despised work and loved leisure and depended on his quick wits and sharp tongue to get him out of a jam. He was the quintessential popular hero who showed time and again that the common people could triumph.[3]

The spiritual needs of slave society had been met within the community until the latter part of the eighteenth century. At that time Baptist missionaries fanned out onto the plantations and began Christianizing the slaves in earnest. The white planters and overseers did not initially approve such missionary work. They were opposed to any movement which sought to make the slaves literate (Campbell 1987:24).

The planters had also fought earlier against slaves practicing African religions. They passed laws against the performance of various African religious ceremonies as well as against the use of drums.

Slaves too resisted the spread of Christianity until former slave preachers began circulating amongst them winning over their trust. These freedmen were literate and so gained prestige amongst the slaves by being able to read and report on events happening all over the globe. This became especially important during the run up to total emancipation during the first two decades of the nineteenth century. At that time all of the slaves depended on the literate few, usually preachers, to keep them abreast of anti-slavery agitation back in London.

The Black preachers played an even more active role in the resistance in that they also began organizing slave revolts. They alone were allowed to wander from plantation to plantation. One such lay preacher, Sam Sharpe, made the whites believe that he was leading prayer meetings. Actually he used the religious gatherings as a time to agitate for revolt. His "missionizing" finally paid off in the form of the 1831 Jamaica slave revolt in which 20,000 slaves rose up and, using conch shells and drums, spread the word of the rebellion throughout the island (Campbell 1987:28-29).

Slavery was officially abolished in all British possessions on August 1, 1834, thanks mainly to the slaves' continued efforts to resist through rebelling and running away. The rise of the anti-slavery movement back in Britain spurred on the emancipation process. The development of the sugar beet industry in Europe proper also played a role for it lessened the European dependence on imported cane sugar from the colonies. The aforementioned 1831 revolt was also sited by the abolitionists in the British Parliament as another of the contributing factors to the ban on slavery throughout the Empire (Holt 1992: 14).

The initial joy of the Jamaican slaves at the announcement was tempered by the fact that their former owners received 20 million British pounds in compensation for their losses while the slaves received nothing. What's worse, the ex-slaves had to go through a four-year mandatory "apprenticeship" before they were completely free (Campbell 1987:31).

Many fled to the Jamaican hills as soon as they were able. A good number took up farming their own individual plots, selling the excess at market, and then working on the plantations to supplement their incomes.

But the plantation economy was slowly grinding to a halt and no other waged labor opportunities were cropping up to take its place. Furthermore, the government passed restrictive laws against vagrancy and loitering aimed at keeping the rural people out of the cities. They also raised taxes in an attempt to make up for the loss of revenue from the sugar industry.

The increasing misery of the common people after emancipation finally exploded in the 1860s into a religious frenzy called "revivalism." The Jamaican poor had by and large practiced African based religions called Myal and Kumina. Onto these bodies they had grafted many Christian religious notions. Let me give you an example of this intermingling as provided by Chevannes (1994:18-19): The dominant Christian route to conversion is through the acquisition of knowledge (transmitted through reading the Bible or taking catechism classes, etc.). The Myal practitioners believed, on the other hand, that the route to god was through possession by the holy spirit. And this, of course, was brought about by means of dancing and music being performed in emotion-packed ceremonies. Myal worshippers even placed John the Baptist above Jesus for a time because he had transformed Jesus by means of baptism, not the other way around. So as you can see, spirit possession became the defining event in their religion. It is interesting to note, parenthetically, that Myal followers also railed against the practice of sorcery and fought against it wherever they could. That set them apart as did their blind devotion to their leaders who they believed to have a special "gift" (Chevannes 1994:19-20).

As the fever of religious revivalism swept through Jamaica in the 1860s, Myal split into what became known as "Zion" and "Pukumina," or "Pokomania" (both going under the name "Revival"). Chevannes (1994:20-21) describes Zion as being more influenced by Christianity, using more of its symbols, depending more on the Bible and staying closer to its core teachings. Pukumina, however, maintained a more African esteem for the powerful spirits that inhabit this world. In Pukumina, spirits were not divided into good and evil, such as in the division represented by the Christian spirit, Satan. Instead all spirits commanded respect.

The Religious Revival of the 1860s finally culminated in another island-wide rebellion. Under the leadership of one Paul Bogle small farmers throughout Jamaica rose up against their landlords and the state. They moved from town to town defying the planter elite. Campbell describes the scene as follows:

> Bogle and his men marched into Morant Bay and on the way they administered the oath and shouted 'Cleave to the Black, color for color,' and that they would kill all white men. Blowing the conch shell as a sign of war and beating the drums, the soldiers of Bogle's army reached the court house, where the planter Baron was trembling as he read the riot act. Before he could finish ordering the police to shoot, Bogle and his men surrounded the vestry. The Baron was killed and his assistants were roasted in the fire which razed the court house. The prisoners, mostly tax defaulters, were set free. (Campbell. 1987:36)

The uprising that accompanied the Revival proved to be very costly. Maroons chose to side with the government against Bogle and played a decisive role in defeating the rebellion. When it was all over, 1,000 rebels were hanged and 400 flogged; all black Haitians in Jamaica were deported; and even the local white assembly was closed down in favor of direct rule from Britain.[4]

In the period after the 1860s, British capital found itself in competition in Jamaica with American firms that bought up sugar plantations and replanted them in bananas. Such capitalist development was spreading throughout the Caribbean. Jamaicans began emigrating to chase that investment. They found work on other islands, they helped clear plantations in Central America, they left to work on the Suez Canal, or they moved to the U.S. to work as agricultural laborers. This pattern of relieving local unemployment via out-migration continues to operate today (Campbell 1987:44).

Those Jamaicans who traveled abroad during the latter half of the nineteenth century and the beginning of the twentieth came into contact with other African communities abroad (the African Diaspora) and learned from them about the great Western imperialist scramble to colonize all of Africa. The most important connections made by Jamaicans abroad may have been those established with Blacks in America where a black Christian religious tradition dating back to the eighteenth century had helped create a strong identification with Africa, particularly Ethiopia. As Campbell puts it, "[A] religious force had developed in the USA which looked to the biblical references to Ethiopia as a means of challenging the myth that Blacks were destined to be 'beasts of burden.'" That formed the foundation of what came to be known as "Ethiopianism."

Ethiopia, or Abyssinia, the names are interchangeable, came to represent a beacon of black pride and independence on an African continent otherwise under assault by whites. Several biblical verses alluded to the power and importance of that realm. Africans in the Diaspora clung to this image of a strong, black kingdom and came eventually to place their hope in one day achieving salvation by returning to this land. Campbell quotes another expert on the subject as stating that:

> Stimulated mainly by references to ancient Ethiopia in the Scriptures and Sermons, Afro-Americans often perceived that African territory, however defined, as the salvation of the race. Some thought that one day a black messiah would emerge from Ethiopia to redeem the African race religiously, socially and politically. So ingrained did these and related views become that New World Africans often thought of themselves as Ethiopians, using that term to describe themselves and their organizations. (Campbell. 1987:48)

The Italians attempted to capture and colonize Abyssinia at the end of the nineteenth century but were repulsed at the battle of Adowa in 1896. The news of the Ethiopian victory electrified the African diaspora. Story tellers from the villages of Jamaica to the newspapers read on the streets of Harlem, all trumpeted the news of this great triumph. Here was actual proof of Africa's might. An African kingdom with a black Christian ruler had defeated a white army! Psalm 68, v. 31 seemed to be a prophecy coming true: "Princes come out of Egypt, Ethiopia stretches forth her hands unto God" (Campbell 1987:48).

So far we have seen that the consciousness being part of Africa developed in Jamaica through folklore, through religious influences, and through the impact of current events. After World War I awareness of and association with Africa deepened even further in Jamaica and elsewhere around the "Black Atlantic," culminating in the development of the Pan-African movement.[5]

Though the Pan-African movement had many leaders and key figures (not the least of whom was the African American intellectual and activist, W.E.B. DuBois, the founder of the Pan-African Congress), Jamaica was most closely associated with her own son, Marcus Garvey, the leader of the United Negro Improvement Association (UNIA, founded in 1914 in Jamaica). Garvey was born in Jamaica in 1887. At the age of 14 he moved to Kingston where he became a printer's apprentice, emerging four years later as a master printer. Garvey then followed the thousands of Jamaicans before and after him in emigrating from the island in search of work. The search took him from Central America to England and then to the U.S. In all of these locations he worked tirelessly to promote the UNIA. Thanks to his abilities to inspire pride in Blacks from all walks of life, the organization "became the largest mass movement among black people in this century, with 996 branches in 43 countries and over 5 million members" (Campbell 1987:54).

Garvey's influence on Rastafarianism and thus on reggae was two-fold. First of all and like the religious preachers before him, he proclaimed Ethiopia to be the home of all Africans in exile in the diaspora. He thus reinforced the centrality of Ethiopia to black identity. As proof of this Ethiopia consciousness, Chevannes (1994:40) points out that at the first UNIA convention in New York in 1920, the members adopted the following poem as the black international anthem:

> The Universal Ethiopian Anthem
> (poem by Burrell and Ford)
>
> I
> Ethiopia, thou land of our fathers,
> Thou land where the gods loved to be,
> As storm cloud at night suddenly gathers
> Our armies come rushing to thee.
> We must in the fight be victorious
> When swords are thrust outward to gleam:
> For us will the vict'ry be glorious
> When led by the red, black and green.
>
> Chorus
> Advance, advance to victory,
> Let Africa be free;

Advance to meet the foe
With the might
Of the red, the black and the green.

II
Ethiopia, the tyrant's falling,
Who smote thee upon thy knees,
And thy children are lustily calling
From over the distant seas.
Jehovah, the Great One has heard us,
Has noted our sighs and our tears,
With His spirit of Love he has stirred us
To be One through the coming years.
(repeat chorus)

III
O Jehovah, thou God of the ages
Grant unto our sons that lead
The wisdom Thou gave to Thy sages
When Israel was sore in need.
Thy voice thru' the dim past has spoken,
Ethiopia shall stretch forth her hand,
By Thee shall all fetters be broken,
And Heav'n bless our dear fatherland.
(repeat chorus)

The second important influence of Garvey on later Rastafarian beliefs was his emphasis on the need for repatriation. So central was this thrust that Garvey was known to most as the leader of the "Back to Africa" movement. He had not initiated the idea. Like the identification of diasporic blacks with the country of Ethiopia, so too the idea of the return to Africa had been developing over a long period of time. Garvey merely took the notion and made it central to his mission. He dreamed of establishing an African nation run by the UNIA which would speak for and protect the interests of Blacks everywhere (Chevannes 1994:41-42). In fact in 1959 a spurious Rastafarian promoter actually sold 15,000 tickets on a nonexistent boat that he claimed would sail into Kingston harbor and repatriate all ticket holders back to the African motherland. Needless to say, the boat never arrived and the hustler was thrown in jail (King 2002:11).

RASTAFARIANISM

Marcus Garvey made a speech in a Kingston, Jamaica church one Sunday in 1927 where he prophesied that Abyssinia would soon rise again to world greatness. He declared, "Look to Africa, where a black king shall be crowned." Lo and behold, three years later in 1930 the prince regent, Ras Tafari Mekonnen, was crowned King Haile Selassie I of Ethiopia. He had many titles and nicknames: King Negus Negusta, Lord of Lords, the Conquering Lion of the Tribe of Judah, Elect of God, Light of the World. He was said to be descended from King Solomon himself. Many thought he must truly be fulfilling scriptural prophecy for his arrival had been foretold in Revelation 5:5, "Then one of the elders said to me, 'Weep not; lo, the lion of the tribe of Judah, the Root of David, has conquered, so that he can open the scroll and its seven seals.'"

During the run up to his coronation, Ras Tafari carried out an extensive publicity campaign to alert the world to the fact that a black king was about to ascend a throne. Hundreds of newsmen and photographers were present to document this historic event when it finally took place. Pictures of row after row of Ethiopian dignitaries bowing to honor the new king flashed across the globe. That kind of coverage fed into the excitement already running high amongst African descendants in the Americas. From Harlem to the villages of Jamaica, black people in the New World invested with renewed vigor the image of Ethiopia as Zion.

The image carried double the force in Jamaica because it presented a challenge to the rule of the white British king. One man in particular, Mr. Leonard Howell, began preaching that Jamaicans could have only one king and that was the black king of Ethiopia. The white elite immediately charged him with sedition, tried him and sent him and his associate, Robert Hinds, to prison for declaring that Haile Selassie was the black messiah. They were growing worried by the size of the crowds that had been gathering to hear him preach. News reports in the establishment press described these gatherings: "devilish attacks are made at these meetings on government, both local and imperial, and the whole conduct of the meeting would tend to provoke an insurrection if taken seriously" (Campbell 1987:71).

Howell is generally credited with being the first in Jamaica to preach on the divinity of Haile Selassie (Chevannes 1994:42). He may well have been one of the first Rasta teachers too, though it is not known when exactly Jamaicans began calling themselves or began being called Rastafari.[6]

In any case, Haile Selassie received even greater public support in Jamaica and elsewhere after the Italians invaded Ethiopia in 1935. Mussolini's fascist forces wanted to turn Ethiopia into an Italian colony. The Italo-Ethiopian War which ensued angered many diasporic Africans who blamed the white-dominated League of Nations for supporting Rome instead of the Lion of Judah. Campbell mentions that:

> Jamaican newspapers printed front page stories of the atrocities which were being carried out by Italy, who tested the latest instruments of death in Africa. Poisonous gas, aerial bombardment, the creation of concentration camps and those barbarous fascist practices which were to become commonplace during World War II were tested on Africans in Ethiopia between 1935-1941.

> Black people throughout the world interpreted the war as a racial war in so far as the European powers of the League of Nations supplied equipment and spare parts for the Italian war machine, while they were refusing to deliver arms to the Emperor of Ethiopia to defend the mass of African people. (Campbell 1987:73)

Some Jamaicans even tried to enlist in the fight for Ethiopia (Chevannes 1994:42; Campbell 1987:74).

Throughout the Americas black identification with Ethiopia increased. It became concretely associated in their minds with the promised Zion with New World Blacks understood to be Jews in exile—associations that are quite commonplace in Rasta circles today. In fact the cousin of Haile Selassie was sent to New York City in 1937 where he founded the Ethiopian World Federation (EWF), with the idea of raising funds for the defense of Ethiopia. The EWF started its own newspaper, *The Voice of Ethiopia*, through which it worked constantly to increase black support for beleaguered Abyssinia and to make the connection between its fate and the fate of Africans everywhere. It also propagated the idea that Haile Selassie was the Elect of God and that "the true Israelites were Black" while also stating that "Africans formed the twelve tribes of Israel." The Falashas [indigenous Jews of Ethiopia], the newspaper claimed, "had carried the Ark of the Covenant back to Ethiopia" (Campbell 1987:77).

Another important moment in the development of Rastafarianism occurred during 1935; namely, the publicity in Jamaica generated by a news story in *The Jamaica Times* about a movement sweeping Africa known as *Nyabinghi*, which called for "Death to White Oppressors."[7] The newspaper article claimed that this movement had now been taken over by Haile Selassie who would henceforth lead a revolt of Blacks against whites. Any who died in the struggle were sure to rise straight to heaven (Campbell 1987:72; Chevannes 1994:43).

That Rastafarianism arose during the 1930s in Jamaica was, of course, no coincidence. Small farm families gave up, packed up and began flooding into the capital of Kingston by the tens of thousands. Urban and rural black Jamaicans were suffering economic hardships made worse by the Great Depression and periodic hurricanes. They were also suffering from social and political subordination perpetuated by the white colonial regime governing the island. No laws existed to regulate working hours or minimum wages so the poor were extremely vulnerable. One government report at the time showed that the standard of living was so low that a worker had to labor for 6 days to afford one loaf of bread (Campbell 1987:80).

So bad had things become that in 1938 an island-wide rebellion broke out in response to the hundredth anniversary of the abolition of slavery in Jamaica. Low-wage workers and small farmers from the country and the city combined to block roads, cut telephone wires, burn plantations and in general demonstrate that they were tired of the near-slavery conditions that continued to hold sway over them (Campbell 1987:81-84).

The spread of Marcus Garvey's message combined with a specifically black Christian inter-pretation of the Bible prepared the Jamaicans to understand events in the 1930s in Jamaica and Ethiopia as earth shaking. Howell and the other preachers provided them with that understanding. In other words, the poor black Jamaicans needed salvation from Babylon at that time; the Rasta preachers proposed to give it to them.

Howell and his followers, who numbered anywhere from 500-1600, moved away from Kingston society and up into the hills above the town in 1940. There they founded the first Rasta community. They named it Pinnacle and patterned it after the earlier Maroon communities. Howell established himself as "chief," also known to his followers as "Gong" (which later became Bob Marley's nickname and the name of his record company) or "Counselor" or "Prince Regent." The members turned to farming. Each family planted what they needed as well as growing cash crops such as marijuana, that is ganja, to sell in town. All forms of livestock were raised except pigs, pigeons and ducks which were taboo. Each family farmed its own plot of land but also worked communally on projects meant to improve life for all at Pinnacle (Chevannes 1994:122).

The Rasta members lived in typical poor peasant shacks of one room with dirt floor and thatched roof, all arranged along a parade ground which was used for the community's celebrations. Of particular importance were the celebrations surrounding Passover and the anniversary of the emperor's coronation.[8]

Howell and his family lived up on a hill overlooking Pinnacle, which was symbolic of the almost absolute control Howell had over the community. He kept all administrative power to himself and would not let his deacons do any more than lead religious ceremonies. He alone meted out praise and punishment (Chevannes 1994:123-124).

Reports filtered out from the area around Pinnacle that its members were urging their neighbors not to pay taxes to the government. The police raided the commune in 1941, probably for this reason, but ostensibly because of ganja sales. Many Rastas including Howell were packed off to prison. They eventually managed to get Pinnacle up and running again, but the police continued to raid it. They finally destroyed it in 1954 and dispersed the Rastas into the slums of Kingston. Splinter groups multiplied during the late 1950's and culminated in the Henry Rebellion in 1960, in which the followers of another self-styled Rasta prophet named Claudius Henry armed themselves and battled with the police and the army leaving middle class Jamaica even more in fear of their "strange" Rasta countrymen (Thomas 2004: 71-72).

The total time Pinnacle was in existence was not very long; however, its impact on the Rastafarian movement was profound for it was here that many of the symbols, ceremonies, beliefs, and practices of the movement were first solidified.[9]

To talk of Rastafari beliefs is perhaps to overstate the case, for Rastafarianism has no central authority or canonical texts or creeds. Stephens (1999:151) states that it exists more as an alternative worldview to the "artificial affluent society of self-absorbed individuals who worship idols and live decadent life-styles at the expense of the poor." In other words, Rasta exists as a critique of "Babylon System." This is the source in Rasatafarianism of the emphasis on peace and love as opposed to selfishness and competitive acquisitiveness.

However, Barrett (1988:104) claims there are six identifiable beliefs forming the core of Rastafarianism.[10] Other scholars do not seem to share his certitude, but caution instead that not only is the religion not organized, but its decentralized nature probably increases the rate at which new ideas get introduced and old ones are discarded, so that what falls under the rubric of Rasta beliefs changes from one decade to the next.

The beliefs are often expressed more through the meaning behind the symbols of the movement than in any spoken or written form (See Bender's [2005] collection of Rastafarian art for some excellent visual examples of the movement's symbols). For instance, the image of the ganja plant— or more exactly the image of the "herb chalice," that is, a special Jamaican pipe—and the practice of smoking ganja is meant to create something more, as Winders (1997:18) puts it, than just a pleasurable state of mind; it is mainly "cherished as a 'righteous' state, prayerful and con- templative," more akin to a spiritual or religious practice. The Bible even sanctioned its use, according to the Rastas, by stating in Psalms 104 that, "All the herbs bearing seeds upon the land are made for man."[11]

Or take the symbol of the lion. That, according to Campbell (1987:99-100) represents at one level the new confidence, self-respect and Black pride Rastas promoted among Jamaica's poor. (Along this line, one of the interpretations of Rasta dreadlocks was that Rastas were the "symbolic reincarnation or imitation of the lion in man form, both in face and body, as well as in the spirit structure.") It captures, too, the belief in the power of the Ethiopian Emperor, the "Lion of Judah" and the deification of that monarch. God for the Rastas, like Ras Tafari, was black. He had always been black (Chevannes 1994:146)

Another example: the red, gold and green colors of the Ethiopian flag and the Garveyites passed into Rastafarian imagery as did the association of those colors with a free Africa and the defense of the black man against racial oppression. Rastafarianism is also indebted to Garveyism for its emphasis on "Africa for Africans" and its belief that "black people are in reality the captive children of Israel in Babylon and that, in repeat fulfillment of history, they will one day be set free. Repatriation is that freedom" (Chevannes 1994:248).

Finally, a word about dreadlocks. They were originally thought to have developed as a form of identification during the 1950s with the Kikuyu people of Kenya who were battling against British colonialism in what became known as the Mau Mau uprising. A famous news photo sent around the world in 1953 showed one of the military leaders of the revolt standing next to Kenya's eventual president, Jomo Kenyatta (whose nom de guerre was "Burning Spear"). The leader, Mwariama, is wearing dreadlocks. When the Rastas saw that, they immediately adopted it as a sign of anti-colonial African solidarity (Campbell 1987:96).

Another version of the story is that dreadlocks arose out of the first reform movement within Rastafarianism, known as the Youth Black Faith. This was a loose coalition of younger members of the movement who had become dissatisfied by the late 1940s with the organization of the Rastas. They believed the movement needed to abolish all hierarchy, dispense with many of their religious rituals adopted from Jamaican Christianity, and above all else, Rastas needed to cut their ties to Babylon, that is, dominant society (Chevannes 1994:145, 208), and develop healthier, more self-reliant ways of provisioning the community—the inspiration for the vegetarian and "ital" foods emphasis in some circles (Campbell 1987:121-124). The younger leaders of the reform movement, men known as Brother Taf, Pete, Brother Firsop, Badaman, and Watson (aka Wato), stood up to denounce the use of candles and oils which they considered to be superstitious holdovers from Jamaican Christianity. They also advocated that males grow beards and that no offices exist other than chairman, who convened meetings and administered the congregation, and tableman, which was the position held by a literate member who was in charge of all texts important to the Rastafari. The Youth Black Faith were also the ones who elevated the use of ganja to a religious practice, calling it the "holy herb" or the "wisdom weed" (Manuel 1995:148). But most importantly the Youth Black Faith adherents began developing an ascetic tradition within the movement which placed increasing value on those "warriors" who achieved great self-control and practiced self-denial (fasting, sexual abstinence, etc.). They, in turn, enforced greater community self-control, seeing to it, for instance, that the weekly Wednesday night prayer meeting (attendance at it being the only "duty" required of the Rasta) started on time, and so forth. For that they became known as "dreadful" in their strictness as applied to themselves and to others; hence, the "dread" name. The growing of dreadlocks seems to have developed more or less spontaneously as a way for these more ascetic members to mark themselves out to the community and to the world at large as forcefully committed members of the faith (Chevannes 1994:152-158).

In sum, Rastas put great emphasis on the symbols and images referring to 1. Ethiopia (lion, photos of the emperor and his queen, Ethiopian flag, etc.); 2. dreadlocks; 3. the herb chalice and standing drums used during *grounations* (explained later on); 4. Africa in general (map of Africa, etc.).[12]

Another important development in Jamaica accompanied the growth of Rastafarianism; namely, the take over of the country's economy by aluminum industries. Shortly after World War II, Jamaica was found to have some of the world's largest bauxite deposits. The discovery of bauxite, being the ore from which aluminum is made, attracted the major American and Canadian firms (Alcan, Reynolds, Kaiser, Alpart, Revere, Alcoa) who began buying up the land and turning it into open pit mines. Between 1950 and 1957 the aluminum industry replaced the sugar cane plantations as Jamaica's leading export. Sadly for the Jamaicans, the mining and processing operations never employed more than 10,000 workers, while the aluminum companies actually displaced over 560,000 people from their small farms and sent them packing into the already overcrowded cities, or else abroad: Close to 200,000 migrated to Britain and the U.S. each between 1950 and 1968 (Campbell 1987:86-87).

So we have seen that Rastafarianism evolved as a response to a number of socioeconomic and historical developments. Perhaps most importantly, it grew out of the Jamaican people's historical resistance and revolt against slavery, colonization, and then neocolonialism. Rastafarianism was the culmination of poor black Jamaican attempts to reconnect with their African heritage from which they had been so brutally torn away. It was an attempt to reassert pride in their African-Jamaican culture after centuries of its being denigrated and even outlawed by the island's white elite and their mulatto flunkies. More specifically, as we have seen, it was also a response to the energizing message of Marcus Garvey and his UNIA movement during the 1920s, as well as to the emergence of the Great Depression, the coronation of Haile Selassie as King of Ethiopia, and the Italian attack on the new monarch during the decade of the 1930s. A good dose of that old fashioned Christian messianic tradition played an equally important role. Most significant, however, as Nelson (1994:67) puts it, is the fact that Rastafarianism "emerged from among the most deprived sector of Jamaican society" making it "an authentic grassroots movement struggling for liberation" against both continuing forms of racial as well as class oppression.[13]

THE ORIGINS OF REGGAE

Rastafarianism would have existed without reggae, but the world outside of Jamaica would probably not have heard of it had reggae not become internationally popular. Reggae is not Rastafarian music just as Rastafarianism does not exhaust the subject matter of reggae tunes. But the two are intricately intertwined in the contemporary period and how Jamaica's most famous music developed such a close relationship with the Rastafarian movement is what we are about to investigate. To do so we need to take a detour back through the historical forms of popular music developed in Jamaica. This is because reggae did not arise out of thin air, nor did it evolve out of Jamaican musicians listening to American rock and roll on the radio. It matured out of a blend of external elements and internal roots, some of which stretched back to before the nineteenth century, as we will see.

At Rasta ritual gatherings called *Nyabinghis* or *grounations*, music is always played and danced to. But it isn't electric; only acoustic. Drums dominate. The drumming style used in Rasta meetings forms a part of Jamaican drumming traditions dating back to the period of slavery. The Rastas use "kete" and "repeater" drums which are variations of the kumina drums played by "Bongo men." Manuel describes the percussive background in Jamaica this way:

> The older musical languages that were available in West Kingston during the formative period of Jamaica's urban musical culture [1960s] were many. Neo-African drumming traditions, some of them going back to the ceremonial and social dances held on slave plantations during the eighteenth and nineteenth centuries, had survived in several parts of the island. Among these were the *etu*, *tambu*, and *gumbe* traditions, concentrated in the western part of the island, and the *buru* tradition, found primarily in the central parishes of Clarendon and St. Catherine. Like *Kumina* drumming, some of these neo-African styles were tied to African-derived forms of religious worship. Most of them employed an ensemble of two or three drums, one of which led with improvisations while the others provided supporting rhythms. (Manuel 1995:152)

[Parenthetically, *Nyabinghi* drumming music, according to Yawney (1994:79-80), is completely opposed to most popular music such as reggae in that it cannot be marketed. It is a performance tied to a specific situation. Unlike a musical event or spectacle, *Nyabinghi* makes no separation between the performers and the audience. They all gather at a *grounation* to chant, drum, dance and perform in the proper clothing and with the proper reverence and respect. So, presumably, *Nyabinghi* rhythms and style of play can influence Jamaican music, but *Nyabinghi* proper occurs only within the confines of the Rasta devotional/ritual ceremony known as the *grounation*.]

As Manuel also mentions, the missionary musical influence continues to have a significant effect on the popular music of Jamaica:

> Much more widespread than these surviving neo-African forms were the musical expressions of Jamaica's hundreds of rural Afro-Protestant churches and sects, most of them variants of the general form of worship known in Jamaica as Pocomania (sometimes called Pukkumina), or 'Revival.' These indigenous religions were forged out of the nineteenth century encounter between the religious concepts brought to Jamaica by enslaved Africans and the teachings of European missionaries. Like their religious practices, which included possession by both ancestral and biblical spirits, the music of these groups blended African and European influences. Many Revivalists used a combination of two or three drums—one or more side drums played with sticks (often equipped with a homemade snare) and a bass drum played with a padded beater—to accompany their singing. Sometimes other percussion instruments and hand clapping were employed as well. (Manuel 1995:152)

But the missionaries were not alone, and perhaps not the most important influence on the origins of popular music in Jamaica is suggested below:

> Not all of the older musical traditions available to Jamaicans during this period were religious. Before the 1950s, the closest thing to an indigenous popular music in Jamaica was the mento. Though its exact origins are obscure, it is clear that the mento was born of a creolizing process that blended elements of a variety of European social-dance musics with African-derived stylistic features. Varieties of European-derived ballroom dances such as the quadrille, the lancer, and the mazurka were popular in Jamaica both during and after the era of slavery, and the instrumentation, harmonic structures, and melodic contours that typified them contributed much to the music played by village bands across the island until recent times. To the fiddles, flutes, and guitars of these rural bands were added banjoes, rhumba boxes (bass instruments with plucked metal lamellae), drums, rattles, scrapers, and other instruments wholly or partly of African origin. This creole social-dance music, originally more European-sounding, eventually acquired a new rhythmic feel, due to the African-derived aesthetic preferences of the musicians who played it. (Manuel 1995:153)

Even that does not exhaust the kinds of musical influences which had an impact on the development of popular music in Jamaica. Think, for instance, of the work songs commonly performed to accompany various labor activities and made famous by Harry Belafonte in the banana boat song called, "Day O!" Even more important was the creation in Jamaica of big dance bands patterned after their African American counterparts in the U.S. They introduced the island to jazz as well as to the sounds from Trinidad and Cuba, all popular with the growing audiences in the big tourist hotels.

The roots of Rasta and reggae music in both earlier secular and religious music continued to have an effect on later developments. Rasta developed two types of drumming with two types of "ridims" (drumming patterns). As Hebdige (1987:58) lays it out, "The religious songs are called 'churchical' and the ridims are slow and ponderous. Listen for instance, to the Wailers' 'Rastaman Chant,' which is based on a churchical ridim. The other type of music is called 'heartical' and refers to songs which carry social commentary. Here the drumming is faster and lighter."

The division went beyond Rasta music. Hebdige (1987:58) claims that non-religious or "heartical" ridims had a shaping influence on early ska and gave it its choppy, uptempo dance music feel. Likewise, as more and more reggae artists turned to Rastafarianism and took up its practices and principles, reggae began to slow down and become more somber in tone, more in line with serious "churchical" ridims.

But we are getting ahead of ourselves. Back in the late 1940s and early 50s Jamaican music was forever transformed by the introduction of the sound system. Club owners just prior to that had been unhappy with the expense of hiring a live band, particularly the big bands popular in the 1930s and 40s. So as an economical response, club owners switched over to playing mainly American r&b using a turntable, amplifier, and the biggest speakers available. Naturally, the man who introduced and played the records became a very important figure.[14] Actually there was a distinction made between the disc jockeys, who merely played records, and deejays who talked over the tunes.[15] The sound systems themselves were also well known and attracted crowds as much as the deejays and record selectors who worked them. One famous system during the 1950s was owned by Clement "Coxsone" Dodd and was called Sir Coxsone's Downbeat; another owned by Duke Reid was known as The Trojan. By the late 1950s to early 60s the owners of these sound systems had started up their own record companies to produce tunes they could then play on their own sound systems. These were often just instrumental tracks laid down by session musicians. The deejays supplied the vocals in the form of short phrases of encouragement to the dancers ("Work it! Work it!") or else they used exclamations from gospel ("Good God Almighty!") or they just screeched (Hebdige 1987:65). Eventually their vocals were recorded and became part of the songs—a promotional innovation that had the unintentional effect of launching the era of Jamaican r&b. This method of song promotion continues to characterize the Jamaican music scene today (Barrow and Dalton 1997:11-21). Think of "talk over" and "dub" as contemporary examples of this Jamaican tradition.

What is really meant by "Jamaican r&b" is what we know today as the precursor of reggae, that is, ska. Perhaps more than any other Jamaican music, ska had its origins in American music. It evolved as Jamaican musicians began to alter slightly the beat of American r&b, to give the driving rhythm to the horn section, to create that characteristic jumping dance sound.

All of that came about just as much thanks to Jamaican roots, however. The original ska musicians, groups like the Skatalites, grew up with Jamaica's rich and varied drumming traditions, many played in earlier jazz big bands, many had been trained in European styles of music, and most all had been studio musicians backing up every group that made it into the recording studios. Several of the founders also jammed with the great Rasta drummer, Count Ossie, and may have been Rastas themselves (Hebdige 1987:59-60).

Ska formed out of that motley mix of sources. We know so little about the specific origins of Jamaica's first big popular music style because it does not have easily identified origins. The other, darker, reason we know so little of the specifics of ska's origins stems from the fact, as Manuel (1995:159) points out, that ska developed out of the poor slums of Jamaica, the "downtown" scene with its impoverished, in-from-the-country immigrants holed up trying to eke out an existence in the shantytowns of Kingston, places like Trenchtown, one of the sorriest slums of the capital, the home of Bob Marley during the late 1950s and early 60s. No one cared where poor country people's music came from so none of the writers and reporters covering music bothered to investigate it at the time.

Jamaica's dance halls, sound systems, recording studios, and record shops remained jammed with the ska sound until mid 1966 when it disappeared almost overnight. Hebdige describes what happened next:

Then the music suddenly began to slow down to a 'stickier,' more sinister rhythm. A completely new dance style emerged. Gone were the fast, jerky movements of ska. Instead, a slinkier, cooler dance called the rocksteady became popular. . . . In rocksteady, ska's rumbling bass lines became deeper and still more noticeable. The brass was phased out to be replaced by guitar and keyboard set-ups. The main solo instrument of early ska—the trombone—disappeared virtually overnight . . . (Hebdige 1987:71)

Hebdige goes on to point out that recording techniques also advanced during this time so that instead of doing a session in just one take, sound engineers learned to lay down different tracks and to play around with them to achieve different results. The emphasis on the vocals characteristic of ska also changed under rocksteady (1966-1969) to the point where the voice became just one more instrument while the guitar assumed primacy.

These changes coincided with the development of a whole new subcultural style in urban Jamaica that proved to be very important. It went by the name of "rude boy" and referred to the very visible presence on every street corner of angry young shantytown males striking a pose and looking for ways to get into trouble. Hebdige again assesses the movement thusly:

There was a certain style to it all. The rudies wore very short green serge trousers, leather or gangster-style suit jackets, and their eyes were often hidden behind moody pairs of shades. If they were 'rough, tough' and rich enough, they would ride around on light, stripped-down motor cycles which were covered in chrome. Apart from stealing, scuffling or hustling, the rude boys might spend their time playing an aggressive game of dominoes or 'tram hopping'—leaping onto the bars at the rear of the trams as they rattled through the city streets. The point was to be as cool as possible. But sometimes, particularly at the blues dances, the 'pressure' would get too much—fights would break out and guns and knives [ratchets] would be drawn. (Hebdige 1987:72)

The rude boy phenomenon was a form of rebellion against the dead end slum existence the young in urban Jamaica knew awaited them. The aggression, petty crime, and arrogant stance signified resistance to the miserable present and untenable future. The famous movie, *The Harder They Come*, did more than anything to broadcast to the world the nature of rude boy consciousness. Though the movie didn't come out until the early 1970s, its soundtrack included two earlier rude boy hits that became anthems of the subcultural movement (words taken from Hebdige: 1987:71, 73-74). The first was "Johnny Too Bad" by The Slickers:

Walking down the road with a pistol in your waist
Johnny you're too bad.
Walking down the road with a ratchet in your waist
Johnny you're too bad.
You're jesta robbing and a stabbing and a looting and a shooting
You know you're too bad.

The second rude boy hit from the movie was a re-issue of "Shanty Town (007)" by Desmond Dekker and the Aces:

And now rude boys have a wail
Cos them out a jail.
Rude boys cannot fail
Cos them must get bail.
Dem a loot, dem a shoot, dem a wail
In shanty town.

The anger and violence of rude boy culture continued in Jamaica (and actually got worse in the 1970s as attested to by the assassination attempts on both Bob Marley and the Prime Minister), but by about 1968 something else was beginning to emerge: "the music shifted down another gear, becoming even slower and 'heavier' with an even greater emphasis on the bass," according to Hebdige (1987:75). Another commentator claims that it was the development of the bass and electric piano that really marked out the arrival of reggae (Bradley 2002: 47). In any case, American influences were still important to Jamaican popular music, but there was definitely a conscious attempt to work with the music's island origins. As Manuel puts it:

> By 1968, when reggae proper became established on the scene, indigenous influences were becoming yet stronger, partly as a result of social currents in the larger society. Class consciousness was converging with increasing cultural assertiveness. The popular expression 'roots' came to refer as much to the downtown ghetto experience of suffering and struggle as to the African sources of Jamaican culture. Linked to this trend was the rapid growth of the Rastafarian movement, especially among poor urban youth. By the 1970s, the Rasta emphasis on African roots, black redemption, and social awareness had become the dominant force in Jamaican popular culture. (Manuel 1995:164-165)

Many varieties of reggae flourished in the Jamaican popular music hothouse of the 1970s, roots reggae was only one of them. Love songs and lighter dance numbers found an appreciative audience. Christian revivalist-inspired reggae did likewise, as did more traditional mento-reggae or "country music." But few of these genres circulated abroad. The greatest export proved to be the Rasta-inspired reggae made famous by reggae's biggest superstar, Bob Marley.

Marley came up through the vibrant Kingston music scene of the 1950s and early 60s. He cut his first record in 1961, but it received little recognition. His abilities remained undeveloped until he managed to hook up with the singer Joe Higgs, who taught him harmony, and Mortimer Planno, who initiated him into Rastafarianism (Hebdige 1987:78). Later, Marley repaid the favor by having Higgs replace Bunny Wailer on the group's musical tour through the U.S. in 1973 (Gooden 2003:238).

Marley first broke into the music scene in 1964 when he teamed up with Bunny Livingston and Peter McIntosh (Tosh) to form the Wailing Rude Boys, aka, The Wailers, later to become the first reggae group composed entirely of Rastas.

The Rasta angle did not really develop fully until the late 1960s. In 1971, the Wailers met the white Jamaican plantation aristocrat, Chris Blackwell, and signed with his new record company, Island. Blackwell respected the political positions taken in the lyrics of Bob Marley and the Wailers' songs. He appreciated that they were authentic, from the heart and Rasta inspired. But his real genius was to realize that the dreadlocks look and politically conscious lyrics would appeal to Anglo-American rock fans. He thus encouraged the whole roots trip as a marketing approach for the Wailers, rather than toning them down to make them seem less strange. He was right. The wild dancing on stage at live performances combined with the dread hair, flamboyant clothing, and the ganja smoking persona adopted by Marley acted as a perfect accompaniment overseas to the pounding music and mystical political lyrics. Blackwell even went so far as to package Marley's first album, *Catch a Fire* (1972), in the form of a giant zippo lighter (Barrow and Dalton 1997:131).

Marley's switch in the late 1960s from the rude boy style to Rasta coincided with a real crisis of law and order in Jamaica. Gang warfare had reached an all time high by this point and the establishment placed much of the blame on the backs of the poor Rastas. In July 1966, the police even bulldozed down a Rasta neighborhood in the Back o' Wall slum section of Kingston in retaliation (Ferguson 1997:53).

This was about the same time that Marley met his second Rasta teacher, Vernon Carrington—Gad the Prophet—who inducted Marley into the Twelve Tribes of Israel branch which he had founded. Members were associated with one of the 12 tribes depending on their month of birth. Marley, born in February, was a member of the tribe of Joseph (Ferguson 1997:54).[16]

Marley's first spiritually conscious songs began appearing in 1968 with the song, "Selassie I Is the Temple." More socially conscious ones soon followed with the appearance of "Duppy Conqueror," Small Axe," and "Trench Town Rock," all songs that railed against the evils of the world. The Jamaican ruling party the JLP, banned such songs from the radio during the national elections of 1972 because they were thought to be inciting the people against the regime. Ironically, reggae protest songs are given credit for having helped throw the JLP out of office that year and thus ushering in the rule of the more populist candidate Michael Manley and his People's National Party (Ferguson 1997:55).

Manley's supporters among the Jamaican poor had hoped his arrival in office in 1972 would mean the decriminalization of ganja, possession being the most common charge brought against the poor by the police. Unfortunately, the criminal underworld in Jamaica had managed to establish links to the American mainland to such an extent that the island was shipping over $400 million dollars worth to the U.S. by 1974, making ganja Jamaica's number one export. The U.S. government began putting pressure on the Jamaican government to curb the traffic. The Manley regime pledged its support and the American DEA took over internal Jamaican attempts to eradicate the herb (Campbell 1987:12-115).

Another interesting ganja trend surfaced during the late 1970s and early 80s; namely, the spread to Jamaica of the Ethiopian Zion Coptic Church. Campbell (1987:115-117) claims that the church was a cover for wealthy white Americans who mainly wanted to set up cannabis growing operations on the island. The group, under its American leadership, bought up huge tracks of land and started promoting a variety of capitalist enterprises, as well as promoting the use of ganja. The group also started a newspaper dedicated to anticommunism which endeared it to American officials and may have helped smooth the way for its various illegal activities.

Bob Marley and the Wailers were joined from the start by dozens of reggae musicians who also made their mark in the "roots" sub genre. People like Jimmy Cliff, who became the first to internationalize the music through his cult film, *The Harder They Come*, and spent most of his musical career singing about the despair of the Jamaican poor. Perhaps his most famous song along these lines is the haunting gospel-inspired lament called, "Many Rivers to Cross," in which he speaks metaphorically of the hardships of surviving. He may be better known today for his famous exhortation to stop "Fussing and fighting, cheating and lying, scandalizing and hating" in the international hit, "Wonderful World, Beautiful People." Though just as important was his 1969 protest song, "Vietnam," which Bob Dylan once called the "Best protest song he'd ever heard" (Erlewine 1997:912). Hearing the same tune caused Paul Simon to fly down to Jamaica and hire the studio, engineer, and musicians that Jimmy Cliff had used. Simon then hired them to make his hit, "Mother and Child Reunion," which became the first U.S. reggae song ever (Erlewine 1997:912).

Jimmy Cliff was not alone, of course. Desmond Dekker and the Aces had a hit in 1969 called, "Israelites," which though bouncy and danceable, actually described how desperate life could be on the edges of complete poverty ("Get up in the morning/ Searching for breakfast/So that every mouth can be fed").

Mutabaruka, the celebrated dub poet, used to perform without shirt or shoes to register his solidarity with the downtrodden of the earth. As Erlewine (1997:927) puts it, "his dub poetry cut through '80s mellow reggae like the blast of an AK-47."

The list could go on and on: Burning Spear, The Abyssinians, Big Youth, the Royals, the Wailing Souls, Bunny Wailer, and many others. Special mention must be made of Peter Tosh who broke with the original Wailers in 1973 and set out on his own roots protest road. His first album, *Legalize It*, established the direction he would be heading in. Like Marley who was shot thanks to his notoriety, Tosh was beaten almost to death three times by the Jamaican police for his outspoken stance in favor of justice and equality, and against poverty and oppression. He stayed militant to the end and was finally murdered in 1987 (Erlewine 1997:933).

Our sketchy "biography" of the politics of Jamaican music winds down at this point. We need to stop and take stock of what roots reggae signifies in this world.

But first I should explain why we are ending here. Marley's death in 1981 did not bring Jamaican music to a halt, as you well know. Pick up any copy of the reggae music magazine *The Beat* and you will see advertisements for dozens of currently popular reggae groups as well as for CD releases of most every reggae album made since 1968. What did happen is that the DJ sound, the musical genre known as dancehall (with famous DJs like Cutty Ranks, Spragga Benz, Beenie Man, Red Rat, etc.), began to take over around the mid-1980s and that marked a break with the past. I know too little about it to be in a position to dismiss or condemn post-1980s Jamaican music, but my initial sense is that it has lost its overtly political edge. 'Slackness' became its defining feature. The glorification of the gangsta and the macho concern with the marks of manhood (guns, cars, girls, money) came to dominate its themes. That development deserves as much anthropological attention as any other, I hasten to add, and for those interested in investigating further, I highly recommend the engaging new study by Norman Stolzoff (2000), called *Wake the Town and Tell the People: Dancehall Culture in Jamaica*. Stolzoff argues that Jamaican dancehall does not deserve to be compared with reggae and that those who see reggae as "noble" and dancehall as "decadent" completely miss the meaning of dancehall in its Jamaican context. He claims that in fact dancehall has fractured into a variety of categories with Rasta-inspired DJs holding their own against gangsta and slackness oriented DJs. Without condemning I am simply pointing out that the political message of the music seems to have altered. Paul Gilroy exemplifies the critical position on the subject:

> Jamaica's DJs steered the dance-hall side of roots culture away from political and
> historical themes and towards 'slackness': crude and often insulting wordplay
> pronouncing on sexuality and sexual antagonism. I am not suggesting a simple
> polarity in which all toasters were agents of reaction and all singers troubadours of

revolution. The Jamaican DJ tradition had been as involved in the spread of Rastafari during the late 1960s and early 1970s as recorded song. The two aspects of reggae culture interacted and combined in complex fashion. Even as slackness achieved ascendancy there remained popular toasters like Peter Metro and Brigadier Jerry who fought to maintain rhymes with a social content in the dances. However, the role and content of reggae changed markedly after 1980. This shift related to the consolidation of Seaga's regime and the consequent militarization of ghetto life. Both were also expressed in roots music and in the social relations of sound systems sub-culture where guns became an increasingly important aspect of the rituals through which the crowd communicated its pleasure to the DJs.[17] (Gilroy quoted in Cooper 1995:141)

Now back to the assessment of reggae's impact. On this subject, Marley invites us to decide for ourselves what to make of his songs. He once said, "You have to play it and get your own inspiration. For every song have a different meaning to a man. Sometimes I sing a song and when people explain it to me I am astonished by their interpretation" (Cooper 1995:118).

Marley is not the be all and end all of reggae—he would never have claimed so himself. But he did ride it to international stardom and he did more than anyone else to associate reggae with liberation from oppression. That is what has given the music its global appeal. Today the Australian aboriginal bands Blekbala Mujik and No Fixed Address play reggae. Alpha Blondy, the world famous reggae singer from the Côte D'Ivoire, calls himself the 'African Rasta.' A reggae band composed of Maoris, Tongans, and Fijians exists called "Herbs." Some of the Havasupai Indian families living at the bottom of the Grand Canyon are reported to have Bob Marley pictures on display in their homes, presumably as a mark of respect and interest in his message and music (Erlewine 1997:907). The CD titled *Reggae Around the World* put out by Putumayo World Music (1998. cat. # PUTU 142-2) includes cuts by reggae bands from South Africa, Australia, Brazil, Sudan, Mali, Nigeria, Martinique, Ghana, the U.S., and of course, Jamaica. So by all accounts the music has touched a nerve the world over. Its calls to resist "Babylon system," to "Chant down Babylon," is understood everywhere as a call to struggle against the forces promoting and profiting from imperialism and racism. It is also a call for radical social and personal change. The title track from Marley's album *Exodus* implies a ready identification of black people the world over with the flight of the Jews from bondage in Egypt to the Promised land, only this time around the Jews are black, the god protector is Jah and the promised land is Ethiopia (Cooper 1995:122):

> Open your eyes and look within.
> Are you satisfied with the life you're living?
> We know where we're going
> We know where we're from.
> We're leaving Babylon
> We're going to our father's land.
> Exodus!
> Movement of the Jah people.

That kind of easy association between oppressed black Jamaicans and the Jews of the Old Testament sprang from the close familiarity of Rasta Jamaicans with the Bible and a keen interest in its messages of apocalypse and salvation. Just as important, as we have seen, were the Ethiopianist and black nationalist influences dating back to the time of slavery, but particularly important from the 1920s to 30s with the rise of Marcus Garvey's "Back to Africa" movement and the coming to power of Haile Selassie. Those influences provided the sources for the Rasta desire to be "going to our father's land," that is, Ras Tafari's Africa/Ethiopia/Abyssinia. Equally important, as we have seen, were the musical influences of Revival ("Pokomania"); *Nyabinghi* drumming; the role of the sound systems and

American r&b in the 1950s to early 60s; early ska; the dancehall and recording studio arrangements—all of these elements had a profound effect on the creation of reggae.

The specificity of the Jamaican history behind Rastafarianism and reggae, one would think, might pose a problem for its global audience. How does the rest of the world "connect" with the music when it is so tied to the history of one particular people and place? How can so many fans outside of Jamaica come to embrace reggae as their own when they have little or no appreciation for its roots?[18]

On the one hand, it must be admitted that the vast majority of reggae consumers, particularly in the middle class, Anglo-American world, will never experience anything remotely like the everyday existence of black Jamaicans. We are able to "consume" Jamaican culture thanks only to the multinational juggernauts that own record companies like Virgin and Island and thus fill the commodity circuits of the West with reggae musical products. We buy those products and then listen to the Rasta message in the comfort of our suburban homes or in our air-conditioned cars and bars, light years away from the dancehalls of Kingston's ghettoes. The difficulty of mastering the Rasta argot of Jamaican English alone acts to effectively block most of the rest of the world from understanding exactly what the lyrics mean.

Yet on the other hand, the worldwide popularity of reggae suggests just as powerfully that the specific issues of class and racial oppression addressed in the music can be transposed so that they resonate in other settings. The specific conditions present in Jamaica that created the music in the first place seem to be universally accessible, at least the oppositional traditions and symbols present in the music seem to strike a sympathetic, universal chord. That is the position of noted music critic George Lipsitz (1994:99-100) and it is seductive. He makes two points that are worth ending this discussion. First, as he says, the plasticity and resilience of socially oppositional popular cultural symbols cannot be overemphasized. Think, for instance, of the way dreadlocks have come to stand the world over for liberation and solidarity, whether it be liberation from stultifying bourgeois cultural norms among, say, middle class white youth, or whether it be a sign of black liberation from racial oppression and black solidarity within the communities of the African Diaspora around the world. The "icons and images encoding oppositional meanings," within a song, Lipsitz suggests, resonate with youth everywhere even though the reality of their day to day existence is quite different.

Lastly, Lipsitz reminds us, the specificity of Jamaican history is based on cultural hybridity. By that he means to underline the fact that Jamaica did not develop culturally in isolation from the rest of the world, but in symbiotic relation to it. The currents that created Rastafarianism and reggae perhaps developed in a unique way in Jamaica, but they were not unique to the island. For instance, Marcus Garvey and Bob Marley both spent time in the U.S. and in Britain, and were profoundly affected by the culture of the Anglo-American world. Leonard Howell, mentioned earlier as the founder of the first Rasta community in Jamaica and the man who first preached on the divinity of Haile Selassie, had worked as a porter and construction worker in New York. Many other thousands of Jamaicans migrated to work in Central America and Florida and so were exposed to a wide variety of political and cultural cross-currents. Even those who never left the islands were deeply influenced by the important role of American r&b in the form of records brought back by migrants, or played in dancehalls, or by listening to it on southern American radio stations whose signals could be picked up in the Caribbean. And so it would seem that, even though it is a cliché, we do all live in the same world.

VIDEOS ACCOMPANYING

Remember, the actual video lectures can be accessed at the following url: http://oregonstate.edu/media/classes/index.php?className=anth210

Scroll down under the "Classes on Demand" heading and select "ANTH210: Comparative Cultures."

Video 7

The video opens right up with the following overhead:
Sources of Oppression Sung about in Jamaican Music

1. *What was this one?*

2. Racism and oppression dating from plantation economy

3. Continuing poverty

4. Colonialism and imperialism

5. Cut-throat record business

6. Local politics

   1. After some introductory remarks on each of these, we took them one by one. The first one we illustrated with overheads which gave us examples of the touristic, folkloric representations of the island, put out for tourists' consumption. It of course has nothing to do with life as led in Jamaica today. The origins of the Jamaica we know today date back to Columbus and the extermination of the indigenous Arawak Indians. We saw an overhead which showed that many of the Indians were fed to Spanish dogs as food. Within a few decades the British took over Jamaica from the Spanish and used it to ambush Spanish ships as they moved in and out of the Caribbean. This loot then provided the capital to buy the slaves and machinery necessary to set up the plantation economy of the island. The next several overheads dealt with the details of the slave trade to Jamaica.

   2. We then talked about the nature of plantation society with its rigid social hierarchy. The tourist industry has even revived some of the old plantations which tourists can rent. To give some idea of the horrors that the slave populations had to put up with on the plantations, we showed a video clip that described what slave life was really like. Then we saw several more overheads describing the daily toil of the slaves.

      We played the Bob Marley song "Slavedriver" to illustrate the extent to which consciousness of the horrors of that time period are still very much with Jamaicans today, and how conditions of poverty, racism, and underdevelopment tie contemporary Jamaicans to their slave ancestors.

      Jamaicans did not just bow down and accept their lot. Many ingenious ways were developed to evade and avoid the lash of the whip. We showed an overhead of one of the most famous figures, the African folkloric figure known as Anancy.

      Another form of subterfuge was practiced by black preachers who, since they were allowed to travel from plantation to plantation, could keep the local slaves informed of external events, and could even organize revolts.

      After the abolition of slavery in the 1830s, two things developed:

      A. Black Jamaican ex-slaves were not a part of Jamaican society, but were Africans in exile in the New World

      B. The spread of Christianity gave them a series of stories and symbols that spoke to them and provided models of the Israelites' bondage in Egypt and their eventual return to the promised land.

      We played "By the Rivers of Babylon" by the Melodians to illustrate the extent to which such Christian stories and symbols have been internalized in Jamaican music and culture.

      We then talked about the development of the Christian Revival Movement of the 1860s culminating in a large revolt at the time. This was followed by the conversion of many sugar plantations into banana plantations owned by American corporations. Little changed for the poor black workers, however, as an overhead of Jamaican peasants from the 1890s made clear.

3. As a response to the poor economic conditions in Jamaica, many emigrated to Britain, the USA and to the Panama Canal. Even today, many Jamaicans emigrate to try to earn a living (including Bob Marley).

4. After WWII, we said that things got worse with the rise of the aluminum (bauxite) boom. Many large multinationals moved in, bought up land, and turned it into open pit mines, putting many more out of work than they ever hired.

5. As for the cut-throat record business, we used a clip from the Jimmy Cliff movie, *The Harder They Come*, which showed how, even though the artist does all of the work, the wealthy producers make all of the money and control who makes it in the business and who doesn't. This state of affairs is sung about in many songs.

6. Finally, the politics of the island have long been a topic for reggae songs. We used a video clip of Peter Tosh who gave a very critical speech at the famous "peace concert" of 1976 where Bob Marley attempted to bring together the two big men of Jamaican politics. The voice over is by Peter Tosh who, some think, may have been killed later for his critical attitudes towards local politics.

Video 8

This video discusses the subject of Rastafarianism.

Rastafariansim developed as:

1. An authentic grassroots movement struggling for liberation from both racial and class oppression

2. An attempt to reassert pride in African-Jamaican culture

These two aspects of Rastafariansim developed out of the experience of Jamaicans abroad as much as anything. While away working they came to rub shoulders with other communities of Africans in the diaspora. Particularly important was the African American community with its strong sense of attachment to Africa. We used the example of the Abyssinian Church in Harlem to illustrate how attached they were to the idea of Ethiopia-Abyssinia (two names for the same place) as the true homeland. The defeat of the Italians by the Ethiopians in the 1890s Battle of Adawa gave Africans everywhere a sense of pride and accomplishment.

The post World War I era saw the development of the PanAfrican Movement. We showed an overhead of the leader of the movement, Marcus Garvey, a Jamaican who established the United Negro Improvement Association (UNIA). He inspired pride in blacks throughout the world. Garvey's influence on reggae was two-fold: Garvey claimed Ethiopia to be home for all blacks in the Diaspora. He probably did more than anyone to instill interest in the country. He was also important in stirring up interest in repatriation to Africa. So strong was the identification of the UNIA with the repatriation idea, that the organization became known to many as the "Back to Africa Movement."

We showed another overhead which listed the various titles of Emperor Haile Selassie. In 1930 he was crowned and took the name "Ras Tafari." His leadership took on almost a divine quality amongst many of Garvey's followers in the New World.

We then talked about Leonard P. Howell who was an important character in Jamaica because he may have been the first man to preach the divinity of Ras Tafari. He of course was also very important as the founder of the first Rasta community.

The attack on Ethiopia by the Italian Fascists in 1935 electrified the Black world and united them in their support for the embattled nation and its leader. Black people everywhere were interpreting the war as a race war of whites against blacks.

Another event in 1935 that attracted a lot of attention in Jamaica was the report from Africa of a new movement known as the "Nyabinghi" movement, which pledged death to all whites. Rumor had it that Ras Tafari had taken over leadership of the movement. On top of these two events, the Depression added to the general sense of misery and foreboding for poor Jamaicans. In response, in 1938 a revolt broke out against the near slavery-like economic conditions being experienced.

Against this background of political and economic events, Howell and other preachers began providing a king of messianic understanding of what these events all meant: Black people needed salvation from this worldly Babylon. Howell and others were going to provide it for them. That became the genesis of the first Rastafarian community, called Pinnacle.

The video clip of Mortimer Planno was used to provide some illustration of the practices and beliefs of Rastas. Planno, remember, was the man who introduced Marley to Rastafarianism. The tape shows the ubiquity of ganja among the Rastas. It also discussed how persecuted the early Rastas were, as well as the extent to which Rastafarianism stood for pacifism.

We then shifted to talk about the following:

Rasta beliefs are often expressed via symbols and images:

1. Ethiopia/ Africa (emperor, lion, flag)

2. Dreadlocks

3. Herb chalice

And via a few ceremonies and practices:

4. "reasoning" ceremony

5. "grounations" with Nyabinghi drumming

6. "ital" diet

   1. We started talking about #3 first and showed a picture of the sacred chalice, or pipe used to smoke ganja, which is understood to be a religious or spiritual practice.

   2. We then shifted back to talking about symbols and began with the symbol of the lion, which represents pride. It also owes its importance to the "Lion of Judah" which is one of the titles of Ras Tafari, emperor of Ethiopia. We also mentioned the flag of Ethiopia with its red, gold and green colors, which were also the colors of Garvey's movement. They passed into Rasta imagery as representing a free Africa. We then mentioned the way Haile Selaisse has been deified by the Rasta movement.

   3. We next turned to the origins of dreadlocks. One explanation traces them back to the Mau Mau uprising in Kenya in the 1950s, where the warriors in the bush wore dreadlocks. Another possibility was that dreads were brought in during the 19th century with Indian indentured servants. The third version says that dreads were the mark of the first reform movement in Rastafariansim. They developed during the 1950s and marked themselves from the rest of the Rastas by growing dreadlocks, which they saw as signifying their African identity and their decision to separate from wider society.

   4. The Nyabinghi ceremony we saw a bit of in the film clip where Rastas were chanting and playing Nyabinghi drums. During these "grounations," the members "chant down Babylon," that is, they protest and cry out against this profane world we live in. The word "Nyabinghi" here refers to this ceremony, which is dominated by the drums of the same name.

5. A Rasta reasoning session has two purposes:

   A. to speak out about beliefs in justice and liberation as related to the black experience of slavery, colonialism, racism

   B. To act as an initiation of a newcomer, questioning him to see what's "in his heart"

6. (not discussed during the video)

We then went back and summarized all of the reasons leading up to the development of the Rasta movement. We listed and discussed them on the following overhead:

Rastafarianism developed in response to:

1. The energizing message of Garvey and his UNIA movement in the 1920s

2. The hardships of the depression era

3. Haile Selassie crowned King of Ethiopia

4. Italian attack on the new black monarch

5. The strong Christian messianic tradition in Jamaica

We next went back to the beginning of the video and put back up the original overhead:

Rastafariansim developed as:

1. An authentic grassroots movement struggling for liberation from both racial and class oppression

2. An attempt to reassert pride in African-Jamaican culture

We played "One Drop " by Marley and the Wailers as an illustration of the extent to which Rasta has influenced reggae, and the extent to which reggae songs celebrate the symbols of Rastafarianism while chanting down Babylon, that is, protesting against racism and oppression. We then played "Jump Nyabinghi" as a song which celebrates and affirms and reasserts pride in New World African diasporic communities and their culture (the good feelings associated with dance, smoking ganja, holding Nyabinghi sessions, etc.). It is more an uplifting song, spreading a message of pride in belonging.

Video 9

This video looks at the musical influences that created reggae; looking at the precursors to reggae, all of the forms of music popular in Jamaica prior to the mid 1960s.

The first kind of music we talked about was Mento, a kind of country dance music, very little of which made it onto records even though it had a strong influence on later Jamaican music. We played the song, "Mango Time" to illustrate what mento music sounded like. We then played the 1964 Eric Morris ska song "Penny Reel" as another example of the influence of mento on later forms of Jamaican music.

The big band sounds that had an impact in the 1930s, 1940s, and early 1950s were expensive. They eventually were replaced, starting in the early 1950s, by sound systems. These were large conglomerations of various kinds of equipment. Two jobs became associated with the sound systems: one was the dj, the man who introduced and talked over the records, and the other was the selector, the man who played the records and minded the volume controls. The sound systems themselves became famous. People would go to a performance just because of the system that would be playing there. By the 1960s, the owners of the sound systems were producing their own records so that they would have total control over the music being played.

Along with the move of Jamaicans from the country into the city after World War II and the development of the sound systems, a new music also came about. It reflected more closely the new urban reality. It also reflected the more cosmopolitan tastes of Jamaicans who had a sense of a larger world, thanks in part to the mass migration of Jamaicans as well as to the growth of American influences on the island. This was the turn to r&b music from the USA. We played Fats Domino's "Shake Rattle and Roll" as an important example of the sorts of influences sweeping over Jamaica during the 1950s. Fats Domino and other r&b musicians had a tremendous influence, as illustrated by the Jamaican r&b song we played called "Boogy in My Bones."

We mentioned that r&b music was a huge category with many subcategories. One of the most popular in the 1950s was what we called today "Doo Wop," characterized by the emphasis on harmony, choruses with made-up words, an interest in falsetto, etc. We played a series of doo wop songs by various artists to illustrate this kind of music. To give you an example of the extent of the influence of r&b on Jamaica, we played a song by the Jamaican group the Jivin' Juniors called "Sugar Dandy" which sounded almost identical to any other American doo wop song.

We next turned to other Caribbean island influences on Jamaican music. The most important, perhaps, for Jamaica was the music of the island of Trinidad, a kind of music called Calypso. We played a song by Lord Creator from 1962 called "A Big Bamboo" as an illustration of the calypso influence in Jamaica. We then went on to demonstrate the influence of calypso on Jamaican music by playing the song by Peter Tosh called "Shame and Scandal."

We then turned to discuss the Jamaican musical invention called "Ska," which we said developed at the same time as the sound systems. The most famous early ska group was called the Skatalites, and was made up of session musicians. They originated the ska sound with its emphasis on the off-beat rhythms and the importance of the horn section and a light, choppy, up tempo, danceable beat. In fact the driving force behind the Skatalites was the trombonist, Don Drummond. We played a couple of instrumental songs by Drummond and the Skatalites to illustrate what early ska sounded like. We played a vocal number called "Rough and Tough" to again illustrate the early sound of ska. We then played the international hit of the early 1960s called "My Boy Lollipop," which was the most famous ska song of the era.

We next turned to discuss the strong influence of Christianity on Jamaican popular music. During the ska era, the influences were quite easily discernible. We mentioned that the preaching style in Jamaica where the pastor and the crowd practice a kind of call and response found its way onto records (but we didn't play any songs to illustrate this). The use of well-known stories and passages from the Bible in songs were also common. We played the 1963 song by Desmond Dekker and the Aces called "Honor Your Father and Mother," which obviously takes its inspiration from the Ten Commandments. We next played a song by Toots and the Maytals called "Hallelujah" which illustrated the influence of traditional Christian revivals on the music. We ended the section by playing Toots and the Maytals' song called "Pressure Drop," which illustrated the influence of religious sermon styles with the format of opening with exhortation, lots of repetition, and then building to a climax of hoarse shouting all meant to whip up the congregation.

We then shifted to talking about the next kind of American influence on Jamaican music; namely, the influence of American media on the island. We played "Bonanza Ska" by Carlos Malcolm and the Afro-Caribs as an example of the influence of American television.

At the end of the ska period (circa 1965) a new trend had developed in ska. The competitive nature of the sound system-based music scene was leading to ever greater violence. Owners of sound systems would hire ruffians (called "dance crashers") to go around and stir up troubles at their competitors' performances. The song "Dance Crasher" addressed this problem and called for a calming down of the competition.

Ska continued to dominate the music scene until the summer of 1966 when the music began to change. It slowed down a bit, got slinkier and "thicker," some said more sinister. The new music came to be known as "rock steady." The horn sections disappeared to be replaced by the guitar and keyboards. The off-bead remained important, though.

We played a rock steady number called "007/ Shanty town by Desmond Dekker (1967) which referred to the increasing crime and violence of the ghetto, particularly to the popular figure associated with ghetto anger and defiance, the "rude boy," otherwise known as "rudie." Jimmy Cliff in the movie, "The Harder They Come," was just such a rude boy: a cool, petty criminal from the slums of Kingston, who wanted the finer things in life and would do whatever it took to get ahead.

We ended with a famous rocksteady number by the Paragons called "The Tide Is High," covered here by Blondie.

Video 10a

This video follows another video, dividing it up into parts so as to illustrate the discussion of the life and times of Bob Marley, following the book "Catch a Fire." We moved immediately to a discussion of the subjects covered in chapters 3,4 with a clip showing Marley's birth place followed by an interview with Marley's mother, Ciddy.

We then put up the following overhead:
1st movie segment and the Marley book chapters 3,4 emphasize
Marley is special almost from birth:

1. From mixed parentage

2. Enjoys magical, mystical powers

3. Familiar with both country and the city

4. musically inclined at an early age

The second segment focused on Marley's move to the Kingston slums and the nature of life in those slums.
2nd movie segment and Marley chapters 4,5,6 emphasize

1. Extreme poverty of Kingston shantytown (areas called Dungle, Trench Town, etc.)

2. Importance of urban housing space for the poor, called the "yard"

We played two video segments to give some sense of the poverty of Kingston life. The second was based around the Jamaican artist, Joe Higgs, who is addressed by the next overhead:
3rd Movie segment (and part of Marley book chapter 7) emphasizes
Importance of Joe Higgs:

1. As positive Rasta influence

2. As musical mentor

3. As general role model

We then saw a tape clip of an interview with Peter Tosh and Bob Marley about the early musical influences on them. We put up the following overhead:
4th Movie segment and the Marley book chapters 6-10 emphasize:

1. Extreme creative musical energy of Kingston Shantytown dwellers

2. Importance of the dance hall and sound systems

3. Influence of American rhythm and blues and pop music

4. Centrality of ska to early Wailers

We then discussed the importance of American rhythm and blues and pop music on the early Wailers and played a 1958 song by Dion called "Teenager in Love." In 1964 the Wailers covered "Teenager in Love," which shows the influence of American r&b on them.

The importation of r&b into Jamaica deeply affected young groups like the Wailers. But they weren't just imitating blindly. They were putting their own Jamaican stamp on the music. We illustrated this process by playing the 1966 Motown hit, "Shotgun" by Junior Walker and the All-Stars, which the Wailers redid as the "Ska Jerk." The point was made that we too often think of Marley and the Wailers as only a reggae group. We forget that they had a history, that they worked hard to make hit records in styles other than reggae. And that many of the earlier influences were from abroad. However, we also stressed the fact that the songs were undergoing a kind of indigenization, that is, being remade as recognizably Jamaican songs.

We next turned to examine the extent to which Christian music influenced the Wailers. They had grown up in the same general Christian milieu as others on the island and so incorporated that heritage into their music. We played the 1967 version by the Wailers of "Go Tell It on the Mountain" as an example of a Wailers Christian song.

The video wrapped up with an overhead listing the styles of music that preceded reggae where we discussed the various songs we had played which represented the different categories:

Genres of Jamaican Music and Influences on Jamaican Music leading through reggae

1. Mento (country-style) ("Penny Reel")

2. American r&b (boogie woogie) (Fats Domino stuff)

3. American r&b (doo-wop) (Dion and "Teenager in Love")

4. American TV and film ("Ska Bonanza")

5. Caribbean music (calypso) ("Shame and Scandal in the Family")

6. "Jamaican r&b" (ska/ rocksteady)

7. Christian Religion ("Go Tell It on The Mountain")

8. Rude boy (taken up in next video)

9. Rastafari (taken up in next video)

Video 11a

We showed the same overhead that ended the last video. This time we will be starting by talking about rude boy and Rasta influences.

We mentioned that the Wailers' big break came when Joe Higgs got them a studio date with Coxsone Dodd, who listened to their songs and then picked the one he liked the best: "Simmer Down." Since Marley had written it, Dodd suggested that the group be known as Bob Marley and the Wailers. The song was a plea to the rude boys to cool it. It addressed the new subcultural emergence of the violent young toughs and the almost undeclared war which was growing between the rude boys and the cops. Though the song cautions the toughs to put a lid on it, Marley and the Wailers identified with the young toughs. We then saw a video clip on the rude boy culture of defiance and rebellion. With a song like 'Simmer Down," Marley and the Wailers were providing a sort of song of solidarity with the community of oppressed youth. Most interestingly, the rude boy character of Jamaica had a lot in common with the Brazilian samba malandro character. Songs about both functioned as creators of identity and solidarity among the poor youth. The very existence of the songs provided some sense of identity and belonging.

Dodd attempted to steer the Wailers away from the tough boy image and tried to get them to be a more r&b/ doo-wop group such as the Moonglows (we played a quick example of The Moonglows' "Ten Commandments of Love").

The "war" between downtown ghetto youth and the civil authorities continued to worsen during the middle 1960s. The uptown elite called for a shoot to kill ordinance to keep the poor in line. Hysterical fear of the 'hooligans" and "delinquents" kept the rich up at night.

The Wailers rode this tide of discontent to fame, if not fortune. Their performances caused crowds to roar their approval. All of this fuss was caused by the 1965 Wailers' song, "Jailhouse," which we played. They were in the process of moving from an insignificant dance band to a nationally acclaimed music group.

We next put up a summary overhead which said:

Chapters 7-10: Importance of the ska & rocksteady years for the Wailers ('64-'68)

1. Wailers begin to develop into a commercially successful group

2. Beginning of Black consciousness movement in the Diaspora

3. Rude Boy movement develops in Kingston ghetto

4. Wailers become associated with Rude Boy movement

5. Wailers begin to develop socially conscious songs and mix them in with lighter songs

We then talked about Marley's emigration in 1966 to Delaware to live with his mother and how this coincided with the visit, back in Jamaica, of Emperor Haile Selassie, one of the most important events in Jamaican history. That was followed by a discussion of how Marley came to Rastafarianism. We read a passage from the book which suggested that Rita, Bob's wife, had been instrumental in getting Bob involved. Bob was then initiated into the faith by Mortimer Planno, who encouraged Bob to pursue his musical career.

Throughout the late 1960s the Wailers did not swing over to roots/ rasta music. In fact much of what they were doing would not even be recognized by us today as reggae at all. Lee "Scratch" Perry helped them to perfect their craft and gave them a cleaner, more commercially successful sound. We played "Soul Rebel" from the 1968-1970 period as an example of the way other sounds were still competing with reggae for dominance of the group and as an example of how far they still were from the sound they are known by today.

We then shifted to talking about another important influence on the Wailers; namely, Chris Blackwell, a white Jamaican record producer who owned Island Records. In a video clip we saw of Blackwell, he claimed to be responsible for turning them into the reggae stars we known them to be. He helped them financially to give birth to the album, Catch a Fire. Blackwell brought his marketing skill to the project and made Catch a Fire and Burnin' into the Wailers first big reggae hits. Both albums were dominated by social protest songs with politically conscious lyrics. Blackwell, instead of trying to tone them down, encouraged the Rasta style and the political protest music the Wailers were capable of putting out. He was correct to believe that Western consumers would go for this Third World sound.

Back in Jamaica, the more political tone of the music continued to develop, particularly on Burnin'. The album was full of politically activist songs while also celebrating ganja smoking and the life of the poor in ghetto Kingston. We played the Wailers' song, "Get Up, Stand Up" off the Burnin' album (1973) as an example of this now mature, politically conscious protest music being put out by the group.

We then talked about the deteriorating state of affairs back in Jamaica as outlined in chapters 14 and 15 of the book, *Catch a Fire*. Chapter 16 adds to the discussion of political events the examination of Marley's deepening faith in Rastafarianism, having even joined a harder core splinter group of Rastas. Marley at this time put out the album, Rastaman Vibration, which was a mix of political protest and Rasta-inspired songs.

Everything Marley did from that point on was a combination of his spiritual and activist motivations. His songs explored repatriation back to Africa, as well as the oppressive nature of colonialism and racism, captured in the idea of Babylon.

Throughout the 1970s, we mentioned how political conditions continued to worsen in Jamaica which led to Marley being shot, Tosh and Bunny being beaten up and jailed several times, and the development of violent gangs working for the two competing political parties. Finally in 1980, the right wing won the national elections. The ganja trade was replaced by the cocaine trade, thanks in large part to official American interference in Jamaica's affairs. Hundreds died in the streets of Kingston during the run up to the election. A year later (1981), Marley was dead.

We closed with the playing of "Rasataman Chant," which was used to illustrate the extent of Rasta influence on Marley at the end. The Nyabinghi drums and the chanting down of Babylon on the song make it an aural equivalent of a grounation ceremony.

We ended with the following overhead:

What Reggae Has Come to Stand for

1. Epitome of protest music providing a message of liberation and dignity and self-affirmation

2. Call for radical social and personal change

3. Unity of struggle of all in the Black Diaspora

4. Utopian idea of a liberated African homeland

5. Symbols of Rastafari/reggae have become world wide symbols of opposition and resistance

6. Provides a sense of belonging to a meaningful community based on shared struggles

7. A popular cultural form like reggae is both specific to a place and a hybrid product of many international influences

NOTES

1. Taken from a poem by Joe Ruglass, poet and musician with the Mystic Revelation of Rastafari (quoted in Chevannes 1994:1).
2. From the lyrics of "Catch a Fire," Bob Marley and the Wailers.
3. See Barrett (1976:34-35). He discusses the importance of Anansi at more length. See also Campbell (1987:22-23).
4. See Campbell (1987:38). The deportation of Haitians was due to the fact that since Haiti had thrown out the French colonizers way back at the turn of the nineteenth century, they were seen as the spreaders of revolution and anticolonial sedition throughout the Caribbean. For a fascinating and famous account of the Haitian revolution see James (1963) *The Black Jacobins: Toussaint L'Ouverture and the San Domingo Revolution*.
5. The Black Atlantic is a reference to the people as well as the common culture of the African diaspora situated around the Atlantic coasts, including Britain, Canada, U.S., the Caribbean, Brazil, etc. The term was made famous by Gilroy (1993) in his study *The Black Atlantic: Modernity and Double Consciousness*.
6. Barrett (1988:82-83) mentions that Howell and Hinds and two other preachers named Joseph Hibbert and Archibald Dunkley were all preaching in Kingston during the decade of the 1930s that Ras Tafari was the Messiah of Black people. Their collective followers, for whatever reason, soon became known as Rastafarians.
7. The origins of *Nyabinghi* are not clear. Campbell (1987:72) gives the most specific description involving a rebellion in southwestern Uganda headed by one Queen Muhumusa. He states that the battle cry from the beginning was "Death to Black and White Oppressors." Chevannes (1994:42-43), writing after Campbell, ignores his work on this point and states that it was called the *Nya-Binghi* movement, which was founded in the 1920s by a Congolese king and which literally meant "Death to the Whites." Stephens (1999:149) states that the movement originated in Kenya and that the original slogan had been "death to the white oppressor,"

which evolved by the 1960s in Jamaica into "death to the black and white oppressors," which suggests a more sophisticated class understanding of domination and subordination. However, Stephens claims that the original slogan more closely approximates Rasta beliefs in a more binary, racialized opposition between white oppressor and black liberator, white demon and perfect black father, and so on. While Stephens take is interesting and provocative, Campbell's more detailed history is borne out by other authorities. For example, Adu Boahen (1985:516) states that *Nyabinghi* started in the Uganda-Rwanda border region in the nineteenth century, but was not entirely crushed until 1934 (the date of its suppression explaining, incidentally, why the article appeared in the Jamaica newspaper at that particular time). In modern parlance, *Nyabinghi* refers to the music played at Rasta gatherings, called *grounations*. The word refers to the mainly drumming and chanting that is relentlessly performed at these meetings.

8. Today those most important dates in the liturgical calendar have changed to include: Ethiopian Christmas (January 7); King's Anniversary Visit (April 18, commemorating Haile Selassie's visit to Jamaica on that day in 1966); King's Birthday (July 23); King's Coronation (November 7) (Chevannes 1994:239).

9. Two of the most important ceremonies being the *Nyabinghi* or *grounation* and "reasoning" sessions. Anthropologist William F. Lewis (1993:25-26) states that, "A Rasta reasoning session is a communal undertaking in which one shares beliefs about liberation and justice and relates them to the black experience of slavery, colonialism and racism." The reasoning session can also operate as a kind of initiation, as Lewis says, "A newcomer who reasons with the brethren is challenged, mocked, berated, instructed and finally welcomed as a brother (women are generally not involved in this), is his heart has withstood the test and proven itself to be black. [Chevannes (1994:208-230) provides a very interesting account of a reasoning he was subjected to as a novice investigator doing fieldwork in a Rasta community.] Lewis provides a sense of a session in the excerpt below:

> The order of the reasoning session is quite spontaneous. The flow of ideas and the topics determine the length of time it will last. On a quiet afternoon in August, I learned how a reasoning session takes on it form. Since the session was to take place at Dread's (a man's nickname) compound, he took the lead. When the brethren gathered, Dread removed from its wrapping a special pipe called the chalice. He filled it with herb and recited the blessing: "Bestow wisdom, knowledge and understanding. May we live to see the testimony come true when the lion and the lamb lie together. Selassie I shall triumph. Is it right for us to uphold the manifestation of the colonial thing, or should we think on our own?" Having blessed the herb, Dread exclaimed with eyes opened wide, "Jah." The rest responded, "Ras Tafari."

> The pipe passed from male to male. Sometimes it was handed over to another with a prayer affirming the power of Jah and at other times it moved through the group very unceremoniously.

> The spontaneity of this particular session was prompted by my visit to the compound. By then my presence was a familiar sight on the beach. The Rastas used the session as an opportunity to test my heart for its worthiness. Not surprisingly, the first topic was the established church. The Rastas scrutinized the Church of Rome, the Episcopal Church and even the indigenous Jamaican beliefs of *pocomania* (possession by spirits) and *obeah* (witchcraft).

> "The churches teach the people about heaven and hell and not how to live." Dread swears neither by the heavens above nor the hell below because they have not been proven. "Earth is abiding. Man is the center. Survival is for everyone. These are central."

> "The churches believe in Christ. This is the part of the Church that is not correct. Christ was in the days of Christ. To this day the house of David continues in Ethiopia. So, let us deal with what is now. Let us not be celestial on this side."

> Dread then drew deeply from the chalice. After that he passed it to the person next to him. Fire took it and spoke: "The concept that the churches teach is not Rastafari. Rastafari means to be more positive about what is going on in each other. Ganja is the Rasta's source of knowledge and intelligence, the sacrament. . . ."

10. 1. Haile Selassie is the living god. 2. The Black person is the reincarnation of ancient Israel who, at the hand of the White person, has been in exile in Jamaica. 3. The White person is inferior to the Black person. 4. The Jamaican situation is a hopeless hell; Ethiopia is heaven. 5. The Invincible Emperor of Ethiopia is now arranging for expatriated persons of African origin to return to Ethiopia. 6. In the near future Blacks shall rule the world.

11. Chevannes (1994:157) quotes a Rasta to this effect. The King James version of the Bible states Psalms 104:14 as, "He causeth the grass to grow for the cattle, and herb for the service of man: that he may bring forth food out of the earth."

12. Yawney (1994b:77) states that there are more "adjunct" symbols which are part of the iconography of Rastafarianism but have yet to be accepted by Rastas everywhere. She is referring to the palm trees and outline map of Jamaica, as well photos of Marcus Garvey and Bob Marley.

13. But not sexist oppression. The topic of sexism within Rastafarianism deserves more than a footnote. For the moment, I can only point you in the direction of a few good sources on the subject: Turner's (1994) article, as well as Yawney's (1994a) (see especially the book's bibliography), along with Burton (1997:135-139). Turner (1994:30) soberly assesses the problem in this excerpt:

> Jamaican Rasta may have believed that the spirit of Nyabingi possessed Selassie and strengthened his fight against the Babylon of Mussolini's fascism. But the women-centred character of Nyabingi in East Africa was lost in its transfer to the New World. At Nyabingi gatherings in Jamaica, women were marginalized and subordinated, at least since the 1960s. Rasta 'queens' could not cook if menstruating, women could not 'reason' with the 'kingmen' nor partake of the chalice (smoke marijuana). Biblical support was found for limiting Rasta women's access to knowledge except through the guidance of their 'kingmen'.... What interventions transformed the independent Jamaican woman...into a domesticated and idealized queen? The explanation suggested here is that some Rasta men were inducted into a colonial male deal which privileged men at the expense of subordinated women.

14. Mentore's (1999) article "Notting Hill in Carnival," describes the impact of such a sound system man. In this case Mentore is remembering his adolescence among London's Caribbean immigrant community:

> The Reggae Dubman: the "Soundman" who, in my youth, was the envy of every schoolboy in our neighborhood. He had the title. He had the car. He had the girls. He had all the charisma. The weekend monarch of a tiny dynasty, he ruled his empire with what seemed like the divine inspiration of a knowledge that allowed him to have all of the most up to date records from Jamaica and the USA, to be the commissioned DJ at a different house party every weekend, to wear the most fashionable clothes, and to own the equipment that could blast the night away. The epicenter of a cult of personality, he inspired others to a total commitment of joy. We loved him and gave him our affection because every weekend he led us to that world outside the mundane, to that place were we could feel the bliss of an earthly freedom: a tight body-pressing freedom, a squeezed-out spiritual liberation in the cacophony of sound, sweat seeping through clothes, perfumed odors trapped in the head, dark figures wedged against each other swaying to the pulse of his nonstop deliverance of music.... Mentore (1999:57)

15. The deejay of the 1950s acted as master of ceremony with his own trademark chatter and slang, precursor to today's rapper, according to Barrow and Dalton (1997:11-12).

16. In "Redemption Song" on the *Uprising* album (1980), Marley sings: "But my hand was made strong/ By the hand of the almighty," which is a reference, according to Ferguson (1997:54), to the biblical verse Genesis 49:24 which says of Joseph: "But his bow abode in strength, and his hand was made strong by the hand of the almighty." This was understood by Rasta fans of Marley as a reference to his tribal affiliation with Joseph.

17. Cooper (1995) from whom the Gilroy quote is taken, goes on to question whether the DJ dancehall style is best characterized as a conservative turn. Particularly when it comes to matters of sexuality and gender relations, Cooper wants to make the claim that DJ preoccupation with 'slackness'(sexual looseness) is also a subversive attack on Jamaican fundamentalist propriety. It is a revolt, as she puts it (Cooper 1995:141) "against law and order; an undermining of consensual standards of decency."

    Parenthetically, Cooper (1995:127-132) is also an interesting source on the problem of sexism in reggae. She interprets Marley's repertoire of romance songs (little publicized in reggae circles but actually quite large; are they an embarrassment to male reggae fans?) as revealing an ambivalence towards women, a complicated swinging back and forth between putting woman-as-lover on a pedestal and aligning all women with Satan and original sin. For more analysis of gender relations in Rastafarianism and reggae, see Turner (1994) and the two Yawney (1994a, 1994b) chapters cited in the bibliography.

18. One sobering answer to this question is that they don't. As an example, Eric Clapton, who has made a career for himself covering the work of African American blues musicians, covered Marley's "I Shot the

Sheriff" and sent it straight to the top of the pop charts around the world. But did he understand or sympathize with the song's message? Did he achieve any kind of sympathetic understanding of the experiences undergone by black Jamaicans like Marley, experiences which might be reflected in the lyrical message? Evidence suggests he did not. According to Frith and Street (1992:67-68), in August 1976 while playing a concert in Birmingham, England, Clapton exhorted his audience to "Keep Britain White!" His remark was meant to throw his support behind the anti-immigrant movement which was then building steam in England. Ironically, the majority of immigrants of color in England at that time came from the island of Jamaica....

MUSIC AND DANCE IN THE CONQUEST AND REBIRTH OF NATIVE HAWAIIAN CULTURE[1]

HAOLE HAWAI'I

Films, television programs, and advertising from the last few decades have worked to reinforce the stereotype of Hawai'i as the land of Mai Tais, beautiful beaches, surf, and sunshine populated by lovely, long-haired, Hula-dancing women with bare midriffs, swaying hips, grass skirts, and easy morals—accompanied on the ukulele as they hula dance by their big, bronzed, lazy, happy-go-lucky brothers. Such is the image of Hawai'i conjured up in our touristic imaginations. It exists for us as a paradise to be consumed. It endures in our dreams as a timeless, South Seas fantasy island without conflict, where stress is unknown, where dramatic historical events seldom if ever impact on the lives of the childlike, innocent locals.

Ironically, if you pay enough money, you can vacation in Hawai'i without having to concern yourself overly with the Native Hawaiians. They will exist more as shadows during your stay. They may be the room service maids, the bouncers at the clubs, or the tourist hotel entertainers. But they won't be running the restaurants where you eat or managing the rental car franchise that provides you with transportation. They won't be owning the tourist shops where you buy souvenirs and they won't be operating the hotels and bungalows where you will be staying—they certainly will not be the owners of the land upon which the whole tourist industry is built.

Today's Hawai'i exists in spite of, not because of, Native Hawaiians. They have been the ones made to endure the invasion of Western outsiders, the *haoles*, who, as Native Hawaiian activist Haunani-Kay Trask (1997:187) put it, brought violence and destruction in the form of:

> disease, mass death, and land dispossession; evangelical Christianity; plantation
> capitalism; cultural destruction including language banning; and finally, American
> military invasion in 1893 and forced annexation in 1898. During the course of little
> more than a century, the *haole* onslaught had taken 95 percent of the Hawaiian
> people, 99 percent the lands and waters, and the entirety of their political sovereignty.

But the Native Hawaiians are fighting back. They have continued a centuries-long struggle against the encroachment of outsiders who would take their land and destroy their culture. The battle has intensified since the 1970s and is now focused on three areas: land rights, language recovery, and political sovereignty (Trask 1997:190).

All of these struggles are intricately associated with Hawaiian performative culture, particularly Hawaiian music, chant and dance. As we will see in this chapter, the struggle to recapture the land, the language, political autonomy, and thus a Native Hawaiian identity, those battles get expressed and fought out through cultural expression. Music and dance especially provide Native Hawaiians with a connection to a pre-invasion past. The Hawaiian language, the hula, and Hawaiian music stand today as defiant symbols of Native Hawaiian values, as rich cultural reservoirs and conveyors of Hawaiian identity. That cultural connection feeds in turn into contemporary struggles over sovereignty and land issues by helping Native Hawaiians form a sense of pride, dignity and solidarity and thus the will to fight against continued marginalization in their own homeland.

To begin to get a sense of how the performance of certain genres of music and dance contributes to Native Hawaiian struggles against oppression and exploitation, we must try to grasp the absolutely central role they play in Hawaiian history and culture. To that end we will begin by briefly exploring the role of song, chant and dance historically, and then proceed to investigate how they operate in contemporary Hawaiian culture.

HAWAI'I BEFORE WESTERN CONTACT

The earliest Hawaiian history recorded the origins of the islands in the form of competing genealogies which traced the archipelago back to various mythic gods and forces. These genealogies, recited in the form of chants, told of the islands being born, depending on the genealogy consulted, from a woman named Kumukumu-ke-ka, or from Ka-mai-eli, or from Papa. Another genealogy stated that they weren't born at all but were made by the hands of Wakea; while still another, the great creation chant called Kumulipo (excerpted below), said that they grew up of themselves, not begotten, not made by hand:

> When space turned around, the earth heated
> When space turned over, the sky reversed
> When the sun appeared standing in the shadows
> To cause light to make bright the moon,
> When the Pleiades are small eyes in the night,
> From the source in the slime was the earth formed
> From the source in the dark was darkness formed
> From the source in the night was night formed
> From the depths of the darkness, darkness so deep
>
> Darkness of day, darkness of night
> Of night alone
>
> Did night give birth
> Born was Kumulipo in the night, a male
> Born was Po'ele in the night, a female
> (Lindsey 2000)

Notice how the Pleiades is present at the creation of the world. The rise at sunset in the late autumn sky of this star cluster marked the beginning of the Hawaiian ceremonial cycle, the beginning of the Hawaiian year, when the Year-God Lono, returned from the spirit realm to renew the fertility of the land once again (Sahlins 1985a:196). Lono, when he returns, is understood by the Hawaiians to be searching for his lost wife taken from him by the human Hawaiian chiefs so that she could sire the succession of human kings to come (his remarriage to his lost wife being symbolic of the fertility cycle recommencing at the start of the new year). Interestingly, as Sahlins (1985b:5) points out, the famous hula dance took place during these New Year festivities (called *Makahiki*) and was meant to sexually arouse the returning god so that cosmic reproduction would again take place. The hula dance performed at New Year may also have signified the god Lono's coupling with the human daughters of the goddess, his lost wife. That helps explain why the hula was so religiously erotic—which is exactly why later American missionaries felt the need to prohibit the dance.

Polynesian pioneers settled the eight island Hawaiian chain in two great waves over a millennium and a half ago. They set out from perhaps Tahiti and used their extraordinary navigational skills to sail thousands of miles to the north, across the equator and into the Hawaiian archipelago. That marked the end of the heroic Pacific voyages for the Native Hawaiians, though they did maintain their boat making and navigational skills to the point where they could effortlessly move from island to island and back again within the Hawaiian island chain. The first settlers stayed along the islands' coasts during the initial settlement period (A.D. 300-600).

The Polynesian colonists who originally settled Hawai'i brought with them pigs, chickens and dogs. Over time, besides such domesticated animals, the Native Hawaiians adopted ever refined agricultural and aquatic food production techniques which marked the second phase of their settlement (A.D. 600-1100). The third phase is known as the expansion period and covered the time from A.D. 1100 to 1650. Diamond provides some sense of Hawaiian agricultural achievements during this third phase of Hawaiian history when he states that:

> Hawaiian labor corvées built elaborate irrigation systems for taro fields yielding up to 24 tons per acre, the highest crop yields in all of Polynesia. Those yields in turn supported intensive pig production. Hawai'i was also unique within Polynesia in using mass labor for aquaculture, by constructing large fishponds in which milkfish and mullet were grown. (Diamond 1997:61)

The large agricultural surplus generated by Hawaiians combined with the large population size living within each political unit (in this case the individual islands of Hawai'i which held upwards of 40,000 inhabitants), led to a complex social structure that was extremely hierarchical. In fact it has been said that the principle that governed and ordered all of Hawaiian life was the principle of hierarchy itself.[2]

There were essentially two kinds of people in ancient Hawai'i: commoners and *ali'i*, or nobles. They were all descended from the same ancestors and a king or high chief ruled over them. He made all decisions in matters of state; he alone could dispossess commoners and lesser chiefs alike; taxes belonged to him; he oversaw the highest rituals; he made up the law as he went along: there were no judges or courts. The king or high chief could not marry a commoner. In fact the most appropriate spouse for a high chief was his sister; their offspring would be divine. He would often have many children with other women and they would be higher in status than their mothers and often form part of the chiefly entourage. He would adopt many children as well, given to him by couples who wanted their offspring to enjoy a higher status than their own (Malo 1951:51-55).

Hawaiian kings did not inherit rights to the land so each one was required to reconquer it anew upon the death of the last leader. In order to conquer and keep land, the leader had to gather around him as many followers, or vassals, as he could. These court followers and the commoners below them were tied to the king or high chief by means of strong bonds of reciprocity. They gave their love and undying devotion to the leader and he in turn pledged his to them. This sentiment of mutual affection and attachment and love was called in the Hawaiian language, *aloha*, the same word we associate with Hawaiian greetings today (Valeri 1985:87).

The constant struggles among the powerful *ali'i* at the top meant that their ties to any piece of land were transitory. The commoners at the bottom of the social pyramid, though not bound firmly to a place, enjoyed a tradition of use rights which meant that most extended families were allowed to continue to work their land because for generations prior their family had worked it. They just had to pay taxes in labor and kind to the *ali'i* in charge of that region who then shipped some of the surplus up the hierarchy to his chief, and so forth. The period of taxation fell, not coincidentally on the New Year, or *Makahiki*, festival when Lono came back to insure the fertility of the land.

It would be a mistake to assume the lowly Hawaiian peasant families automatically bristled under the inequality built into the system. As Buck (1993:9) describes it: "While little probably filtered down to the [commoners], their benefit, however symbolic, was nonetheless real. Their land had been revitalized by the God in whose honor they had given tribute."

THE CONCEPTS OF *MANA* AND TABOO

The Hawaiians, like all Polynesians, judged their kings on the basis of their *mana*. The word as it has come down to us has lost much of its original meaning in the ancient Hawaiian context. Back then it referred more or less to "outstanding effectiveness in action;" it was a procreative power transmitted from its divine source out across the universe. *Mana* could be fickle; it was unstable; a good chief did not possess it so much as take it or wrench it away from its godly source. It obviously had deserted the chief who failed in battle (or even the land which failed to produce). This emphasis on the visible, measurable efficacy of *mana* probably led to the association in Polynesia of nobility and status with sheer size. As Shore (1989:138-139) noted, "Whether through height or girth, brightness or generosity, chiefly *mana* in Polynesia is expressed through images of abundance. Distinctions in quality manifest themselves in distinctions in quantity, but always as indications of spiritual luster."

The potency that was *mana*, that divine force, that power, was constructive only when contained or channeled. When in the wrong hands or when handled improperly it was a dangerous force that threatened human existence. So, understandably, many Polynesian spiritual beliefs and practices centered on how to be careful around *mana*.

The term that refers to the danger of mishandled *mana* has passed into English as the word "taboo," which in Hawaiian was pronounced *kapu*. Shore (1989:144) glosses the term taboo as originally meaning "dangerous," or "marked," or "set apart," implying the need to "pay attention." He clarifies it thusly:

> The divine, pure or impure, is *kapu* [taboo] to persons or things that are not divine. This means that the latter have to pay attention and relate to the former in a prescribed way. Inversely, things or persons that are not divine are *noa* [common, polluting], because the divine beings are not supposed to be careful with them. Moreover, persons or things that are closer to the divine are *kapu* to those that are less close to it. Vice versa, the latter are *noa* to the former. (Shore 1989:144)

Malo (1951:27-30) provides some interesting examples from ancient Hawai'i of what kinds of practices were taboo. He mentions, for instance, that men and women had to eat separately, even their food had to be prepared separately. Eating together was taboo. Additionally, women were isolated during menstruation; a man's sanctuary and eating house couldn't be entered by his wife while he was there on penalty of death. He could enter her eating house while she was eating, however. Women's places where men were forbidden included the menstrual hut; men were forbidden upon pain of death with having sex with menstruating women. Women were also forbidden from eating pork, bananas, coconuts, certain fish, shark, sea turtle, porpoise, whale, and stingray upon pain of death. Oddly enough, doorsteps were very taboo places in ancient Hawai'i. It was highly improper to sit or stand on one—a taboo which is still respected today (Malo 1951:85).

Another interesting example of the concept of taboo comes from the world of ancient Hawaiian medicine. In the old days the priest, when called to a sick person's bedside, would taboo certain foods for the duration of the illness. He would then perform his priestly duties and try to cure the patient (he would sleep at the patient's shrine, look for omens that would tell who or what had made the patient sick, he would pray for the patient, give the patient fever reducing drinks, enemas, a steam bath, bed rest, or whatever was required). Then, if the patient recovered, the healing ceremony ended with the patient eating the foods which the priest had originally made taboo (Malo 1951:107).

Many taboos also surrounded the interactions of chiefs and commoners. If a commoner's shadow fell on a chief's house, his robe, his back, or on anything belonging to the chief, the commoner was to be killed; when a chief ate, people had to kneel and if anyone raised a knee, they were killed. Wearing the clothes of a chief meant death. High chiefs moved about only at night to spare the population, but if they did move in the day, a messenger went ahead crying his presence and all had to prostrate themselves while he passed, or be killed (Malo 1951:56).

So we can see from the above examples that the concept of taboo was complex and multifaceted with at least two usages of the term co-existing, the one active and the other passive. Shore again:

> As an active quality, *tapu* [taboo] suggests a contained potency of some thing, place, or person. In its passive usage, it means forbidden or dangerous for someone who is *noa*. Moreover, it seems to combine contradictory properties, suggesting on the one hand sacredness, reverence, and distinctiveness and, on the other, danger, dread, and pollution. (Shore 1989:144)

What is perhaps most important to understand about this complex system of *mana* and taboo was that it justified the rigid social hierarchy that dominated Hawaiian society. *Mana* and taboo controlled and constrained all human interactions and practices. Since it was a divine force, it shed divine light on those who possessed it; and those who possessed it were, of course, the rulers. Buck explains its force in human society this way:

> *Mana* was the positive manifestation of spirituality and power—power that emanated from the gods and was channeled through the *ali'i* [nobles], power that was embedded in the forces of nature (weather, volcanoes, the fertility of crops), in human knowledge and skills, in procreation and fertility, in cycles of birth and death; and power that was evident in the social well-being of the community. *Mana*, the life force that came from the gods, infused all of nature—plants and animals, sky and water, places and people—but the greatest concentration of *mana* was in the highest *ali'i*, the most divine and most powerful chiefs, who received it through their sacred genealogical links to the gods. (Buck 1993:33-34)

CHANT AND HULA IN ANCIENT HAWAI'I

The varieties of chants recited in the past were numerous. There were genealogy chants; chants praising the gods; and prayer chants which sought protection from evil, or divine inspiration, or appealed to family gods, or were prayers of thanksgiving. Secular chants existed as well. They were not all sacred. Many dealt with trickster figures or tales of enchantment or horror; some dealt with games and sporting events and so forth (Kanahele 1986:53).

Not surprisingly, the greatest patrons of the dancers and chanters in old Hawai'i were the highest *ali'i*. They kept around them chant and hula composers and performance specialists whose jobs were to produce and perform chants and dances that celebrated the high chief's sterling character and his genealogical connections with the gods. Whole schools (*halau*) of hula and chant were established to teach selected individuals how to properly perform them. The performers trained long and hard because the chants and hula were varieties of religious ritual that had to be executed according to very formalized rules covered by taboos. An eighteenth century observer of a hula performance provided the following report of its meticulous concern with detail:

> The entertainment consisted of three parts, and was performed by three different parties consisting of about two hundred women in each, who ranged themselves in five or six rows, not standing up, not kneeling, but rather sitting upon their haunches ... The whole of this numerous group was in perfect unison of voice and action, that it were impossible, even to the bend of a finger, to have discerned the least variation. Their voices were melodious, and their actions were as innumerable as, by me, they are indescribable; they exhibited great ease and much elegance,

and the whole was executed with a degree of correctness not easily to be imagined.
(Buck 1993:45)

Since in general high chiefs as a class remained dominant over commoners while individual
chiefs vied with each other for power, the chants were called upon to illuminate the spiritual
stability of the social hierarchy in general while incorporating modifications to reflect the constantly
changing contemporary political scene. The chants were thus constant in their expression of the
"naturalness" of dominance over the many by the powerful, noble few, but they were constantly
reworked to incorporate new genealogies so as to legitimize the political claims of newly powerful
chiefs (Buck 1993:43-46).

Hulas, like chants, were performed at many different functions and came in many different
varieties. There were mourning hulas performed when an *ali'i* died; there were prayerful hulas of
purification and consecration; hulas were performed at the birth of a royal child; hulas were
performed at ritual feasts; before entering battles; and even to welcome the return of a traveling
relative (Kanahele 1986:132-133).

Hulas and chants worked to reinforce the Hawaiian status quo. In this they were joined by
other aristocratic rituals, particularly the periodic crowning of a new ruler. Since as mentioned
earlier, Hawaiian noble families had no inherited rights to land, each time a great *ali'i* died, all the
land which he had bequeathed to his followers returned to his successor alone. The new ruler then
reapportioned the land to his followers as he saw fit.

The act of restoring the land was meant to reenact creation itself. For just like creation, the
redivision of the land involved making differences and distinctions where none had previously
existed. Those who received the land were in turn distinguished as superior to those who did not
and thus the social order with all of its attendant taboos and *mana* was re-established. Each king,
upon accession to power, literally recreated the world and established his own order in it. The
primordial state of undifferentiated sludge, or darkness, or water, or confusion was transformed by
the creative power of the ruler as he established his reign, just as it had been at the dawn of the
world (Sahlins 1992:25).

CONSOLIDATION OF *ALI'I* POWER AND THE ARRIVAL OF FOREIGNERS

The ritual and mythical celebration of aristocratic power did not occur in a vacuum. Throughout the
period from 1650 to the end of the 1700s important historical changes were taking place. For
example, competition among the nobility to expand their chiefly status system meant more intense
wars of conquest and greater exploitation of land and labor. The chiefs were vying with each other
to concentrate power and wealth in fewer and fewer hands. As a consequence, more marginal land
was brought under cultivation and the common people (*maka'ainana*) suffered from greater
demands on their resources in the form of ever greater demands to send tribute to the *ali'i*.

The arrival of the outside world in the form of Captain Cook and other European sailing vessels
after 1778 introduced the market economy to Hawai'i, which the nobles also worked hard to
monopolize to their favor (Sahlins 1992:27, Buck 1993:51-52). That Hawaiian society did not
explode into open rebellion attests in part to the power of the performance of Hawaiian cultural
practices which effectively legitimized and rendered natural for commoners and nobility alike this
increasingly onerous state of affairs.

THE FUR TRADE

Cook's voyages to Hawai'i and the Northwest Coast starting in 1778 opened up an extremely
valuable trade network. Furs from the Northwest were exchanged in Canton, China, against silks

and other products bound for Europe and colonies in the New World. Hawai'i became the main stopover in the trade where ships could be reprovisioned and crews rested.

The consequences for Hawaiians proved to be dramatic. They benefited economically from the trade—at least the nobles did—but the commoners paid a horrific price in the form of venereal and other infectious diseases introduced by the sailors against which the Hawaiians had no immunities.

Perhaps the greatest side effect of Hawai'i being pulled into the capitalist world market was the spread throughout the islands of firearms. *Ali'i* who were savvy enough to establish good trade links with visiting merchant ships amassed arsenals which allowed them to conquer ever wider territories.

As mentioned earlier, increased rivalry between various high nobles in the Hawaiian islands and greater pressure to produce surpluses had begun to mark Hawaiian history before the coming of Western contact. However, that trade certainly accelerated the trend, so much so, that from the 1780s on, the goal of several powerful Hawaiian leaders became for the first time the unification of all of the islands under one ruler. The great king Kamehameha I of the island of Hawai'i eventually achieved this unprecedented goal in 1810 when, thanks, 1. to his many and various trade contacts, 2. to his ability to increase agricultural productivity, and 3. to his army of over 15,000 warriors, he became king of all of the (then called "Sandwich") Islands (Sahlins 1992:40-44).

THE SANDALWOOD AND WHALING ERAS

The Northwest Coast sea otter skins began to disappear by the 1810s to be replaced by Hawaiian sandalwood, an aromatic tree which grew wild in Hawai'i and was used to make Chinese fans. This meant that Hawai'i was now the source of goods bound for world trading networks—instead of just a resting place for traders.

The sandalwood period (1812-1830) as Sahlins (1992:57) makes clear, saw the strong monarchy set up by Kamehameha I slowly replaced by an oligarchy of aristocrats. Sahlins is referring to the fact that the king's favorite wife, Ka'ahumanu, managed, after his death (1819), to raise her own family to positions of great prominence from which they more or less ruled the island until the 1850s, even though the king's own sons were nominally in charge.

The queen mother and her family made monumental changes in Hawaiian culture during their rule. They first abolished the traditional religion in 1819 by annulling the customary taboo system. They then adopted Christianity and began encouraging the spread throughout the islands of American missionaries. In reality, as Sahlins (1992:57) argues, they revived the taboo system but in a puritanical Protestant form (prohibited dancing, games, activity on the Sabbath; adopted Western dress codes; cracked down on extramarital sex, etc.). They also elevated the missionaries to the position of quasi-priests of the state.

The competition among the *ali'i* at this time to monopolize trade with the outside world turned from the amassing of arms to the race to acquire prestige goods. Sandalwood traders encouraged them in this and supplied all manner of luxury items, particularly silk clothing and china tableware. By diverting labor from agriculture to sandalwood tree cutting, and by causing the nobility to accumulate huge debts, the trade nearly bankrupted the islands by the late 1820s, about the time the sandalwood supplies gave out.

Hawai'i was "saved" from reverting back to a subsistence economy in the years after the sandalwood gave out by the rise in the Pacific of the American whaling industry. Over 700 whaling ships visited Hawai'i during 1847, along with 70 merchant and naval vessels. They bought all manner of provisions from Hawai'i and caused the island's merchants to prosper like never before. That lasted until the 1860s when the American Civil War and the rise of the petroleum industry put an end to the trade (Sahlins 1992:101).

INCREASING FOREIGN POWER AND THE GREAT *MAHELE* REFORMS

Much changed in Hawai'i during those decades. Whereas foreign missionaries had come to exert significant influence over the islands during the earlier decades, so during the middle decades of the nineteenth century did foreign merchants and diplomats begin to acquire power. The local Hawaiian nobles could not compete with foreigners when it came to capitalist commercial arrangements. Consequently they began to lose control over the island's economy, and then over its administration. The monarchy continued in place, but the minister of foreign relations, the attorney general, and the chief justice had all fallen into the hands of foreigners by the 1850s.[3]

The Hawaiian people did not sit still while their country was overrun by outsiders. They held mass petition-collecting drives and made pleas to the king and the *ali'i* to rid the government of foreigners, to prohibit the sale of land to foreigners, and to halt the practice of making foreigners naturalized citizens of Hawai'i. Sahlins sums up the period:

> From all over the Islands, the countryside as well as the towns, the people deluged the king, the legislature, and various government ministers with a stream of petitions and letters of grievance. There were protests against abusive taxes, the forced labor system, and the highhanded activities of Hawaiian tax collectors, magistrates, land commissioners, *konohiki* [middle level Hawaiian land officials], and owning chiefs. More than once the political consciousness rose to the level of the people as a whole and the survival of the nation. As for instance in 1854, in response to a movement in favor of annexation to the United States bruited in Honolulu and the U.S. Congress: 'Your hereditary people from the time of your ancestors,' read a petition from Ka'u addressed to the king, nobles, and representatives, 'refuse to have you consent to join with American, lest you ... become as nothing, like the Indians in America.' (Sahlins 1992:130)

The common people's complaints against the *haole* (white) and Hawaiian elite increased but were ignored. Ironically, just as their protests reached a crescendo in the middle 1840s, the Hawaiian government began passing a series of land tenure reforms known as the *Mahele*. The king and merchants and other capitalist investors claimed land had to be privatized to allow for the massive capital investment needed to improve agricultural production further. The missionaries in the countryside advocated the commodification of all land because they believed that private property was the key to civilization and the advancement of the Hawaiian people. The ruling chiefs advocated the switch because, they claimed, the *Konohiki* (land stewards) were pocketing the profits from taxes and gifts and not sending them on up the ladder to them. So the switch came about. Between 1846 and 1855 the laws of private property spread across the land and effectively ended the traditional Hawaiian land system (Sahlins 1992:132-134). From then on foreigners could buy land in Hawai'i.

In fact the *Mahele* divided the land of Hawai'i into several different types. First there was the land of the king, which was divided into his private land (Crown Lands: one million acres) and into Government Lands (1.5 million acres). The *ali'i* received another half million acres. The rest, less than 1% of the land, went to commoners. This was rectified somewhat in 1850 by the passage of the *Kuleana* Act which gave commoners the right to petition for access to their traditional lands, and gathering and watering places (failure to do so meant loss of ancestral claims to the land), though many commoners found that even after they gained title to their land they could not hold on to it because they could not pay the taxes. Thus by 1886, two-thirds of allotted Hawaiian land was in the hands of foreigners (Buck 1993:69-71).

The destruction of the older Hawaiian system of communal land and tribute to ruling chiefs led to the ever greater shift by commoners to wage labor to survive. Many left the land all together and migrated to Honolulu and other towns. Many began to migrate to the large sugar plantations being created under the new laws that allowed large, private land holdings to develop.

SUGAR COMES TO RULE THE ISLANDS

The American Civil War had ruined the sugar production capacity of the South, so a large market for Hawaiian sugar existed on the mainland. In the beginning, the plantation workers were mainly Hawaiian nationals. But the Hawaiian population was actually declining just as the plantations were expanding, so thousands of foreign laborers were imported to work in the fields. The largest numbers of workers came from China, Japan, and the Philippines with smaller contingents from Europe Asia and the Pacific islands.[4] The U.S. guaranteed the profitability of the Hawaiian sugar industry in 1876 by signing the Reciprocity Treaty which allowed for the duty free importation of Hawaiian sugar (Buck 1993:73-74).

The spread of the sugar plantation industry throughout Hawai'i marked the end of the island chain's autonomy. Foreign interests, already well ensconced in positions of power, came to dominate completely. From 1840 on, according to Sahlins (1992:126) the king became little more than a constitutional monarch who shared power with a Privy Council dominated by whites and a bicameral legislature composed of a House of Nobles and a Chamber of the People's Representatives. Buck sums up the decline of autonomy:

> As sugar became the mainstay of the islands' economy, Hawaiian control and sovereignty were increasingly jeopardized. A Hawaiian nationalist movement began in the 1870s, marshaling Hawaiians under the slogan 'Hawai'i for Hawaiians.' Feeling their economic and political control threatened, the *haole* elite turned on Kalakaua [king at the time] and became very vocal in their criticism of his style of government. They wrote newspaper editorials castigating his 'extravagant' expenditures on the 'Iolani Palace, on his coronation and birthday jubilee, and other perceived evidences of his unfitness to rule. But the major point of controversy was Kalakaua's opposition to the ceding of Pearl Harbor to the United States in return for the renewal of the Reciprocity Treaty, which had expired in 1886. To get their way on this and other matters affecting their position in the islands, members of the economic and political elite (second-generation missionary families, plantation owners, sugar and trade agents) forced Kalakaua to sign a new constitution that greatly limited the powers of the monarchy. The 'Bayonet Constitution' of 1887, the same year the Reciprocity Treaty was renewed and the United States acquired exclusive rights to Pearl Harbor, was the primary focus of Hawaiian dissatisfaction until Kalakaua's death in 1891. Realizing that Queen Lili'uokalani would continually oppose their plans for economic and political expansion, the Americans organized and eventually effected, in 1893, the overthrow of the Hawaiian monarchy backed up by the threat of American marines. A provisional government was set up, followed by a republic in 1894 and annexation in 1898—the same period in which the United States acquired Cuba, Puerto Rico, Guam, the Philippines, and the Virgin Islands as a result of the Spanish-American War. The result of annexation was the total appropriation of the Hawaiian islands by American economic and political interests. (Buck 1993:75-76)

The loss of Hawaiian sovereignty over the islands continued during the twentieth century by means of: 1. the spread of American education and the English language; 2. the centrality of Pearl Harbor to the Pacific theater during World War II; and 3. the culmination of American dominance in 1959 with Hawai'i becoming the fiftieth state of the U.S.

THE CHANGING ROLE OF *MELE* (CHANT) AND HULA DURING THE NINETEENTH CENTURY

As mentioned earlier, the rise to positions of importance of American missionaries under the patronage of the female chief, Ka'ahumanu, wife of the first islands-wide king, Kamehameha I, during the 1820s and 1830s meant that traditional Hawaiian performance cultural forms were discouraged. Chants were at first demoted to being accompaniments to hulas. They had traditionally been a form of poetry that was chanted, retelling the genealogical and mythological past in a particularly "literate" style of Hawaiian language said to be full of double entendres and multiple layers of symbolic meaning. Now with the coming of the missionaries and the rise of Protestant/ Puritan Christianity, chanting and hula were considered inappropriate behaviors, a sign of backwardness "and a disgrace to the age" (Buck 1993:108). In decline, too, was the Hawaiian religion and the system of *ali'i* patronage which kept the hula schools and teachers operating and provided the incentive for the handing down of the ancient chants from master to apprentice. By 1883 the islands had to be scoured to find the old people who remembered how to perform the ancient chants and hulas and who were still conversant in the older language forms. By 1924 only 17 old men could be found who knew the ancient chanting styles (Buck 1993:111).

Hulas were dances that accompanied the poetry of chant. They did not exist apart from the chants. That relationship was inverted during the decline of traditional Hawaiian culture during the nineteenth century. As Buck (1993:112) describes it: "Even when performed with chant, hula gradually became the dominant element, body movements overshadowing the poetry and its poetic-religious concepts and connotations. As a result, the meaning of chant and hula changed for performers and audiences."

Ironically, contemporary commentators argue over whether knowledge of the text sung as part of a hula is absolutely necessary to capture the meaning of the dance, that is, the story it tells. So removed has hula become from the ancient chants that it is possible for experts to argue that the body movement of the dance alone holds its key today. Kanahele represents this approach:

> Hula is mimetic, that is, it imitates actions, events, phenomena, persons, animals, and so forth. When we say hula tells a story we mean that it speaks through its body language, as this is expressed by physical movements and gestures. As in ritual, so in dance; Hawaiians believed that the hula possesses *mana*. But why did Hawaiians think that a certain set of rhythmic motions had such power? Quite apart from its mythic origins, the answer lies in the ancient belief that by imitating something, one can possess it or control it. Contemporary *kumu hula* [hula teacher] John Kaha'i Topolinski writes that 'the dance is based on the assumption that by presenting an act, one gains power over it. Thus one can govern the outcome of a future act or cause a past act to happen again. By imitating a person or object, moreover, one can possess it or control it. It is sufficient, therefore, to reproduce, say in dancing, the wished-for events: the victorious battle, the successful hunt ... ' (Kanahele 1986:130-131)

Of course the association of hula with chants was not what attracted the hostility of the missionaries. They targeted the dance because of its sexual connotations. The lack, by Western standards, of "decent" clothing combined with the sensuous body movements drove the missionaries to distraction. A more blatant example of sinful behavior could not have been invented. They refused to acknowledge any of the religious beliefs behind the cultural practices but labeled them instead as mere superstitions.

RESISTANCE TO MISSIONARY ATTACKS ON TRADITIONAL CULTURE

The assault on the traditional Hawaiian cultural forms of chant and hula did not go unchallenged. The first sign of resistance arose almost immediately during the reign of Kamehameha II (Liholiho 1819-1825) who, when confronted about the "idolatry and licentiousness" of the hula by the powerful leader of the missionaries, Pastor Bingham, said of the hula, "This is the Hawaiian custom, and must not be hindered" (Buck 1993:155). The missionaries persisted and the king compromised by banning hulas on Sunday.

This and other bans on the hula were honored mainly in the *haole* areas, such as around Honolulu on the island of Oahu. The prohibitions had much less of an impact on the other islands. This was because unorganized but effective resistance to the spread of missionary culture was strongest among the common people in the countryside. As evidence of this Sahlins (1992:124) mentions that in spite of over 10 years in which to spread their religion and language through missionary station schools, by the middle of the 1830s, over half the missionaries in the stations were reporting zero school attendance.

Remember we mentioned earlier that a kind of female regency developed during the early nineteenth century based on the power accumulated by Ka'ahumanu and her female descendants. That competition for power between the kingship and the female regency, was manifested at the ideological level in the struggle between Christianity and traditional Hawaiian culture. The female regents backed Christianity and were probably responsible for the overthrow of the old Hawaiian religion in the form of the official breaking of the taboos in 1819. That behind-the-scenes power struggle continued throughout the reigns of the next several kings who were in fact no more powerful than the female premiers who essentially ruled alongside them.

What is of interest to us here is that those kings appear to have adopted a kind of grudging defense of traditional Hawaiian culture as a way of distancing themselves from the female premiers, as a way of symbolically combating their influence. The missionaries with the backing of the premiers did much to cripple traditional culture; yet they were not completely successful—even in the capital of Honolulu—thanks to the on-again, off-again support of the kings.

For example, after the death of Ka'ahumanu in 1832, Kamehameha III (Kauikeaouli 1825-1854) supported the hula. It is hard to say whether this was a conscious act of defiance or more the playing out of a kind of renegade persona on the part of the young king. Whatever the motive, hula festivals enjoyed a brief period of royal patronage unknown during the life of the first female regent (Buck 1993:108).

By the time of King Kalakaua (ruled 1874-1891), American influence was so strong that support of traditional Hawaiian expressive cultural forms was understood to be a symbolic act of defiance against Uncle Sam. The days of direct missionary cultural authority were more or less over, but the threat to Hawaiian political autonomy was growing ever greater. King Kalakaua recognized this when he ordered the performance of the ancient Kumulipo chant and the accompanying hula at his coronation in 1883. The master chanters, evoking the long genealogy that connected the new king with the ancient *ali'i* and then with the gods, publicly chanting the hallowed history that was about to come to an end.

That end occurred in the form of American annexation of Hawai'i in 1893, during the reign of Kalakaua's sister, Queen Lili'uokalani. Like her predecessor she continued to patronize chant and hula as symbols of resistance to increasing American dominance. What is also interesting about her case is that she actually composed a song of quasi-resistance that stressed the importance to Hawaiian identity of the ancient chiefs and the land—at a time when both were being eclipsed by the growth of American influence. The song is the famous "Aloha 'Oe."

The resistance of the Queen to American annexation inspired other Hawaiian musicians to follow suit. The Royal Hawaiian Band, Hawaiian musicians who played primarily western music on formal occasions and for private parties, steadfastly refused to honor annexation. They resigned en masse rather than be associated with the new regime. As a form of cultural protest they composed a song to commemorate their mass refusal to serve the new government of annexation. The song, "Kaulana Na Pua" (Famous Are the Children), goes like this (Buck 1993:115-116):

'A 'ole 'a'e kau i ka pulima	No one will fix a signature
Maluna o ka pepa o ka 'enemi	To the paper of the enemy
Ho'ohui 'aina ku'ai hewa	With its sin of annexation
I ka pono sivila a'o ke kanaka.	And sale of native civil rights.
'A'ole makou a'e minamina	We do not value
I ka pu'ukala a ke aupuni.	The government's sum of money.
Ua lawa makou i ka pohaku,	We are satisfied with the stones,
I ka 'ai kamaha'o o ka 'aina.	Astonishing food of the land.

Both the Queen's and the Royal Band's songs were composed in modern styles that did not predate the nineteenth century. They represent early examples of the extent to which Hawaiian expressive culture remade itself during that century, incorporating new influences from the outside in the process of redesigning indigenous Hawaiian culture. The best examples of this process would probably be the importation and then rise to prominence in Hawaiian music of the ukulele and the guitar. Foreign cowboys from Mexico, Puerto Rico, Spain, Portugal, and the Philippines shipped in to tend Hawaiian cattle herds taught the locals how to play. But then the Hawaiians took the instruments and modified them to meet local tastes, creating in the process the famous Hawaiian slack key guitar sound achieved by loosening or "slackening" the strings. Hawaiians also developed the steel guitar and exported it back to the U.S. where it became a mainstay in country and western music (Buck 1993:102-103).

Hawaiian music also became crucial in the development of Hawaiian struggles against American hegemony because of its continued use of the native Hawaiian language. As Buck mentions,

> Words and their meanings have been the only things that Westerners could not totally appropriate, could not buy like they bought land, or remake into their own as they did the political system. Even though wedded to Western forms and the capitalist incentives and constraints of the music market, the continued use of the Hawaiian language in Hawaiian songs is a statement of pride and ethnicity that still inspires the writing of Hawaiian music. (Buck 1993:119)

THE TOURIST INVASION OF THE TWENTIETH CENTURY

Hawaiian music is more important today than ever before in the struggle to maintain a space for a Hawaiian culture that keeps alive a utopian image of an autonomous and sovereign native Hawai'i. Contemporary music (in English but especially in the Hawaiian language) creates a culture that reminds Hawaiians of their honored heritage as a once free and proud people. It provides an alternative to the tourist culture which denatures Hawaiian song and dance, packaging them as harmless pastimes indulged in by the adorable natives.

That tourist culture is not something to sneeze at. Within two decades of annexation Hawai'i started attracting the attention of tourists on the continent. Broadway musicals about "Hawaiian life" became popular as early as 1912. Touring Hawaiian musicians the next year sparked a national craze for Hawaiian music and so Tin Pan Alley got busy cranking out dozens of songs with lyrics that supposedly mimicked the Hawaiian language. The 1919 hit, "Oh How She Could Yacki Hacki

Wicki Wacki Woo (that's love in Honolulu)," or the song, "Princess Poo-Poo-Ly Has Plenty Papaya," epitomized this trend towards the creation of a bastardized, artificial Hawaiian music. These U.S. versions of supposedly Hawaiian songs made their way to the islands on the back of the development of the tourist industry. The famous hotel complex at Waikiki began in 1901 with the construction of the Moana Hotel, but peaked in 1927 with the opening of the "world's most beautiful hotel," the Royal Hawaiian. These big hotels contracted for their own house orchestras and dancers to entertain cruise line customers with the commercialized songs and hulas the tourists had come to associate with the islands (Lewis 1992:174-175). The post war American economic expansion and the development of air transport in the 1950s caused Hawai'i to become an even bigger American tourist Mecca. The impact proved catastrophic as witnessed to by the fact that figures such as Don Ho and his trademark tune, "Tiny Bubbles," became synonymous with Hawaiian culture. Talking about that time, Hawaiian Entertainer Kahawanu Lake said, "We could always sell the 'Hawaiian Wedding Song,' 'Beyond the Reef,' 'Little Grass Shack,' but that was it. Singing something really Hawaiian … to sing something really important, something you really enjoyed, just wouldn't sell" (quoted in Lewis 1985:189).

The Rebirth of a Native Hawaiian Culture

But things were beginning to change by the late 1960s and early 70s. Local radio stations played an influential role—still do—in the revival of interest in traditional Hawaiian culture. One station, KCCN, began mixing traditional music into its play lists as early as 1966. In 1971 the station sponsored a concert at Waikiki with over 50 local musicians. Many played in older styles and the fans went wild. Lewis (1992:177) mentions that the concert marked a watershed in the revival of interest in traditional Hawaiian music by exposing a whole new generation to the possibilities lying dormant in the older forms.

From that point on local groups of young musicians began to search out and learn from the elders who still knew how to play the slack key guitar and how to sing in older styles. The most influential of the elders was probably Phillip ("Gabby" or "Pops") Pahinui. Though he was one of the last masters of older Hawaiian musical genres, he was forced to work for the Honolulu street department to put bread on the table.

A half dozen young musicians gravitated to Pahinui to learn the trade. They then formed their own early and influential pop/jazz rock group known as the Sunday Manoa.

The musical revival set in motion during the 1970s coincided with a general cultural and political awakening among native Hawaiians. The tremendous growth in both tourists and residents had squeezed everybody to the breaking point. As one commentator put it:[5]

The stress was felt most by rural Hawaiians who were still living in close contact with the land and sea, on the fringe of the expansion. Suddenly, their lives were shaken by eviction notices and 'No Trespassing' signs as exclusive condominiums and hideaway resorts reached the most remote and untouched corners of the islands. Lands that had languished for years were suddenly targets for speculation and development. Title to *kuleana* [ancestral] lands was challenged and lost.

Often farmers and fishermen had no place to go. Some decided to organize and fight eviction. For the first time in almost 200 years the *maka'ainana* [commoners] stood up for their way of life. Their battles, now legendary, meant Hawai'i would never be the same. Joining in the life-and-death-struggle around them, Hawaiian musicians, dancers and artists rescued a civilization that had almost disappeared, and from its remnants crafted a powerful renaissance.[6]

Many groups followed in the wake of Sunday Manoa in the 1970s and 1980s. Like Sunday Manoa, they refused the touristic names associated with Waikiki groups (Royal Hawaiian Serenaders, for example) but chose, instead, names associated with Hawai'i and the land (Ma Kapu'u Sand Band, Hui Ohana, Hokule'a, the Makaha Sons of Hi'i'hau, etc.). They did not, however, play in a strictly traditional acoustic style. They blended traditional themes, such as love for the land and the ancestors, with contemporary, electrified instruments playing at faster than traditional tempos (Lewis 1992:178-179).

Speaking of traditional themes, at least three important ones dominate contemporary Hawaiian protest music. They are: 1. love for and celebration of the land and its beauty as well as lament for its destruction; 2. hostility towards the impact of American tourism and the American military; and 3. concern for the preservation of traditional Hawaiian beliefs and practices (Lewis 1992:180-181). These themes have remained important from the 1970s, when the famous musician George Helm lost his life at sea protesting against the American military exploitation of Kahoolawe Island, until the late 1990s when the huge, wildly popular, singer Israel Kamakawiwo'ole combined the three in his song "Hawai'i '78" with the following lyrics:[7]

Chorus:
Ua mau, ke ea o ka aina, i ka pono, o Hawai'i
Ua mau, ke ea o ka aina, i ka pono, o Hawai'i

If just for a day our king and queen
Would visit all these islands and saw everything
How would they feel about the changes of our land

Could you just imagine if they were around
And saw highways on their sacred grounds
How would they feel about this modern city life

Tears would come from each others eyes
As they would stop to realize
That our people are in great great danger now
How would they feel, could their smiles be content, then cry

Chorus:
Cry for the gods, cry for the people
Cry for the land that was taken away
And then yet you'll find, Hawai'i

Could you just imagine they came back
And saw traffic lights and railroad tracks
How would they feel about this modern city life

Tears would come from each others eyes
As they would stop to realize
That our land is in great great danger now

All the fighting that the king had done
To conquer all these islands now these condominiums
How would he feel if he saw hasai'i nei
How would he feel, would his smile be content, then cry

Chorus:
Ua mau, ke ea o ka aina, i ka pono, o Hawai'i
Ua mau, ke ea o ka aina, i ka pono, o Hawai'i

THE REVIVAL OF THE HULA

The increasing militancy and political awareness of native Hawaiians set in motion during the late 1960s and early 70s affected the hula as much as it did song traditions. The Merrie Monarch Festival of hula held in Hilo, Hawai'i every year since 1963 has become almost as important as the music/ language revival in marking out the distinctive territory which constitutes native Hawaiian culture. The words of King Kalakaua spoken over 100 years ago continue to express dominant sentiments today: "Hula is the language of the heart, and therefore the heartbeat of the Hawaiian people."

But this is not the hula of the Waikiki hotels. These are not the movements of bare midriffed tourist hostesses beckoning island visitors out of their night club seats to learn the dance steps of love. The Merrie Monarch Festival is a ferocious competition between reconstituted hula schools (*halau*) directed by famous and revered hula masters. Both men and women perform older styles of dance (*Hula Kahiko*) to illustrate accompanying chants (*mele*) that praise the beauty of the islands or recount the myths and legends of Hawai'i's past and the exploits of its royalty. Percussion instruments always accompany the older hula style and the male and female dancers are almost always clothed in some form of pants or skirts. Some of the schools will also perform *hula kuhi lima*, that is, hulas danced from a sitting position which depend on only hand signals and torso movements (or *hula ki'elei* performed by a dancer squatting on haunches). Others will perform *hula ku'i Moloka'i* which are from the island of the same name and are famous as fast, very athletic dances marked by rapid feet stamping and mimed sporting or fishing moves, often accompanied by verbal taunts but without percussion. Some hulas honor specific gods (*hula Pele*, for instance, danced to honor the volcano goddess Pele) or are quite sexual in nature (*hula Pahua*). And last but not least are the *hula hapa haole*, or Westernized hula accompanied usually by English lyrics; and the modern day, more informal hula known as the *hula 'auana* which we mentioned earlier as having evolved during the nineteenth century as a more self-contained hula that does not accompany a chant so much as tells its own story, often accompanied by instruments, singing, and with greater audience participation and comprehension.[8]

THE STRUGGLE ENTERS THE TWENTY-FIRST CENTURY

Powerful American and Japanese economic interests control the Hawaiian economy. American cultural production overshadows and dominates native Hawaiian culture. Native Hawaiians are a minority in their own islands and inhabit the lowest rungs of the socio-economic ladder. Yet for all of that they are fighting back, clearing a space within which they can perform their own cultural expressions. Their identity as a people rests on a growing recognition of the foundational importance of creating their own culture and achieving sovereign control over their land. Dance, music and the Hawaiian language are the elements which evoke profound emotional attachments in native Hawaiians today and provide them with the means of expressing themselves.

In the earliest times, chant and dance were sacred activities; during the time of the missionaries they became shameful, prohibited practices; towards the end of the Hawaiian monarchy they became vehicles of protest against the looming loss of autonomy; during the decades after annexation music and dance became commercialized products accompanying tourism. Then, finally, starting in the 1970s music and dance became the harbingers of a cultural renaissance. They were used to express the resurgent pride in a new-found native Hawaiian identity. The practice of these traditional forms had changed but their significance, if anything, had increased. Native Hawaiians began investing them with symbolic value and using them to protest against their marginalization in their own land. They began to use them to recapture a sense of themselves in opposition to the dominant culture that was choking out indigenous alternatives. In short, they used music and dance to assert their right to control their own destiny. Buck sums it up succinctly:

> In effect, the Hawaiian political movement has again reconstituted and
> reappropriated Hawaiian music as a symbol of a recovered history, a
> representation of contemporary Hawaiian identity, a vehicle of public protest, and
> as a voice for Hawaiian sovereignty. The performance of Hawaiian music has taken
> on an explicit political message by practice, if not always by content, becoming part
> of a politicized discourse about Hawai'i that challenges the dominant myth of
> paradise. (Buck 1993:190)

VIDEOS ACCOMPANYING

Remember, the actual video lectures can be accessed at the following url: http://oregonstate.edu/media/classes/index.php?className=anth210

Scroll down under the "Classes on Demand" heading and select "ANTH210: Comparative Cultures."

Video 16

We had an OSU student guest expert for this video, named Mauna Kea Higuera-Trask. He guided us through a discussion of Hawaiian history from the earliest times until the present.

We talked first about the migrations from the Marquesas and Tahitian Islands that first populated the Hawaiian islands. He talked about how most all Polynesians are mutually welcoming, with the exception of the Tahitians, who, since they were colonized by the French, they have a different colonial background.

We then used the following overhead to talk about early Hawaiian culture:

1. Early Hawaiian history told in form of mythic genealogies that were chanted

2. Late Autumn marked beginning of Hawaiian ceremonial cycle and new year

3. New year (*Makahiki*) ceremonies revolved around return of Lono, god of fertility; involved *hula*

We then talked about the early migrations and first periods of settlement using the following overhead:

1st period [settlement] (300-600 A.D.)

2nd period (600-1100 A.D.)

3rd phase (1100-1650) most impressive:

1. built irrigation systems

2. Intensive pig production

3. Built aquaculture systems

We next discussed the nature of Hawaiian hierarchy with this overhead:
Large agricultural surplus and population size led to extremely hierarchical society:

1. Two kinds of Hawaiians: commoners (*maka'ainana*) and *ali'i* (nobles)

2. Society ruled over by great chiefs or kings

3. **Chiefs didn't inherit the land, they "recreated" it**

We now turned to the important notion of Mana with this overhead:
Concept of Mana
Mana = potency, virility, divince force, power
Mana was also fickle, threatening
As an illustration of the way mana and size were connected we played the song about the Sumo wrestlers. The song, called "Tengoku Kara Kaminari (Gentle Giants)" performed by Israel Kama-kawiwo'ole (1995). This illustrated the almost revered status of big people in Hawai'i.

Next, we talked about taboos using this overhead as a guide:
Concept of Taboo
Taboo = dangerous, marked, set apart
Taboos were rules governing the proper ways to deal with mana so that danger or pollution did not occur
Taboo also suggested sacredness, reverence
We saw a photo of a Tahitian chief which showed that it was taboo for leaders to touch the ground. Mauna Kea also told us that you weren't allowed to look at leaders in the old days, to touch their clothes, etc.

We shifted at this point to talk about traditional chants and hulas with this overhead:
Chant (*Mele*) and *Hula* in Ancient Hawai'i

1. Many varieties of chants and hulas

2. Nobles were patrons of chants and hulas

3. Rigid rules governed proper, sacred performance

4. Many schools (*halau*) arose to train performers

5. Hulas and chants worked to maintain social hierarchies

We saw a video clip of a traditional chanter and then some Hawaiian students today learning to chant.

Next we took up the issue of Capt. Cook and talked about the competing beliefs about what Cook stood for. The most common belief is that Cook was mistaken by Hawaiians as the returning god Lono. The minority view is that Capt. Cook was actually used by one faction against another in the internal political struggles within the islands. We then talked about what happened to Hawai'i after the arrival of foreigners. We put up this overhead:

Impact of the arrival of Capt. Cook and foreigners starting in 1778

1. They introduced:

2. Market economy to Hawaii

3. infectious disease

4. Firearms

5. Increased noble rivalry

6. Increased pressure on commoners to produce

Very soon after contact with the West, Hawaii was unified, as this overhead suggests:

Unification of the islands under Kamehameha I in 1810

Thanks to:

Many and various trade contacts

Increased agricultural productivity

Large army (15,000)

Almost immediately after the death of Kamehameha, Hawaii was taken over by the queen's family, as this overhead outlined:

The rise to power of Queen Ka'ahumanu

1. King died in 1819, queen began to put her own family in charge

2. She abolished the old religion (system of taboos)

3. She adopted Christianity

4. She promoted missionaries to positions of authority

Along with the queen's family, the whites also began to take control, as this overhead discusses:

Hawaiian monarchy begins to lose control

1. Foreign diplomats, merchants gain power

2. Hawaiian elite cannot compete

3. Some govt. positions go to foreigners

4. Missionaries, Hawaiian and foreign investors push thru the Mahele reforms

5. Sugar industry and labor importation begin

We saw an overhead photo that showed Honolulu in the 1830s, which looked to be still a fairly modest settlement, though Mauna Kea told us that the city actually got electricity before the White House in Washington, D.C.

We mentioned how Hawaiians didn't take the encroachment of outsiders lying down, as this overhead suggests:

Hawaiian resistance to foreign influences

1. In the 1840s, locals across Hawai'i held mass petition drives to halt land sales to foreigners

2. In 1850s they protested against idea of annexation to US

3. In 1870s a Hawaiian nationalist movement began with slogan, "Hawai'i for Hawaiians"

4. In 1880s, 1890s King Kalakaua (the Merrie Monarch) and Queen Lili'uokalani lead opposition to US influence

We then talked about the political events that led up to the loss of the islands, as this overhead outlined:

Loss of Hawaiian sovereignty over the islands

1. 1887 Bayonet Constitution & loss of control over Pearl Harbor

2. 1893 *haole* overthrow of Hawaiian monarchy

3. 1898 U.S. annexation of Hawai'i

We closed with an overhead which shows how the process of loss has continued:

Loss of sovereignty continues in 20th century

1. Spread of American education and English language

2. Increasing military significance of Hawaii to US during and after WW II

3. American dominance leads in 1959 to Hawai'i becoming a state

Mauna Kea ended the session by doing a traditional chant that he had been taught.

Video 17

This video, again with Mauna Kea, went back to the 19th century to pick up the story of what happened to Hawaiian song and dance as foreigners took over. We mentioned that, though song dominates today, there are still chanters performing, though hula dominates. We played an example of a chant which we described in the following overhead:

'Au'a'ia is an ancient chant from the collection performed during the celebration of the 50th birthday of the last King of Hawaii, David Kalakaua (1836-1891). The text was translated by his sister, Lili'uokalani, who said that it was originally written for her grandfather, Aikanaka, at his birth (mid-1700s?). The song appears to be a prophecy of foreign domination. The chant is addressed to Kamapua'a (Kama) who was the pig god. Recorded in 1935 by Ha'aheo accompanied by a sharkskin drum and knee drum.

We then saw some video footage of a hula done to the chant we just heard.

We then turned to a discussion of the ways the Hawaiian music has influenced other musics around the world. The ukulele is a good example of this. It originated from a Portuguese instrument brought to the island. The name, "Ukulele" means "jumping flea," which refers to the way the fingers jump on the strings. The last king of Hawaii was very fond of the ukulele.

We then played a song by the Hawaiian performer, King Benny Nawahi (song not mentioned) to demonstrate what the instrument sounded like closer to the turn of the last century.

We then talked about the slack key guitar tuning that was developed in Hawaii. The lap played, acoustic steel sliding guitar is another instrument developed in Hawaii. We played the song, "May Day is Lei Day in Hawaii," by Benny Nawahi, as an illustration of what early slide steel guitar music sounded like in Hawaii.

We also mentioned that high tenor and falsetto singing were another characteristic of Hawaiian music that marks it out.

We next took up the influence that the tourist industry had on the islands' music. In fact, music about Hawaiian beaches really started the tourist fascination with the islands. We played an example of the tourist influence as represented by the song, "My Girl from the South Sea Isles" by Benny Nawahi and the Hawaiian Beach Combers, 1928.

In some ways the 1920s to 1940s became the golden age of Hawaiian musical influence. We played a Bing Crosby movie clip to demonstrate the extent of the effect Hawaii was having on Hollywood.

We then talked about the decline of the music during the 1950s and early 1960s, as characterized by the rise of Don Ho and "Tiny Bubbles." Everything was geared towards tourists.

This was followed by the first revival, started by Gabby Pahinui. It climaxed in the early 1970s with the return to traditional music, reborn interest in the Hawaiian language. We played, as an illustration of this 1970s development, a song by Gabby (song not mentioned) opened with a chant, which was unheard of at the time. They also revived men's hula, which no one living had ever seen. This explosion of interest in more traditional Hawaiian culture became known as the Hawaiian Renaissance.

The next song we played was "The Beauty of Mauna Kea" by Keola Beamer (early 1970s) which we discussed as not a particularly protest-oriented song, but a kind of romantic, nostalgic song which longs for an earlier time, for rural Hawaii and its beauty which the singer misses now that he lives in the city. He is remembering the traditional Hawaiian good old days. It was also showing respect for the past by including a nose flute at the beginning. Our guest, Mauna Kea is named after the same mountain.

We then talked about the emphasis on traditional, back to the Hawaiian basics educational movement that developed during the 1980s. We saw a video clip on this school movement. (Before 1987, you weren't allowed to speak Hawaiian in a public school).

In the 1990s the developments in Hawaiian music crystallized in the form of Israel (IZ) Kamakawiwoʻole. He followed in the Hawaiian tradition but became very popular with the youth of today. We played "Hawaiʻi ʻ78" by Israel (IZ) Kamakawiwoʻole (1993) as an example of the kind of overtly political, confident protest song of the 1990s era. He sings in Hawaiian and English, he opens with a kind of chanting, he uses the high tenor and ukulele connected with Hawaiian music, and he uses lyrics that criticize the contemporary scene. We the played another song called, "Living in a Sovereign Land" by IZ Kamakawiwoʻole (1996), which again illustrates the kind of confident, more straight-forward form of Hawaiian protest against their marginalization, poverty, etc. Finally, we closed with another song that mixes politics and music called, "E Ala E" by IZ Kamakawiwoʻole (1995). Mauna Kea closed by discussing how central Hawaiian music has been throughout the modern period, particularly in the contemporary movement of Hawaiians fighting for their rights and to define who they are.

NOTES

1. I want to thank OSU student, Mauna Kea Higuera-Trask for stimulating my interest in Hawaiʻi and for teaching me about the love and affection Hawaiians have for the islands' music and dance.
2. Buck (1993:48-49), citing Kirch, states that during the first phase, "Although the first settlers brought with them Polynesian-wide concepts of chiefly hierarchy, first-fruits tribute, and chiefly intercession with the gods, the early chiefs were senior members of a descent group and not a separate class, as later

developed." Then, during the second phase, "The gap between chiefs and commoners widened, but still it was not distinct enough for the two groups to be considered separate classes." And then finally during the third period (1100-1650), the division was completed and chiefs became a separate class from the commoners.

3. Sahliins (1992:106-107) says that the population of Honolulu increased from 6-7,000 in the middle 1820s to 14,000 by the 1850s, with perhaps around 700 foreign merchants and craftsmen and a couple of thousand whalers present at any given time. The town also boasted 4 papers, 8 hotels, 15 eating houses, 7 bars, 5 wharves, 5 markets, 4 churches and several public buildings, including the palace.

4. Maxine Hong Kingston's *China Men* (1989) has a fascinating section called "The Great Grandfather of the Sandalwood Mountains" which is about the life and times of her ancestors brought from China to work on Hawaiian plantations.

5. Quoted from the web site "Office of Hawaiian Affairs." (http://hoohana.aloha.net/~oha/). See the "about OHA" subsection.

6. The spirit of resistance and rebirth led to the holding of a Hawaiian constitutional convention which in turn gave birth to the Office of Hawaiian Affairs. The OHA was set up in 1978 to administer the original public lands ceded to the state of Hawai'i by the U.S. government after it became a state in 1959. The OHA's mission required that it place any revenues from the land in trust to be used, among other things, to better the conditions of native Hawaiians, understood to be people with at least 50% or more Hawaiian blood. The OHA since its inception has been governed by a board of trustees voted into office by native Hawaiians. Hawaiians with less than 50% native blood could not vote. The exclusive arrangement went unchallenged until 1996 when a non-native Hawaiian, Mr. Harold Rice, filed suit to have the exclusive OHA voting regulations ruled unconstitutional. On February 23, 2000, The U.S. Supreme Court sided with the plaintiff and struck down the OHA exclusion. See the web site at http://hoohana.aloha.net/~oha/ devoted to the case for more information.

7. From the CD titled: "Facing Future." (1993) Composed by Mickey Ioane; performed by Na Wai Ho'olu'u O Ke Anuenue/Makaha Sons of Ni'ihau/Israel Kamakawiwo'ole. (Lyrics taken from: http://Hawai'i-nation.org/hawaii78.html).

8. I have taken these hula descriptions from the web site called "Different Types of Hula" to be found at http://hawaiianlanguage.com/o-h-hula.html.

The Music and Politics of Punk

CHAPTER 5

ARAB NOISE AND RAMADAN NIGHTS: RAI, RAP AND FRANCO-MAGHREBI IDENTITIES[1]

CAN'T TAKE NO MOOR

For two thousand years, essentially the same people have posed the same dangers to us. Aren't the Iranian mujahidin the descendants of the Persians who were defeated at Marathon; isn't the Islamic World, now striking at Europe's frontiers and slowly penetrating her, composed of the sons of the Ottoman Turks who reached Vienna, and the Arabs who Charles Martel routed at Poitiers?
Jean-Marie Le Pen[2]

In the aftermath of the Berlin Wall's collapse, Western Europe has been forced to rethink its identity. If in the recent past its conception of itself as a haven of democracy and civilization depended—in part—on a contrast to the evils of the Communist Empire, today an idea is being revived of Europe as "Christendom," in contradistinction to "Islam." Only this time around, the Islam in question is not being held back at Europe's Spanish or Balkan frontiers but has penetrated its very core, in the shape of new "minority" populations of Muslim background. Questions about the nature of Europe's identity and the place of Muslim immigrants within it are now among the most contentious on the Continent (Morley and Robins 1990). So acute is the anxiety about the 10 to 12 million "immigrants" that many white Western Europeans feel that they are living under cultural and economic siege (Miller 1991:33).

Spanish novelist Juan Goytisolo brilliantly lampoons this European hysteria about "foreigners" in his hilariously provocative *Landscapes after the Battle*. It opens with the inexplicable appearance of unintelligible scrawls on the walls of the Parisian neighborhood of Le Sentier. At first the natives assume the marks are the secret language of a gang of kids, but then someone spots a man with "kinky black hair" inscribing the mysterious messages. The natives conclude that the scrawls are written in a real alphabet—but backwards—and are the handiwork of "those foreigners who, in ever-increasing numbers, were stealthily invading the decrepit buildings abandoned by their former tenants and offering their labor to the well-heeled merchants of Le Sentier" (1987a:3). Then one morning, a working-class native of Le Sentier drops in at his local bar for a pick-me-up of Calvados, only to discover that the sign identifying his tavern has been replaced by one written in that incomprehensible script. Wandering through the neighborhood, he is horrified to find that every marker—the Rex cinema's marquee, McDonald's, streetsigns, the placard on the district mayor's office—has been transformed. Even the sign outside the office of the newspaper of "the glorious Party of the working class," *L'Humanité*, now reads *al-Insaniyya*.

A catastrophic, cacophonous traffic jam has broken out, for drivers cannot decipher the street signs, and the traffic police are no help. "Trying to hide his laughter, a swarthy-skinned youngster with kinky hair purveyed his services as guide to whichever helpless soul bid the highest" (1987a:7). "Colonized by those barbarians!" the unnerved Le Sentier native thinks to himself (1987a:5).

Goytisolo's 1987 send-up of the French nightmare about *immigrés* seems remarkably prescient today, almost two decades after its publication, for French antipathy is especially virulent toward those "foreigners" who have been coming from North Africa for decades and who utilize that "backward" script, Arabic. French society has never come to terms with the legacy of colonization or its bloody war against the Algerian national liberation movement, which cost 1 million Arab and 10,000 French lives.[3] Instead, one might imagine, from the frenzied reactions of so many white French men and women to all things "Arab" and "Islamic," that colonialism had been a magnanimous and bloodless project and that the Arabs in France are living in the lap of luxury and have nothing to complain about.[4]

So severe are apprehensions about the *immigré* "problem" that during the *"hijab* affair" of 1989, when nine female Franco-Maghrebi students in state-run *lycées* demanded the right to wear Islamic headscarves, the media fused the signifiers "immigrant," "Muslim fundamentalist," and "invasion" together into a specter of an eventual Islamic France—a vision that horrified a good portion of the French population, on both the left and right (Koulberg 1991).[5] Even President François Mitterrand, who postured as an antiracist, was prompted to assert that the country had gone beyond "the threshold of tolerance" (Riding 1990:I16). Jacques Chirac, ex-prime minister, mayor of Paris, and leader at the time of the right-wing Rally for the Republic (RPR), complained about the "overdose of immigrants"—a codeword for "Arabs"—while Valéry Giscard d'Estaing, the former president, warned of a foreign "invasion" (Gorce 1991:30; Singer 1991:814). These elite opinions lent legitimacy to widespread popular sentiments. Two surveys in 1991 indicated that 71% of the French populace thought there were too many Arabs in the country and that over 30% of the electorate supported the platform of Jean-Marie Le Pen's far-right National Front which calls for the expulsion of *immigrés* (*Le Monde*, March 22, 1991; Riding 1991;).[6] And Chirac, in a now-infamous statement, expressed his sympathy for the decent French working people who are being driven "understandably crazy" by the "noise and smell" of foreigners (Drozdiak 1991; Hall 1991b:18).[7]

"Noise and smell"—music and cuisine—are crucial cultural forms of expression, essential vehicles through which North Africans assert, sustain, and reconfigure their identities in France. And probably the most well-known type of "Arab noise" blasting out of boomboxes in Maghrebi neighborhoods in Paris and Marseille at the end of the twentieth century was *rai* music, a genre which arrived in the U.S. under the category of "World Music" in the late 1980s.

This chapter tracks this brand of Arab noise through its origins and evolution in Algeria and examines how its uses and meanings were transformed as it crisscrossed the Mediterranean along with North African migrant workers. It assesses rai's significance within the Maghrebi community and its role in the construction of Franco-Maghrebi identities, particularly with regard to gender, tradition, and religion. We stress rai as an exemplar of the hybrid cultural practices that typify the integration of Maghrebis into French life. The rather defensive cultural identities associated with rai are compared to the more assertive and multiethnic ones that accompany rap, the music currently in vogue with young Franco-Maghrebis. Finally, we will argue that, despite their marginal status, Franco-Maghrebis and their expressive culture are integral to an understanding of contemporary French identity. Because the assimilation of Maghrebis into French life "is not a process of acculturation but of cultural syncretism" (Gilroy 1987:155), French culture is being "thirdworldized." Against its will, the country is gradually shedding its Europeanness and becoming "mestizo, bastard, [and] fecundated" by formerly victimized civilizations (Goytisolo 1987b:37-38). Franco-Maghrebi expressive culture proposes a model of decentralized plurality and multiple affiliations as a means of recasting contemporary French identity and undermining French exclusivism.

ALGERIAN RAI: FROM COUNTRY TO POP, BORDELLO TO PATRIMOINE NATIONAL

Modern rai emerged during the 1920s, when rural migrants brought their native musical styles into the growing urban centers of north-western Algeria, particularly the port town of Oran (Wahran in Arabic), Algeria's second-largest city. In the new urban settings, rai developed as a hybrid blend of rural and cabaret musical genres, played by and for distillery workers, peasants dispossessed by European settlers, shepherds, prostitutes and other members of the poor classes (Virolle-Souibès 1989:51-52). Oran's permissive atmosphere proved congenial for rai artists, who found spaces to perform in its extensive network of nightclubs, taverns, and brothels, as well as in more "respectable" settings like wedding celebrations and festivals. Women singers were prominent from the genre's beginnings; and unlike other Algerian musical genres, rai performances were associated with dancing, often in mixed-gender settings (Benkheira 1986:174).

Due to its location (close to Morocco and Spain) and its port economy, Oran was permeated by multifarious cultural influences, which permitted rai musicians to absorb an array of musical styles: flamenco from Spain, *gnawa* (a musical genre performed by Sufis of West African origin) from nearby Morocco, French cabaret, the sounds of Berber Kabylia, the rapid rhythms of Arab nomads. Rai artists sang in Orani (*wahrani*), an Arabic dialect rich with French and Spanish borrowings and liberally seasoned with Berber.

As early as the 1930s, rai musicians were reportedly being harassed by the colonial police for singing about social issues of concern to Algeria's indigenous inhabitants, such as typhus, imprisonment, poverty, and colonial oppression. Likewise, during the independence struggle, rai artists composed songs that expressed nationalist sentiment (Virolle-Souibès 1988b:184-186). But throughout the period, rai's main themes were wine, love, and the problems and pleasures of life on the margins. One of the most renowned, and bawdy, rai singers was Cheikha Rimitti, one of whose songs went:

> Oh my love, to gaze upon you is a sin,
> It's you who makes me break my fast.
> Oh lover, to gaze upon you is a sin,
> It's you who makes me "eat" during Ramadan.[8]
> (Virolle-Souibès 1988a:208)

Elsewhere, Rimitti sang: "When he embraces me, he pricks me like a snake," and "People adore God, I adore beer" (Virolle-Souibès 1988a:211, 214).

After Algeria won national independence in 1962, a state-sponsored Islamic reformist chill descended over all manifestations of popular culture, which lasted throughout the 1960s and 70s. In the wake of official puritanism, drastic restrictions were imposed on public performances by women singers (Virolle-Souibès 1989:54). But the genre flourished on the fringes, at sex-segregated events like wedding parties and in the demimonde. Meanwhile adolescent boys with high-pitched voices replaced female rai vocalists in the public arena. At the same time, musicians were gradually supplementing and even replacing the *gasba* (reed flute), the *rbaba* (single-stringed instrument played with a bow), the *gellal* and *derbouka* (Maghrebi drums)—the instruments that had typified the genre for decades—with the more "modern"-sounding *'ud* (Oriental lute), violin and accordion.

In 1979, rai reemerged from the shadows, following President Chadhli Benjedid's loosening of social and economic restraints. By now, rai artists had incorporated more musical influences—from the pop musics of Egypt, India, the Americas, Europe, and sub-Saharan Africa—and were performing and recording with trumpets and electric guitars, synthesizers and drum machines. A new sound known as "pop rai" was inaugurated, whose stars were a generation of young singers known as *chebs* (young men) and *chabas* (young women). In its "pop" incarnation, rai shed its regional status, and massive cassette sales made it the *national* music for Algerian youth. Its popularity derived from its lively, contemporary sound and its raciness. Pop rai lyrics, just like "traditional" rai, dealt frankly and

openly with subjects like sex and alcohol while challenging both official puritanism and patriarchal authority within the family. The "modernity" of its musical texture and the insubordinate spirit of its messages earned pop rai a substantial audience among a generation of disaffected and frequently unemployed youth, chafing at traditional social constraints and the lack of economic opportunities.

As cassette sales soared, producers tried to boost profits by insisting on more risqué lyrics from their artists (Virolle-Souibès 1989:59). The pop rai star Chaba Zahouania, whose ruggedly sensual voice earned her the sobriquet, the Billie Holiday of Oran (Virolle-Souibès 1988b:197), sang: "I'm going with him, Mamma, I'm climbing in next to him," and "Call Malik so he'll bring the beer" (Virolle-Souibès 1988a:211, 213). In a similar vein, Chaba Fadela spiced up her lyrics: "I want to sleep with him, I want him to open up his shirts" (Virolle-Souibès 1988a:210).

If racy lyrics spurred sales, they incurred government wrath in the early 1980s. The association of rai with dancing, particularly in mixed-gender company, also provoked the hostility of state officials who adhered to orthodox Islamic views that dancing is obscene (Benkheira 1986:174-176). But even more importantly, the government felt compelled to suppress an increasingly influential cultural practice that seemed to articulate the sentiments of insubordinate youth claiming new sexual and cultural freedoms—the so-called "rai generation." Police rounded up single women patronizing nightclubs featuring rai, while the government denounced rai as "illiterate" and lacking in "artistic merit," banned it from the state-run airwaves, and prohibited the import of blank cassettes in an attempt to halt distribution (McMurray and Swedenburg 1991; Bizot 1988:89).

But in mid-1985 the government abruptly reversed its position. In part, the volte-face was due to lobbying by a former liberation army officer turned pop music impresario, Colonel Snoussi, who hoped to profit if rai could be mainstreamed. Another factor in officialdom's shift was the music's growing popularity in France, where the diasporic Maghrebi community provided an expanding market for the music, as well as facilities for production and a distribution network (via the massive to-and-fro movement of immigrants who smuggled cassettes). Pressure was also brought to bear by the French minister of culture, Jack Lang, who urged Algerian officials to grant exit visas to rai stars wishing to perform in France. Some sectors of the Algerian nomenklatura, moreover, argued for promoting rai as a counterweight to the growing militant Islamist trend (Benkheira 1986:177).

So the government relaxed its opposition, rai festivals were duly organized in Oran and Algiers, and the music began to receive radio and television exposure. But at the same time that officialdom brought rai in from the periphery and claimed it as part of the national patrimony, it attempted to tame, contain, and mainstream it. A line sung by several chebs as "we made love in a broken down shack" was diffused on Algerian radio as "we did our military service in a broken down shack" (Bizot and Dimerdji 1988:133). The police tried to prevent audience members from dancing at the first Oran festival in 1985 (Benkheira 1986:176). Under this pressure, the music industry began practicing self-censorship. The same producers who so recently were promoting bawdiness started vigorously cleaning up rai lyrics in order to get their product played on radio and television and to make it palatable to a wider audience. Rachid Baba, the producer of *Rai Rebels* and other acclaimed rai releases for the U.S. market,[9] explained without a hint of irony: "In the beginning, I let a *cheb* sing the words as he wanted. Now I pay attention. When he sings a vulgarity, I say stop. If he doesn't obey, I cut it during the mixing" (quoted by Virolle-Souibès 1989:60). And the mainstreaming did succeed in increasing rai's audience, as many who were previously put off by rai's "dirty" reputation now found it pleasantly acceptable.

RAI AND THE DISCOURSE OF WORLD MUSIC

U.S. World Music publicity—the CD or cassette jackets, the record reviews, and the critical articles—never tells such stories about rai's self-censorship. Instead, the World Beat discourse which has promoted rai since its U.S. arrival in 1988 generally presents the music as a vehicle of resistance, comparing its role within Algerian society to that of U.S. or British rock music at opposi-tional moments—the mid-1950s (Elvis), the late 1960s (Beatles and Stones), and the late 1970s (Sex Pistols). Rai is frequently advertised as "The music of . . . Algerian rebel youth,"[10] and commentators claim that Cheb Khaled "is to rai what Elvis was to rock" (Bizot and Dimerdji 1988:93) or that rai is a kind of "North African punk" (Eyre 1992:19). While partially true, such claims are based on a projection of a (white, eurocentric) version of the culture wars onto the Algerian scene. Such a move allows us—World Music fans—to identify with the Algerian rai audience by assimilating their struggles to our models. We can sympathize with rai audiences because they seem to be fighting battles we have already fought—as teenagers demanding more sexual freedom—or are still fighting—as rockers against religious fundamentalism or official puritanism.

This is not to deride the positive effects of rai's late-1980s arrival on the U.S. World Music scene, which until then had largely ignored or excluded Arabo-Islamic musics. The repute that Arab musicians like Palestinian-American *'ud* and violin virtuoso Simon Shaheen, the Sudanese singer Abdel Aziz El Mubarak, and Moroccan *gnawa* artist Hassan Hakmoun have recently gained in the West was greatly enabled by rai's breakthrough. But that opening depended in part on a crucial discursive absence. For World Music publicity treats rai as a strictly Algerian phenomenon, as a musical genre that has merely *absorbed* Western influences, rather than viewing it as part of a wider endeavor to bring about what Goytisolo calls "the gradual dissolution of 'white' culture by all the peoples who, having been forcibly subjected to it, have assimilated the tricks, the techniques necessary to contaminate it" (1987b:38). World Music publicity has crucially ignored the role of rai in France, where it has served as a central mode of cultural expression in minority struggles. Perhaps this silence can be attributed to the fact that it is easier for white World Music fans to align with young rockers or punks fighting the same battles as "us" than to identify with a racialized Other combating European racism.

THE VARIETIES OF FRANCO-MAGHREBI IDENTITY

> The diaspora experience is defined, not by essence or purity, but by the recognition of a necessary heterogeneity and diversity: by a conception of 'identity' which lives with and through, not despite, difference; by hybridity. Stuart Hall (1989:80)

As pop rai won over Algerian youth, it simultaneously gained adherents among Maghrebi immi-grants in France and their offspring—the *Beurs*, as the second generation had come to be known. Rai emerged as a crucial cultural vehicle for a minority striving to carve out a space for itself in an inhospitable, racist environment. Rai became a veritable token of Maghrebi ethnic identity, and very presence, in France.

In the summer of 1981, a series of dramatic events involving young Franco-Maghrebis, which the media rapidly transformed into staged spectacles that variously stunned, scared, and titillated an uncomprehending French public. Known as *"rodeos,"* they took place in the impoverished *banlieues* (suburbs) that encircle French cities, where the bulk of the Franco-Maghrebi population is concentrated. Young *banlieusards* heisted big-engined cars and proceeded to race and perform stunts at dusk for enthusiastic banlieue spectators. Before the police could catch them, they would stop, douse the vehicles with gasoline, and torch them. During July and August some 250 vehicles were immolated in these dramatic moments of defiance that were aimed at the hated police and that represented an angry affirmation of the minority's ghettoized existence (Jazouli 1992:17-22).

This startling display of the drastic problems and incendiary mood of young banlieue Franco-Maghrebis was followed by a flurry of organizing and networking by Arab militants. Grass-roots groups proliferated, as the massive demonstrations organized in 1983 and thrust the socio-economic problems and the racist treatment of *Franco-Maghrébins* were thrust upon the national. The French public could no longer pretend that the Arabs living in their midst were simply immigrant workers whose presence would be temporary. Here was a militant, visible generation of Maghrebis who spoke French fluently, who were not visitors but permanent residents in France, who were laying claim to full citizenship rights and equal participation in French cultural life.

But who precisely are these Franco-Maghrebis, whom French racist discourse usually lumps together into a single category—immigrants, Muslims, Maghrebis, Arabs, or foreigners? In fact they are very heterogeneous, encompassing Algerians, Moroccans, and Tunisians; Arabs and Berbers; citizens, "legal" non-citizen residents, and "illegals;" immigrants born in the Maghreb and their offspring born in France; *harkis* who fought for France during the Algerian War and their descendants as well as Algerians who backed the FLN. An estimated 1.5 million North African "foreigners" (non-citizens) live in France, and tens of thousands more (no one is sure of the total) reside there without legal permission.[11] About 1 million French citizens are of Maghrebi origin, including from 400,000 to 600,000 harkis and their offspring (Lanier 1991:16-17; Etienne 1989:107). If Jews of North African ancestry—many of whom still identify with the Maghreb—are included, that adds another 300,000 persons (Morin 1991:535). We are speaking then of between 2.5 and 3 million persons, out of a total French population of 60 million.

Economic Conditions The bulk of the Franco-Maghrebi population, immigrant and citizen alike, is concentrated in the multiethnic banlieues. These isolated modernist architectural nightmares, bleak zones of high-rises, minimal public facilities, substandard schooling, and exceptional rates of unemployment—70% of the children of immigrants in Lyons between 16 and 25 have no jobs (Begag 1990:6)—are the true loci of the "immigrant" problem.

Conditions in the banlieues are closely tied to the recent restructuring and "rationalization" of the French economy. The country has entered a "post-Fordist" phase characterized by gradual state disengagement from economic affairs and the privatization of former state enterprises; the decline of trade-union influence as well as local administrative effectiveness; the swelling of the service sector; the diminution or flight of industries dependent on massive employment of unskilled labor; and the rise of industries employing little unskilled labor.[12] The impact of these changes on the immigrant work-force is revealing: between 1973 and 1985 the proportion of working "immigrants" employed in industry fell from 45% to 36% and in construction from 35% to 26%, while "immigrant" participation in the lower-paying service sector rose from 20% to 37.5% (Lanier 1991:20).

The spatial marginalization of the Maghrebi population in France also reflects a socioeconomic shift towards the "ethnicization" of the labor force and an increased dependence on undocumented and "reserve" labor, in the new era of "flexible specialization" (Naïr 1992:39-46).[13] One facet of this shift is the fact that the total number of working North African male employees has actually decreased by about 5% since 1975, while the number of Maghrebi women workers shot up dramatically (by over

150%) during the same period. The fall in male employment and the coincident rise in the female work-force is integral to a process of economic restructuring, in which employers tap a "reserve army" of women and youth in order to maintain profits and ensure flexibility of labor allocation. This transformation in the makeup of the labor force is due in part to the government's halting of immigration in 1974 (until then predominantly a Maghrebi male activity) and its shift to a policy of family reunification (mainly involving Maghrebi women and youth). So sharp was the demographic turnabout that by 1982 more than 44% of the Maghrebi population in France was under 17 years of age, compared to 22% for the population as a whole (Talha 1991:497-499).

Authenticity and Hybridity We employ the name Franco-Maghrebi here as a convenient descriptive device. Although one occasionally encounters the designation "franco-maghrébin," ethnic groups in France typically do not define themselves in terms of hyphenated identities. Whether one's background is Italian, Spanish, Jewish or Polish, one is simply expected to be assimilated, to be "French." This requirement has proved difficult for residents and citizens of Third World origins to live up to. The stipulation is particularly problematic for North Africans, because memories of recent colonial violence in Algeria remain so vivid and because so many French people regard Maghrebis' Islamic heritage as making them unassimilable. Hence, citizens or not, French Arabs tend to be regarded as foreigners.

Many first-generation immigrants would agree, at least in part, with this designation. They will never feel "at home" in France, and dream of returning to their villages of birth as they slowly lay aside savings to build homes there for comfortable retirement. Such *immigrés* often retain an image of an Algeria or Morocco that still upholds the revered traditions and Islamic values. There are also those Franco-Maghrebis, both immigrant and citizens, who have reacted to French exclusivism by practicing their own form of isolationism. These are the ethnonationalists, most prominent among them the militant Islamists.

But advocates of a separatist "authenticity" are probably a small minority. Most Franco-Maghrebis, particularly the younger generation and especially those with citizenship, dream neither of returning to the motherland nor of establishing an isolated Maghrebi or Islamic enclave in France. Although all have felt the sting of racism, few have contemplated departing France for a "home" in unfamiliar North Africa. Instead, their project is to create a livable zone for themselves within French society. Therefore, most favor some form of integration, but not through total assimilation and the abandonment of "Arabness." They seek to negotiate integration on their own terms, maintaining their right to be different.

In the wake of the upsurge of Arab militancy in the early 1980s, Franco-Maghrebis born in France began to be known as "Beurs," a *verlan*[14] term made by reversing the sounds of *arabe*. Today many educated French Arabs consider this tag pejorative and lacking in geographic specificity. They prefer the cumbersome appellation, "youths originating from North-African immigration" (*jeunes issues de l'immigration maghrébine*).[15] Others simply refer to themselves as Algerians or as French. But none of these terms seem able to capture the complex positionality of those who feel located somewhere "in-between." As one educated young Franco-Maghrebi told us:

> We don't consider ourselves completely Algerian or completely French. Our
> parents are Arabs. We were born in France (and only visited Algeria a few times).
> So what are we? French? Arab? In the eyes of the French we are Arabs. But when
> we visit Algeria some people call us emigrants and say we've rejected our culture.
> We've even had stones thrown at us [in Algeria].

Such ambiguity is expressed in the various avenues of integration Franco-Maghrebis have chosen to travel, all of which could be considered, in their different ways, paths of hybridity.[16]

At one end of the hybridity spectrum are the quasi-assimilationists, who tend to see France as the height of civilization, who frequently change their names from Karima to Karine or Boubker to Bob, and who practice a kind of hyper-conformism to French societal norms. Members of this group tend to be successful, upwardly-mobile, and educated, and frequently of harki or *kabyle*

(Algerian Berber) background. But they have also organized politically, most notably within the framework of France-Plus, an electoral pressure group that pushes for Franco-Maghrebi electoral representation on all party tickets except Le Pen's National Front and the Communists. Even Franco-Maghrebis who disapprove of France-Plus's middle-of-the road orientation admit it has markedly increased Arab visibility and influence in the political arena. France-Plus managed to get 390 Beurs elected, about equally divided between parties of the Right and Left, in the municipal elections of 1989, a major gain over 1983 when only 12 Beurs were voted in (Begag 1990:9). Two "Beurettes," Nora Zaïdi of the Socialist Party and Djida Tazdaït of the Greens, were even elected to the European Parliament in 1989. France-Plus, however, lacks a social base in the banlieues, and is often viewed as representing the interests of the *"beurgeoisie"* (Aïchoune 1992:15).

SOS-Racisme, France-Plus's chief competitor in the political sphere, occupies an intermediate position. Founded in 1985 by activists with close ties to the ruling Socialist Party, SOS-Racisme built on the wave of Beur militancy of the early 1980s, channeling and neutralizing its energies. The emergence of this multiethnic organization, according to many militants, represented a blunting of the Maghrebi-Arab specificity and orientation of the earlier antiracist struggle (cf. Jazouli 1992; Aïchoune 1991;. SOS-Racisme quickly deployed its connections with officialdom, superior organizing skills, media savvy, and ability to attract the financial support of government agencies, in order to position itself as *the* hegemonic group within the antiracist movement. It gradually shifted the concerns of the antiracist movement away from a platform focused on the rights of immigrants to one that emphasizes individual ethics and diffuse "multiculturalism" (Jazouli 1992). SOS-Racisme is now the mediagenic organization of the antiracist "establishment," the favorite of the ruling (until March 1993) Socialist Party. Although a vocal critic of racism, SOS-Racisme often takes quasi-assimilationist positions. Like France-Plus, it enjoys little grass-roots support in the banlieues.

Those who have felt defeated or overwhelmed by an impossible social and economic environment have followed yet another route. These are the "delinquents," who are chiefly from the impoverished banlieues and whose response to the lack of decent educational or employment opportunities has been a resort to petty criminality, random acts of violence, angry rage, and drug use. Many of these Franco-Maghrebis regard the battle to establish a meaningful identity and comfortable space of existence as utterly hopeless. Yet the position of this group is unstable and contradictory, its members capable of actions, like the "rodeos," at once nihilist and oppositional.

The opposite end of the spectrum from the "beurgeoisie" is populated by a diffuse array of community-based political and cultural groups, operating fairly autonomously, outside the framework of any overarching umbrella organization. It is these groups which carry out much of the organized activity with a specifically Franco-Maghrebi character. Franco-Maghrebis who share this perspective aggressively assert their right to a place in France, regarding racism as French society's problem and rejecting out of hand the notion that they, the Arabs, are the "problem," as racist discourse would have it (see Gilroy 1987:11). They regard themselves as French citizens, just like anyone else, and they lay claim to the French heritage of democracy and freedom of speech. Their attitude might be summed up by the slogan, "We're here, we're Beur, get used to it!"[17] They advocate a kind of affirmative identity politics that, at the same time, promotes syncretizing rather than essentializing practices.

HYBRIDITY IN PRACTICE (1): RAMADAN NIGHTS IN THE DIASPORA

Rai has played a significant part in the story of Franco-Arab mobilization and identity formation. It was aired widely on the local radio stations, such as the celebrated Radio Beur in Paris, that sprang up to serve and instill pride into French North African communities in the early 1980s. Rai gained greater public visibility as a consequence of the upsurge of Franco-Arab struggles against racism, and particularly when SOS-Racisme sponsored multi-cultural concerts featuring rai. Prominent Algerian rai performers started touring France, while young Franco-Maghrebis began forming their own rai bands.

Salah Eddine Bariki's study of Franco-Maghrebi radio stations, carried out in Marseille—the site of France's largest concentration of Arabs—in 1984, highlights rai's role in the complicated, syncretic processes of Franco-Maghrébin identity formation (Bariki 1986). The most popular radio programming, he discovered, was during Ramadan Nights, the evenings of feasting and celebration that follow daytime fasting during the holy month, when airwave listeners stayed up late and called up radio stations to request songs, tell jokes, engage in political or religious debates, or discuss the meaning of Ramadan for North Africans in France. Almost all callers to Arab stations spoke in "Musulman," as they termed the Arabic spoken in France (meaning they were probably immigrants rather than French-born). Bariki's survey of everyday practices and beliefs of Marseille's Arab radio audience showed that most drank alcohol, few condemned mixed marriages (with non-Muslims), about a third had eaten pork, and less than half fasted during Ramadan. But most of them still observed Ramadan, if rather idiosyncratically by orthodox standards. Many made special efforts to buy meat that was *hilal* (slaughtered according to strict Islamic precepts) during the holidays, while a large number claimed they did not drink alcohol for 40 days prior to the holy month. Both practices were immigrant innovations.

Participants in the survey described Ramadan Nights radio programming as a nostalgia-laden return to an ambiance resembling what they had heard of or remembered about Ramadan celebrations in the home country—a time of plentiful food and pleasant relations between parents and children. The evenings of North African entertainment reduced the "burden of exile" by establishing a mood of community closeness. By far the most common way that radio listeners reaffirmed their ethnic presence was to phone up and dedicate a song to a relative or friend. In the early 1980s, the near unanimous choice of Ramadan radio audiences was Algeria's "King of Rai," Cheb Khaled.

That Arabs of Marseille selected Cheb Khaled as their favorite vocalist during Ramadan merely underscores the complicated and contradictory nature of North African identity construction in France. For ever since launching his career at the age of 14 in the mid-1970s, Cheb Khaled has cultivated the image of a swaggering, dissolute, worldly cabaret singer. "When I sing rai," Khaled proclaims, "I talk about things directly; I drink alcohol; I love a woman; I am suffering. I speak to the point. I like Julio Iglesias. But he just sings about women, whereas [I sing] about alcohol, bad luck and women" (Eyre 1991:44; Bizot 1988:88).

Although not sentiments one normally associates with Ramadan observance in the Arab-Islamic countries, they are consistent with rai's demimonde, antipuritanical heritage in Algeria. (Recall Cheikha Rimitti's song about "eating" during Ramadan.) According to Benkheira, Cheb Khaled typically opened his concerts in Algeria during the mid-1980s with a number about Muhammad, followed by songs about drink, women, and so on. Whether Khaled's subject was whiskey or the Prophet, the Algerian audience danced—no one present considered this blasphemous (Benkheira 1986:176). Such attitudes corresponded with cultural life in a tolerant country where, despite official puritanism and a growing Islamist movement, mosque attendance remained comparatively low and alcohol was consumed in open view of the street at the numerous taverns of central Algiers and Oran (Kapil 1990:36).

In spring 1992, we made friends with the 23-year old Sonia, "modern" in outlook, a student of English at the Université d'Avignon, and recently married to Jeannot, the son of a harki. Her father left Algeria at age 14 to work in France. Sonia is in charge of the family grocery store, and supplements her income by flipping Big Macs at Avignon's golden arches. She sells liquor in her shop—located in a rundown Maghrebi district where the usual clientele includes addicts and prostitutes—reasoning that although the Qur'an forbids handling alcohol, it is permissible to dispense wine sealed in glass or plastic bottles. But she does not peddle pork, which she would have to touch, an act that would be *haram* (morally prohibited). Sonia fasts during Ramadan, but finds Islam's five daily prayers too cumbersome to integrate into everyday activities. "You've got to adapt to the society where you live," Sonia asserts, "but if I didn't observe Muslim holidays, there would be nothing to set me apart from any other French person."

Her syncretizing attitudes and practices reflect a general secularizing trend within Franco-Maghrebi communities, in the course of which Islam—like cuisine, language, and music—has become for many more a question of ethnic identification than of belief (Jazouli 1992:133-34). Despite unceasing alarms raised by the mainstream press, the extent of militant Islamist mobilization in France is actually quite limited, and by some estimates, only 5% of the "potential" Islamic population are actually practicing, orthodox Muslims (Singer 1988:861; Etienne 1989:259-260). Islamic observances like Ramadan, however, are widely commemorated—but in novel "ethnicized" forms (Safran 1986:104). The focus of Ramadan has shifted away from daily fasting and praying to the celebratory nighttime meal. In this regard, the Franco-Maghrebi community resembles French society at large, for which all former religious holidays are observed chiefly as secular feasts. The head of the Paris Mosque, for instance, has suggested that on 'Id al-Kabir (the commemoration of Abraham's sacrifice of a lamb instead of his son) Muslim families slaughter chickens in the privacy of their homes rather than violate health laws and offend popular prejudice by slaughtering rams according to orthodox precepts (Brisebarre 1989). Lacoste-Dujardin (1992) reports that it is increasingly common for Franco-Maghrebis to drink champagne on festive occasions, including religious feasts like 'Id al-Kabir.

The secular, modern, and socially progressive lyrics and ambiance associated with rai therefore continue to appeal to young Franco-Maghrebis like Sonia, who desire to belong to a collectivity within France that shares a tolerant Arabo-Islamic identity. Singers like Cheb Khaled articulate the younger generation's rebellion against the restrictive mores of both the older generation and the younger Islamist militants:

> I am against Islamic fundamentalists. Young people want to progress. Even now, I can't smoke in front of my father, not even a cigarette. Young people who want to speak with a girl or live with her can't talk about it with their parents. In rai music, people can express themselves. We break taboos. That's why fundamentalists don't like what we're doing (quoted in Eyre 1991:45).

But Khaled is not anti-Islam *per se*. "I'm a muslim man, I love God, but I don't practice and I don't pray," he explains (Goldman 1993). Meanwhile other rai artists incorporate religious themes into their songs. Cheb Anouar's "Bi'r Zem Zem" (from the video album *La Ballade d'Anouar*), for instance, refers to the famous well in Mecca which figures prominently in the *hajj* ritual. Anouar sings to his mother about leading the proper life and one day making the *hajj*. The vendors at Avignon's weekly Arab *suq* (open-air market) who sell rai cassettes and videos claimed that "Bi'r Zem Zem" was merely Anouar's attempt to cash in on the heretofore ignored Islamic market niche. Many stalls in the *suq* carry Islamist cassettes featuring Qur'anic recitations, sermons, and how-to guides for proper Islamic conduct hard by the recordings of Cheb Mami or Chaba Fadela that extol the virtues of libertine lifestyles.

HYBRIDITY IN PRACTICE (2): WOMEN AND RAI[18]

Most of the women were sitting on the low cushions along the walls at one end of the rented room in the Avignon banlieue. Those who felt uncomfortable squatting close to the floor were supported by chairs on the other side of the room. Older women were decked out in long, empire-waisted, shiny polyester Algerian dresses and gold marriage belts. Some younger ones were similarly clad in "traditional" outfits; others sported slacks or miniskirts plus accessories like new-wave geometric earrings or necklaces hung with miniature pastel-colored pacifiers (a 1992 teenage fashion craze throughout Europe). Some women had flown in from Algeria specially for the wedding, while others had traveled north from Marseille or south from St. Etienne. Only five of the 60 women at the wedding were not of North African origin.

Rai provided the soundtrack for the wedding festivities, but no one was paying much attention to the singers or the lyrics. If you want to know the name of the singer or the song, they said, go look at the cassettes. I picked up a bag full of home-dubbed tapes. Many contained minimal or no information, but several Cheb Khaled tapes were clearly marked. When Khaled's 1992 hit "Didi" came on, many younger women jumped up to dance. The room was hopping when a power outage stopped us short.

The windows looking onto the courtyard where the men were gathered were thrown open. A rai singer named Cheb Kader[19] started his set, accompanied by a single instrumentalist on keyboard synthesizer. The dancing inside took up in earnest: a throng of shimmering sequins and beads, provençal skirts, satin and linen, bare shoulders and legs. The dance styles resembled what I had witnessed in northeastern Morocco in 1986, but occasionally younger women broke into disco steps and some girls seemed to be imitating cabaret belly dancers.

After midnight, over bowls of *chorba* and *tajine*, I asked some chicly-accoutred lycée girls whether they liked the music. Not very much. What did they listen to? Funk—African-American. But they supposed that when their turn came, they would have weddings like this one. I tried to imagine James Brown's "Funky Drummer" blaring out amidst the crowd of matrons who had flown in from Algeria to a gender-segregated event.

Rai was passé for but tolerated by the under-20 set. But to the 23-year-old bride and her generation, it signified a strong attachment to Algerian roots. The older women regarded rai as merely familiar Arabic music—perhaps not their first choice, but what people enjoyed dancing to. Rai was the form of cultural expression uniting the generations in this community celebration.

Weddings, therefore, remain a major site for rai performance and consumption. Beur radio stations in the major cities also continue to serve up rai on a regular basis, often as part of astonishing sets that also feature African-American funk, tunes from Berber Kabylia, Caribbean reggae, rap, and Zairian soukous. Rai is also disseminated via video technologies. Several videotapes sold in Arab stores and market stands feature live concert footage of *chebs* (male rai singers) at festivals in Oran or on European tour. Others show *chabas* or older *cheikhas* in staged settings, like Cheikha Rimitti's television-studio "wedding" performance, and often feature female dancers in "traditional" dress.

Another video genre, the narrative music videos featuring visual and lyrical representations of romantic love, provides interesting commentary on gender relations. Cheb Anouar's above-mentioned video, *La Ballade d'Anouar*, not only pays homage to Mecca but features tunes where teenage dating and the pain of separation from one's lover are acted out. Videos from the famous married couple of rai, Chaba Fadela and Cheb Sahraoui, depict romantic relationships between boyfriend and girlfriend, in stereotypically western settings.

Such videos advocate a rejection of the "traditional" and patriarchal family power relations that continue to define the lives of so many young Franco-Maghrebi women. In fact, differences of opinion on *how* to integrate into French culture seem to focus on the question of gender. The controversy about the appropriate behavior for women seems exacerbated both by the preference of French employers for female as opposed to male Franco-Maghrebi labor and the tendency of French society and media to treat young Franco-Maghrebi women as "model" citizens while subjecting Arab men to overt discrimination and denigration (Jazouli 1992:179). Many ostensibly "integrated" Franco-Maghrebi males, who haunt the nightclubs and have white girlfriends, invoke traditional values when dealing with their own sisters and zealously police their movements in and outside the home. Parents too often attempt to uphold ethnic identity, at least within the domestic sphere, by insisting on controlling their daughters' extra-domestic activities, choosing their marriage partners, and requiring that they perform servant-like duties in the home and wait on their brothers and fathers hand and foot. Even young, unmarried Franco-Maghrebi women who appear completely at ease in French society assert that they would face tremendous problems if their family were informed that they had been sitting with a man at a café. And for such young women, marriage to a non-Muslim would automatically cause a radical break with their families.[20]

Hence romantic love, involving dating before marriage and the option of choosing one's marriage partner without the interference of kin, is seen as offering liberating potential for many Franco-Maghrebi youth (as well as young people in North Africa).[21] But paradoxically, while many rai songs and videos promote romance and more freedom for women, the jackets of most rai cassette seem governed by traditional codes which would confine Maghrebi women to the private realm. The cheb's photograph almost invariably adorns his cassette, but tapes by chabas typically feature picturesque Algerian countryside vistas or photographs of women—often lissome surfer girls with lush blonde hair and deep tans—who are more "conventionally" beautiful—by Western standards—than the chabas who sing the music contained within.

Before going to France we found several explanations for this absence in the World Music publicity on rai. An Algerian student told us that the celebrated Chaba Zahouania, with the distinctive, vigorously husky voice and ribald lyrics, was unmarried, and forbidden by her family in Algeria to perform in public or be photographed for album jackets. She began to acquire a certain mysterious quality. What resemblance, we wondered, did Zahouania bear to the exquisitely beautiful and exotic chiffon-draped belly dancer on the cover of her suggestively titled U.S. release, *Nights without Sleeping*?[22] We came across another explanation: Zahouania did not sing in public because she was a divorcée with four children who did not want her ex-husband's family to be able to argue in court that she was an unfit mother and thereby win custody of the children (Rosen 1990:23). Wandering Paris' Goutte d'Or in summer 1992, we found dozens of Chaba Zahouania cassettes for sale, none with a photograph of the elusive singer. But we did discover a video featuring Chaba Zahouania performing live before a television studio set. Zahouania looks about 40 and wears a modest, Western-style dress. Thick, clunky glasses magnify her conventional plainness. Later, acquaintances from the Netherlands tell us that, in an interview with a Dutch paper, Chaba Zahouania explained that her picture was not displayed on cassettes because she considered herself ugly! So perhaps rai's advocacy of greater freedoms for women is held back as much by Western standards of beauty as by "traditional" constraints.

We met rai artist Chaba Aicha after her performance—complete with disco globe and fog machine—held in a modest hall near Avignon in August 1992. She claimed that rai is the music of women with a great deal of experience in life, and that mothers with no husbands have traditionally sung rai to support their children. The youthful Aicha is a spirited singer, whose repertoire includes a tune dedicated to undocumented immigrants. Her close-cropped hairdo and butch outfits are unlike any other *chaba* we have come across and remind us of kd lang. Yet even the androgynous, progressive Chaba Aicha did not want her photo to appear on the cover of her first release—but the Marseille-based recording company insisted.[23] One other female of rai, the chubby—by Western standards—Chaba Fadela, shows up on cassette photos, usually in unassuming dress (although once in a black leather jacket) and always accompanied by her husband, Cheb Sahraoui.

In marked contrast to the chabas' public propriety, Franco-Maghrebi *rappeuse* Saliha strikes a pose—at once defiant and seductive—on the cover of her 1991 recording, *Unique*. Saliha is fitted out in a sleek black mini, hands encased in black leather half-gloves. Romantic love as liberation does not feature prominently in the hip-hop emanating from the banlieues, nor does a wholesome image "sell" in the ghetto. Yet French rappers also appear unable to escape conventional expectations regarding female looks.

FROM RAI THING TO RAP THANG

By the mid-1980s, rai was beginning to break out of the strictly "ethnic" boundaries that characterized its uses in the Marseille of Bariki's study. Rai gained greater public visibility during the upsurge of Franco-Arab struggles and through SOS-Racisme's concerts, which gained it an audience among antiracist whites. In the late 1980s and early 90s, rai's star rose in French World Music circuits and, via Paris, it was propelled into the international world beat market.[24] By 1990, when Islamist campaigns against rai, as well as the lure of higher earnings and global exposure, had prompted several of its leading figures (Cheb Khaled, Cheb Mami, Chaba Fadela and Cheb Sahraoui) to relocate from Algeria to France, Paris became a major rai center.

More recently, rai's fortunes in France have varied according to the different trends within the Franco-Maghrébi community. For their part, the "beurgeoisie" and their benevolent white liberal and Socialist allies sponsor concerts and festivals featuring Arab music (including rai) that celebrate the "authentic" culture or folklore of "the people," a strategy which simply disguises their lack of a social base in the banlieues. State monies for such concerts were abundant under Socialist rule.

At the grass-roots level, by contrast, rai's core audience has been somewhat diminished—it is now the music of choice principally for recent immigrants and "les jeunes issues de l'immigration maghrébine" over the age of 25. Rai performers continue to tour the French-Arab communities, performing at modest local dance halls and at weddings. But none of the major figures—Cheb Mami, Cheb Kader, Chaba Fadela and Cheb Sahraoui or Chaba Zahouania—have been able to capitalize on their momentary successes on the World Music scene between 1988 and 1990, when their recordings were released on various U.S. or international labels. Crossover success, therefore, has been limited.

Except for Cheb Khaled, who after years of performing for adoring Franco-Maghrebi audiences has finally, and spectacularly, "crossed over" into the French and international pop scene. His latest long-playing album, *Khaled*,[25] at base a rai recording, incorporates an impressive mélange of styles—traditional "folk" and "pop" rai, funk and reggae, flamenco and cabaret. But it is Khaled's hit single "Didi" which propelled him onto the international pop arena. Opening to *derbouka* rhythms, "Didi" switches to a deep-bass hip-hop underpinning, and is constructed around an instantly recognizable instrumental hook and a hummable chorus. During spring 1992, it was a dancehall favorite throughout France.[26] The "Didi" video, aired frequently on French television and a key ingredient in the song's success, is a rapid-fire, MTV-style, cut-and-mix of images of a Moorish *mashrabiya* (wooden latticework screen), evocations of a Sufi music circle, and hip-hop steps performed by a multiethnic team of miniskirted dancers.

In July 1992, some Franco-Maghrebi women we met in Avignon told us that mainstream French nightclubs and discos had, in the past two or three months, begun playing Arab music—and then only Khaled. The Franco-Maghrebi men sitting with us had to take their word for it, for Arab men are still regularly turned away at the doors of French clubs. The first Arab voice to penetrate French discos had yet to open the gates either for his Arab brothers who wished to dance there or for the discs of the other chabs and chabas. But it should be stressed that a key ingredient in the success of "Didi"—besides its undeniable intrinsic qualities—was Barclay's heavy promotion. A subsidiary of Virgin Records, Barclay is one of the big six recording companies (along with BMG, EMI, PolyGram, Sony, Warner) which control 83% of the French market (Laing 1992:129). Without similar backing, commercial triumph is likely to elude other rai artists.

As Khaled (who has dropped the title Cheb, with its rai associations) captivated non-Arab music fans in France and elsewhere in Europe, he lost some of his original devotees. Like every new star in France, Khaled was interviewed on television, where he expressed the same views about wine and women he voices in his songs. Some Franco-Maghrebis who did not object to Khaled *singing* about such subjects were offended when he *discussed* them on the air. Others asserted that Khaled had demonstrated disrespect for the community's values after he cancelled a number of concerts scheduled for Arab audiences—reportedly due to drunkenness—and released a music video featuring "scantily-dressed" dancers. Still others claimed that Khaled had "sold out" to Western commercialism.

Although such complaints were voiced frequently in summer 1992, *Khaled* appeared to be selling briskly in the music stores we visited in Arab quarters like the Goutte d'Or in Paris and the Cour d'Aix in Marseille. Meanwhile, "Didi" went high in the charts elsewhere in Europe, sold well in the *suqs* of northern Morocco, and ruled the airwaves in Israel, Jordan and Lebanon. In October and November of 1992, "Didi" occupied the Number One spot on Egypt's official Top 40; in May 1993 Khaled was said to have sold 2.5 million tapes in Egypt (de Neys 1993). By spring 1993, "Didi" was a certified global phenomenon (which seems to have bypassed the U.S., however) and with the aid of European and Asian MTV, was reported to have sold 4.5 million copies (Dickey and de Koster 1993). It is not yet clear what this unprecedented international popularity for a Franco-Maghrebi singer will ulti- mately mean. But we wonder whether Khaled's move out of "ethnic" space will contribute to a corrosion of dominant/white French identity, or will hegemonic Western forces try to deploy Khaled as a convenient spokesman against "backward" Algerian traditions and "fundamentalism?"

But ironically, even as Khaled's reputation soared, French Arab youth had already largely abandoned rai for rap. The following conversation with a group of 20-something Franco-Maghrebis in Avignon suggests some of the continuities and differences between Khaled's rai and the new *rap français*:

> Mehmed: Everyone listens to rai. It creates a festive atmosphere. Rap is for adolescents, 15 to 20 years old, who have hard lives and feel lost. Rap is for their generation. Rai only talks about love, but rap speaks about society and how to change it.

> Malika: I object. Rappers talk about their society because they are not doing well. Rappers are guys who don't have work, who don't have much, and they project messages about changing society. But in certain songs of Cheb Khaled, when you see that he speaks of love, of alcohol, of everything that is taboo in our culture, well, it's clear that he also wants a change. They're not only love songs. If they were, why would some of them be banned in Algeria? Umm Kalthum sings love songs and they're not banned.[27] Rai songs evoke emancipated, libertine women. They too contain messages.

> Salah: Rap tries to change daily life, but rai tries to change a culture. Both rap and rai reclaim something which has been kept from us.

On a number entitled "Do the raï thing," Malek Sultan of the rap group I AM also equates the social significance of the two genres when he dubs Cheb Khaled "le Public Enemy Arabe."[28] But this resemblance was all but lost on the second-and-third-generation Franco-Maghrebi boys, ages between six and ten, at a birthday party Joan Gross attended in an Avignon banlieue. "No Arab music!" the boys yelled, whenever their mothers put "Didi" on the tape recorder. The moms appeased their demands for hip-hop, but periodically snuck the funky "Didi" back on the player. Eventually the boys started breakdancing to the arabesque grooves of "le Public Enemy arabe."

RAPATTITUDE

The late 1980s found the French media once again training their lenses on the menacing youth of the banlieues. The focus of their new concern was not on "rodeos," but the apparent danger that of suburban ghettos going the way of southcentral Los Angeles and the south Bronx. What had become visible to the media, particularly after a wave of riots in *"banlieues chaudes"* like Vaulx-en-Velin and Sartrouville during 1990 and 1991 and the banlieusard-organized *lycée* strikes, demonstrations and attendant "anarchic" violence in fall 1990, were the gangs (*bandes*) and their associated practices: "tagging," drug use, petty crime, and rap music.[29] The right-wing press sounded the alert, luridly suggesting links between banlieue youth and crack, AIDS, gang warfare, and welfare scrounging—all the press suggested, inhering in immigrant culture. There were even intimations that the big (immi- grant) drug dealers of Marseille were using profits from heroin sales to finance "certain Arab movements in France."[30] And in the latest version of the French nightmare, it was the illegible "tags" (*le graff*) of the banlieue posses which now threatened to deface all the walls and monuments of *la civilisation française*.

For their part, most members of the French gangs or "posses," who give themselves names like Black Tiger Force or Black Dragons and turn out in continental hip-hop garb—Air Jordans, baseball caps, and baggy pants—regard themselves as part of an oppositional youth movement whose sonic expression is rap music. This new multi-racial orientation reflects the ethnically diverse character of the predominantly "immigrant" banlieues. The bandes, whose argot is a distinctive blend of French *verlan* and unitedstatesian hip-hop vernacular,[31] often include Arabs (*rebeus* or *beurs* in verlan), Jews (*feujs*, from *juifs*), blacks (*renois*, from *noires*), Portuguese (*tos*) and white French. The posses are vigorously antiracist, and many try to project a positive image to mark themselves off from the so-called *cailleras* (from *racailles*) or "riffraff," those gangs involved in criminal activities like drug dealing and theft (Aïchoune 1991:79, 89). The bandes of the 1990s therefore represent a marked departure from the early 1980s, when Adil Jazouli (1982) described the Maghrebi banlieue "delinquent" youth as incapable of fashioning coherent identities, as trapped between two distinct cultural poles (French and Arab), neither of which could accommodate them.

French rappers had achieved a remarkable proficiency (by unitedstatesian standards) and media visibility by the early 1990s.[32] Coming from banlieue backgrounds, *rappeurs* and *rappeuses* attempt to express as well as shape and mobilize the sentiments of ghetto youth.[33] Their most salient message is antiracism, the assertion of the need for interracial solidarity, the unity of "black, blanc, beur." French rap groups, like the bandes and unlike groups or gangs in the U.S., tend to be multi-racial; Marseille's I AM, for instance, includes whites, blacks and Arabs. Nonetheless their messages and historical sensibility tend to be pro-black African; the backing tracks, like in unitedstatesian rap, are composed primarily of sampled African-American riffs and beats. Yet while articulating pro-black sentiments, French rap is largely devoid of the kind of black nationalism so hegemonic within African-American hip-hop. Saint Denis rappers Supreme NTM have even criticized Louis Farrakhan (a black nationalist-Islamic leader promoted by unitedstatesian rappers Public Enemy and Ice Cube), asserting that he is an agent of hatred just like Le Pen ("Blanc et noir"). Such a claim would be virtually unthinkable in the unitedstatesian hip-hop nation.[34]

But although they are anti-Le Pen, French rappers refuse to define themselves in terms of a hegemonic political discourse of Right, Center, or Left, manifesting the disdain for traditional "politics" that is typical of the "new social movements" (see Mercer 1990:44). They propose multiracial alliance and antiracism as an alternative to the "old" politics. Music and dancing are often viewed as the chief means available today for achieving such utopian trans-racial unity. According to Beurette rapper Saliha's "Danse le beat," "Seul le beat aujourd'hui nous lie et nous unit" ("Today only the beat links and unites us"). Rappers express total disdain for the state—"ce putain d'état," as I AM dubs it (on "Non soumis à l'état")—and the police. They dream of more money allocated to the banlieues and a cut-off in funds to the army, while advocating equal rights for immigrants (I AM's "Le nouveau president" and "Red, Black and Green"). French homeboys and homegirls refuse all media discourses which brand them as criminals and barbarians. These hip-hoppers promote a renewed spirit of militancy, anger, and menace—self-consciously distinguishing themselves from the pacifistic and mediagenic image projected by state-positive antiracists like SOS-Racisme (on NTM's "Freestyle").

The largest single constituent of the multiethnic banlieue posses and rap audiences are probably Franco-Maghrebi youth. Arab rappers (like Saliha, Malek Sultan of I AM, the members of MCM 90 and Prophètes de Vacarme) occupy a significant position in the movement, although black rappers seem to be preeminent. Rap numbers, whether by black, white, or Maghrebi artists, are typically peppered with samples from Arabic music, positive references to Palestine and Islam, and the occasional Arabic expression ("Allahu akbar," "Salaam"). The name of one of the foremost rap groups, Supreme NTM, is short for "*Nique ta mère*" or "fuck your mother." The designation is symptomatic of the degree to which French street slang has been penetrated Arabic terms (*nique*, sometimes spelled *nik*, is Arabic for "fuck").

But despite Maghrebis' significant involvement, French rap lyrics make few references to the history of French colonialism in Algeria. Instead, like Unitedstatesian hip-hop, French rap expresses a hegemonic Afrocentric historical sensibility concerned mainly with sub-Saharan, not

North or Arab, Africa. North Africa is only mentioned in the context of claims about African civilization's origins in ancient Egypt. (Most of I AM's members carry Pharaonic names: Kheops, Akenaton, Imhotep, and Divin Kephren.) Rappers compose rhymes about the history of slavery, humanity's origins in Africa, Europe's destruction of African civilizations, and the struggle against apartheid—but almost never about Arabo-Islamic civilization,[35] the French colonial violence in Algeria, or the independence struggle led by the Front de Libération Nationale (FLN).[36] Perhaps this absence stems in part from rap's roots in a diasporic, Afrocentric form of cultural expression that does not usually deal with specifically "Arab" subjects.[37] This hesitation on the part of otherwise-militant rappers seems to echo French society's incapacity to confront the bloody colonial history which still poisons race relations in the metropole. The fact that a significant portion of rap's audience is composed of descendents of harkis—who fought on the side of the *colons* in the Algerian War—also no doubt contributes to *rappeurs'* reticence to discuss colonialism in Algeria.

While the Right has fulminated about crack, rap, and immigrant hordes, the Socialist establishment's tactic was to attempt the co-optation of youth subculture. "Le rap, le graff; I believe in this generation," intoned Jack Lang, hip-hop's loudest elite cheerleader, during his tenure as culture minister. Lang's attempts to appropriate rap ranged from arranging museum space for graffiti artists to subsidizing NTM tours to inviting rappers to perform at a prime minister's garden party before nonplussed National Assembly members (Riding 1992; James 1991). His justification was typically elitist: "A man of the theater such as myself would tell you that rap bears a relationship to *la commedia dell'arte* as it was practiced in the sixteenth and seventeenth century" (Labi 1990:40-41).[38] But if such elite sponsorship gave hip-hoppers greater publicity, there are few signs that banlieusard youth are about to be tamed. "What gratitude should I have for France," raps NTM's Joey Starr, "I who they consider a barbarian?" ("Quelle gratitude?").

MOOR BETTER BLUES

Beyond the realms of raï and rap, Franco-Maghrebis have also actively invaded, created or influenced an impressive range of expressive forms, from the humble local supermarket—where canned couscous or tabouli may be purchased—to the pinnacle of high culture, the Paris Opera—where we find the star dancer Kader Bélarbi (Videau 1991:39). The fiction of Tahar Ben Jelloun

(1987 winner of France's most prestigious literary award, the Prix Goncourt), Driss Chraïbi and Abdelkebir Khatibi crowds the "Francophone" shelves in the bookstores (cf. Hargreaves 1989). Arab comedians are making inroads as well. The Tunisian-born Lilia is a prominent figure on the Paris stage, and the well-known trio Les Inconnus perform television and video comedy sketches which frequently revolve around the misadventures of Beur characters.[39] The 1990-91 television season was enlivened by *La Famille Ramdan*, a Cosby-ish sitcom (the oldest son was a doctor) about a Beur family (Hargreaves 1991). The most successful French Arab comedian, Smaïn, is often described as the successor to the late, and now canonical figure, Coluche.[40]

But it is in popular music, and not just in genres like rai and rap, where the Franco-Maghrebi contribution has been especially complex and contradictory. Among cultural forms, popular music in particular seems to lend itself to syncretization and cross-fertilization—especially because it is relatively unconstrained by the generic rules that fetter traditional or elite genres (cf. Malkmus and Armes 1991:23; Barber 1987). Take heavy-metal band Dazibao, who performed in June 1992 at Zik à Ouf, a free outdoor music festival organized to keep Marseille's heavily "Maghrebized" 13th and 14th arrondissements "cooled off."[41] Dazibao's speed guitars inspired white head-bangers to thrash about wildly but left inner-city North Africans unmoved. This even though Dazibao's Moroccan-born vocalist, Jamil, sang only in Arabic and (in French) exhorted his audience between songs to be proud of their Arabic heritage. Dazibao's startlingly innovative sound—screeching Arabic vocals cascading over grunge-metal—seems to find no significant audience among Arab youth.

During the same month Radio Beur in Aix-en-Provence held a fundraiser on its first anniversary, which was attended by a casually-attired but well-heeled, college-town, Maghrebi crowd able to pay the 100 Francs (approximately $20) admission. The show's emotional peak was Parisian-Algerian blues-jazz-funk crooner Jimmy Oihid's performance (in French) of "Ballade pour les enfants," his famous tribute to the Palestinians.[42] The spots dimmed as hundreds of Bic lighters flickered on. Those who knew the words sang along with the chorus; the dance floor swayed solemnly to the lament's measured beat. Hybridized Franco-Maghrebis may care little for Arab nationalism or Maghrebi "traditions," but even the beurgeoisie often identify strongly with Palestinian militancy.

Other figures represent still other styles and cultural tendencies. Sapho, a French new-wave jazz/rock singer raised in a Jewish Moroccan household in Marrakech, actively celebrates her "Oriental heritage" as the source of her musical inspiration and performs with North African string musicians and sub-Saharan percussionists (Billard 1987). Mano Negra, whose members are of Spanish, Corsican, and Moroccan backgrounds, belt out polyglot (Arabic, French, Spanish, and English) tunes to a frenetic bouillabaisse of punk, rockabilly, reggae, flamenco, and rai styles—something like The Clash gone pan-Mediterranean. Until recently there was Carte de Séjour (meaning "residence card"), Franco-Maghrebi rockers who vocalized in both French and Arabic and turned out guitar riffs tinged with subtle arabesques.[43] And finally there is the Franco-Tunisian Amina, France's representative at the mainstream 1991 Eurovision contest, who sings cabaret ballads and disco-funk in French, Spanish and Arabic and is backed by a band composed of Euro-French, West African, and North African musicians.[44] Amina proclaims, "I will continue preaching for the mixture of cultures...The more hybridization we have, the less we'll hear about claims to [a pure] culture" (Attaf 1991).

EL HARBA WAYN? (TO ESCAPE BUT WHERE?)

Franco-Maghrebis are deploying such syncretizing mechanisms to carve out a space for themselves where they can identify simultaneously with French and Arab cultures while rejecting French ethnocentrism and Algerian conservatism. Yet at times the pressures from both French racists and Algerian traditionalists seem overwhelming, and the Franco-Maghrebi border "zone" shrinks to a "line" (Lavie 1996). Potent memories of racist brutality, colonial and post-colonial are re-lived with each new threat and attack. Older Maghrebis still recall the horrific police massacre of 300-400 Algerian immigrants in Paris in October 1961, after a demonstration organized in favor of the FLN— probably the century's bloodiest racial atrocity against immigrants to occur in the West. The younger generation remembers Habib Grimzi, an Algerian killed when French soldiers tossed him from a speeding train in November 1983, and carried his picture at the head of the 100,000-strong antiracist march on Paris in December 1983. Similar incidents are a constant feature of Franco-Maghrebi existence, with over 250 Arabs killed in racist attacks between 1985 and 1993 alone (Alcalay 1993:12).[45]

Franco-Maghrébins felt especially vulnerable and beleaguered during the 1991 Gulf War, when French newspaper headlines howled about "The Arab Threat in France" and "Arab Terrorism in France," and Michel Poniatowski, interior minister during Giscard d'Estaing's presidency, suggested the mass expulsion of immigrants (Attaf 1991:55). A poll in *Le Figaro* taken during the war showed that 70% of all French "Muslims" (i.e. Arabs)[46] feared they would become targets of terrorist attacks, and more than half felt that the war could lead France to deport Muslim immigrants (LaFranchi 1991; see also Ben Jelloun 1991). Rumors raging through southeastern France, declaring that Arab immigrants were arming themselves and attacking whites, caused a run on guns and ammunition by panicky French natives (Leblond 1991:61; Cambio 1991). During this period of heightened tensions, France-Plus urged Franco-Maghrebis to remain calm and not to organize demonstrations. Arab stations like Radio-Gazelle in Marseille and Radio-Soleil in Paris decided not to air "Vas-y Saddam!"—Algerian Mohammed Mazouni's recording that was so wildly popular across the Mediterranean (Bernard 1991). To its credit, SOS-Racisme came out against the war, but lost many liberal supporters as well as significant financial backing (Lhomea 1991).

Meanwhile, back in Algeria hybrid cultural forms were also under assault from conservative forces who branded popular music—especially rai—not merely as "noise," but as "illicit" and "immoral." Rai artists and consumers came under intense pressure in the wake of the sweeping municipal electoral victories of the Islamist party, Le Front Islamique du Salut (the Islamic Salvation Front, known popularly as FIS) in 1990. The FIS-dominated city council of Oran cancelled funding for the annual rai festival scheduled for August 1990, and its mayor banned a Cheb Mami concert on the grounds that his lyrics were offensive. Cheb Mami and other rai artists like Cheb Sahraoui who returned from France to perform that summer were harassed and sometimes physically threatened by Islamists. As the Islamist movement emerged as a significant forum of expression for alienated Algerian youth in the late 1980s and early 90s, it reportedly cut into rai's audience, reducing it, by some accounts, by over 50%.[47]

During Ramadan 1991 (which fell during March) FIS mounted a vigorous campaign against the public performance of music (rai and other genres). Fourteen persons were injured in Algiers on March 21 when young Islamists, attempting to torch a performance hall and halt a music concert, clashed with police. On March 24, crowds led by FIS activists threw bottles and stones at another concert audience, injuring several fans.[48] An anti-rai plank was a central ingredient of FIS's successful platform in the December 1991 elections (Ireland 1992:8). Franco-Maghrebi writer Mohamed Kacimi, attending a Friday prayer service in late 1990 at an Algiers mosque, reports hearing FIS second-in-command Ali Benhadj make the following remark: "As for the secularists, pseudo-democrats, atheists, feminists and francophones, and other evil-doers [*suppôts de Satan*], the day we gain power we'll put boats at their disposal which will take them to their motherland— France."[49] The crowd, according to Kacimi, was entranced. Writing during the Gulf War, Kacimi wondered where—given virulent French anti-Arab sentiment and the rise of religious-based intolerance in Algeria—*Franco-Maghrébins* should go (Attaf 1991:55)?

Kacimi's question recalls Cheb Khaled's celebrated song of alienated fury "El Harba Wayn?" (To escape but where?), released when rai was at its peak of popularity in Algeria. It was taken up as an anthem by rioting Algerian youths during the violent October 1988 urban insurgencies that resulted in over 500 civilian deaths (Rosen 1990:23). (Many disaffected rioters have since been won over by FIS.) It goes:

Where has youth gone?
Where are the brave ones?
The rich gorge themselves,
The poor work themselves to death,
The Islamic charlatans show their true face.
So what's the solution? We'll check it out.
You can always cry or complain
Or escape. But where?
The good times are gone,
With their celebrations and prosperity.
Baraka[50] has fled
And selfishness destroyed solidarity...
Where in this organized chaos
Are the men of yesteryear
And the proud women?
Youth no longer answers,
This life is nothing to smile about.
Let's stop saying: everything's all right.
Gold has turned into worthless lead
Whose cover stifles all understanding.
There's only flight. But where?[51]

Rai and rap are both possible lines of flight (cf. Deleuze and Guattari 1983) for Franco-Maghrebis, cultural border zones of syncretism and creative interminglings of French and Arab. At once "ethnic" and French, they are fronts in the wider cultural-political struggle to recast French national identity and force a kind of genetic mutation in French culture. Both are practices of "interculturation" (Mercer 1987) or "transculturation"—which George Yúdice describes as "a dynamic whereby different cultural matrices impact reciprocally—though not from equal positions—on each other, not to produce a single syncretic culture but rather a heterogeneous ensemble" (1992:209).[52]

We should make a distinction, within this heterogeneous ensemble, between the relatively "defensive" and "ethnic" deployment of rai by immigrants and 20-plus Franco-Maghrebis and the more assertive and multiethnic uses of rap by the younger generation. Rai is more "cautious," more "separatist" insofar as it reproduces cultural linkages with a remembered Algeria. With its cultural roots in Algeria, rai provides a kind of protective shield for immigrants experiencing the disruptions, dislocations, and insecurities of migration, who feel vulnerable to racist discrimination and economic marginality, and who wish to maintain an originary/imaginary communal identification. Rai is a tool in immigrants' attempts to "widen the margins" (Anton Shammas, quoted by Lavie 1996), to expand the sphere of existence and identity beyond the claustrophobic confines imposed by their status as manual laborers (Balibar 1992). Its performance and consumption recreate a relatively free and protected cultural zone, not unlike contemporary Oran or Algiers, in which Algerians in France can relax and feel "at home." Rai performances are also ritual occasions of pride and protest where, as when music is performed in African-American and Black British communities, a "moral, even a political community" is defined (Gilroy 1990:275, 277).

It is rai's association with a progressive vision of Algeria—the contemporary, relaxed, sophisticated, tolerant, and urban image of the homeland rai audiences selectively privilege—that attracts over-20, non-immigrant French-born Maghrebis. Equally important is rai's modern, syncretic-pop sound and its danceability. The synthesizers, drum machines and advanced production techniques combine to produce a musical texture which audiences see as a demonstration that Euro-Arab music is not quaintly "folkloric" but is as modern and sophisticated as any popular European music. As Khaled remarked about his "American sound" on the album *Khaled*,

I said to myself, if rock musicians in Europe can take our instruments and rhythms for their music, then why can't I do the same? I wanted to show people in France, where there's a lot of racism—they don't like us there, and that's a fact—that we can do anything they can, and better (Goldman 1993).[53]

On the other hand, because rai is (virtually) always sung in Arabic and every recording is recognizably "Arab" in instrumentation and melody it always carries an unmistakable air of "otherness." Today's rai combines cosmopolitan "modernity" with a distance and distinction from Euro-pop (cf. Urla 1990). Franco-Maghrébins' attachments therefore also stem from rai's functions as a marker of ethnic difference and its ability to evoke solidarity. Rai therefore manages to be at once "ethnic" and "inter-cultural."

Rap is deployed in more volatile and intrusive ways, while expressing new forms of identity. It serves as a kind of badge of a *multiethnic* minority youth subcultural movement whose development has contributed to the struggle against the new racism's attempts to impose rigid boundaries around French national culture. Rap is a key weapon in minority youths' attempts to invade from the margins and "de-homogenize" the French cultural core. (Khaled has invaded too, but in a less threatening or incendiary manner.) Unlike the sometimes nostalgic and community-based appeal of rai, rap is aggressively deterritorializing and antinostalgic, even as it reterritorializes a multiethnic space. Rappers combine elements of the African-Caribbean musical diaspora with the specific concerns of the multiethnic French minorities, linking the diasporic Mediterranean and the diasporic Atlantic (cf. Gilroy 1992). It remains to be seen whether rap will fully open up to assertions of Maghrebi identity, or whether it will remain an ensemble which is weighted towards the diasporic African cultural matrix.

The cultural milieux associated with both rap and rai provide alternative heterogeneous discourses, clearing larger spaces in which formerly colonized subjects can live the multiplicity inherent in diasporic existences. And in some inter-cultural zones, they are contributing to the corroding and mutation of dominant French identity. Maybe one day the "decent" people in France will be those who listen avidly to the sounds of Chaba Zahouania or I AM and who consider the speeches of Le Pen and Chirac to be obnoxious "noise;" and maybe one day French natives will decipher the graffiti, and learn that *l'humanité* and *al-insaniyya* are synonyms, not mutually exclusive.

FRANCO-ALGERIAN HIP HOP AND THE "ISLAMICIZATION" OF THE DIASPORA INTO THE 21ST CENTURY[54]

As has been briefly alluded to, the rise of rap music in France in the 1990s coincided with two traumatic developments for the Algerian diaspora: the outbreak of the horrible, dirty war back in the homeland (having cost over 100,000 lives by the end of the 1990s), and the media- and government-driven demonization of Islam in the metropole. As a consequence, many Franco-Maghrebi community members began to identify more consciously with the practices, symbols, and beliefs of what they understood to be an Islamic way of life (not necessarily consistent with what was practiced back in the old country). Islamist missionizing as well as transnational Muslim involvement in the fighting in Algeria, Afghanistan, and the Balkans also played a role in attracting some of the more alienated banlieue male youth to identify as Muslim. Within France itself, the exposure of the 1980s secular beur organizations (SOS Racisme, France Plus, etc.) as extensions of the government cost them their credibility and left the field free to the Islamist groups that cropped up in the 1990s. The "foulard affair" which broke out in 1989 over the wearing of religious garb in the public schools, added to the growing importance of Islam as a marker of North African identity in France. A couple of years later in 1994, two Franco-Maghrebi youths from a Parisian suburb were sentenced to death in Morocco for their participation in an armed Islamist attack on a tourist hotel in Marrakech. Then in November, 1995, a highly sought after terrorist ringleader from the immigrant Lyon suburb of Vaux-en-Velin was hunted down and shot on national television. In the words of anthropologist, Paul Silverstein, "[These two acts] appeared to confirm the existence of a international terrorist network that supposedly linked Algiers to Cologne to Sarajevo to Kabul, via France's immigrant suburbs (Silverstein 2000: 30). In other words, members of the Algerian diaspora, in the minds of many in the academy, the government, and amongst the public at large, were potential fifth columnists. Their Islamic identities were not reconcilable with French Republicanism.

These two traumatic developments (the blood bath in Algeria and the demonization of Islam), created rather faint musical echoes in France in the beginning. The assassination of entertainers certainly received an enormous amount of press, as did the killings in general and, of course, the martyrdom of Kelkal in France. Yet the music of the first and second generation North African immigrants only slowly began to respond to them.

However, even if the music of the Algerian diaspora did not comment on events back in the homeland in the first half of the 1990s, other aspects of second generation Franco-Maghrebi culture in France were becoming more consciously "North Africanized." The more secular cultural trends of the 1970s and 1980s represented broadly by the rise of "Beur"-based movements gave way in the 1990s to a more conscious association with Arabo-Islamic heritage. Immigrant identity at this time became more closely associated with various signifiers of Maghrebi culture and various forms of popular Islamic beliefs and practices. In an especially insightful piece, Rabah Mezouane, one of France's most industrious commentators on the hip hop scene, chronicles the way this occurred during the decade. He sites, for example, several new verbal expressions of surprise or appreciation based on Islamic imagery that began to circulate in Maghrebi immigrant neighborhoods during the decade ("Sur le Coran de la Mecque," is one such oath). He also mentions how the second generation Maghrebi youth began to imitate the African American practice of associating Islam with resistance to the culture and religion of "the oppressor." No one like a Malcolm X or a Louis Farakhan emerged in France, and nothing similar to a "negritude" movement developed among Franco-Maghrebi youth. Nonetheless, the missionizing group, Jama'at al Tabligh, present in France since the 1960s, began to make real headway. At the same time, groups such as the Union des Jeunes Musulmans and Groupement found a ready supply of converts within the swelling ranks of Franco-Maghrebi youth in French prisons (Kelkal was converted while in prison, which has become something of a traditional source of converts in both France and the US [Herzberg 2001: 34]). These groups also gained some notoriety and publicity by targeting drug dealers in Franco-Maghrebi neighborhoods (Mezouane 1999a: 45-47). In 1994, a survey done by *Le Monde* found that 27 percent of Muslims in France (the Interior Ministry estimates that there are 4 million French Muslims, two million of them citizens) were practicing their religion, compared to the below 5 percent figure for French Christians. In a Harris poll conducted in 1995, 76 percent of Muslims in France stated that they would like to send their children to state supervised religious schools, an arrangement only available to Christians and Jews (Caldwell 2000: 22, 30).

References in French rap in the earlier '90s to the Islamic heritage of any group members tended to refer to popular Islamic symbols or other broad cultural signifiers of Arabo-Islamic or North African origins. The song, "La Main de Fatma," by Siria Khan on the "Rapattitude! 2" album released in 1992 (Labelle Noir) is illustrative of this. Khan sings of the famous hand of Fatima as a talisman which protects her, not just from bad luck and jealousy, but also from forgetting who she is and where her people came from. The hand of Fatima guides her, she claims, and helps her remain strongly identified with her Islamic cultural roots (which are never specifically identified). In a more humorous vein, Malik Sultan, a Franco-Maghrebi youth in the Marseille group IAM, lampoons the growing international identification of *rai* music with Algeria. In his song, "Do the *Rai* Thing," on the album "IAM . . . de la Planete Mars" (Labelle Noir, 1991), he comically boasts in a thick Franco-Arab accent of the growing fame of the "King of rai," Cheb Khaled, and then claims affinity with him as another equally great Algerian singer. Malik Sultan's song is interesting because of the way it suggests how conscious diasporic youth had become of the dominant culture's stereotyping of certain cultural markers of "Arabness," in this case, rai music and a Maghrebi accent in French.

IAM's identification with Arabo-Islamic culture extended beyond Malik Sultan's satire. The words to the song, "Red, White, and Blue" on the same 1991 album even asked for Allah's protection while claiming that the band members were Islamic scholars, "souls of Islam." Two years later, in 1993, IAM's lead singer, Akhenaton, officially converted to Islam, an act which he made much of in print, but which little affected the group's lyrics (Swedenburg 2001). Instead, IAM's more political musical subject matter (as well as Akhenaton's solo efforts) tended toward protests against immigrant immiseration, racism, and abuses by the French state.

The tendency on the part of rappers to identify as Muslim continued to evolve as the 1990s wore on. This was particularly true after the spate of bombings in 1995, culminating in the death of Kelkal. As mentioned earlier, the French state and major media launched a ferocious assault on Islamic fundamentalists in France that year. Under the guidance of the right-wing Interior Minister, Charles Pasqua, and the conservative prime minister, Alain Juppé, Operation Vigipirate was launched. French troops were stationed on the streets and around schools, public buildings and transportation centers for the first time since the Occupation. State agents carrying out surveillance measures and other forms of anti-terrorist actions descended on immigrant neighborhoods. North African immigrants became synonymous in the eyes of many French citizens with radical Islamists bent on destroying the French secular nation.

The 1996 release by the former NTM member, Yazid, of the CD entitled, "Je suis l'Arabe," (Play It Again Sam Records) is illustrative of the general pattern of the times among hip-hop groups of immigrant descent in that it protests mightily against abuses of power while embracing immigrant heritage. Interestingly in Yazid's case, that heritage is identified as Arab and Islamic as opposed to Beur, suggesting the now conscious attempt to put distance between those who would embrace some form of secular, mixed heritage, and those who take pride in their North African/ Arabo-Islamic roots.

The year 1996 also saw the release by the lesser-known Strasbourg group N.A.P. (New African Poets) of the song, "Le monde est à nous" (CD title: La racaille sort un disque. [Night and Day]), which attests to their religiosity (Je cherche ma vérité alors que je l'ai déjà trouver/ Seul l'Islam aujourd'hui peut me sauver. I am looking for my truth even though I've already found it/ Only Islam today can save me). The group of three subSaharan and three North African immigrant youth hail from the tough immigrant quartier of Neuhof, which provides the subject matter of a couple of their songs ("Je viens des quartiers" for instance). What is of note about NAP is their avowedly Islamic lyrical stance as well as their reputation as an outspoken Islamic group. The Islamic symbol of the crescent and star is even woven into the cover design of their 1998 CD, La fin du monde (High Skills/RCA/BMG). In more than one chat room conversation dedicated to the group the possibility of their disbanding was discussed in light of what were presented by participants as anti-music statements found in the Qu'ran. A true Islamic rap group, some thought, was a contradiction in terms and so they would logically have to call it quits. Apparently NAP do not see it that way for they released a new CD in 2000 called, A L'intérieur de nous (High Skills/RCA/BMG).

Several other Franco-Maghrebi Muslim rap artists disagree completely with the assertion that Islam and rap must be mutually exclusive. At the same time, though, Muslim artists make it clear that religion comes first, music second. Faouzi Tarkhani represents this tendency. Well known for the antiviolence crusade behind his hit 1999 CD, "Guerier pour la paix" (warrior for peace [Polydor]), he said in an interview (Mezouane 1999a: 47) that, "Pour moi, la religion est au-dessus de tout. Il faut faire sortir l'Islam des sous-sols de France, lui rendre sa visibilité" (For me, religion is above everything. Islam must be taken out of Fench basements and made visible). In the same interview Kamel, one of the lead singers (of Moroccan parents but raised in Blois) of the group Sawt El Atlas, made a similar claim when he said, "La croyance est dans le coeur et la religion donne un sens de ma vie, m'apporte un certain équilibre. Quand je quitterai cette terre, c'est le respect envers Allah que je voudrai emporter, pas mon passe musical" (Faith is at the heart of religion and religion gives meaning to my life and supplies me with a certain balance. When I leave this earth, It's respect for God that I would like to take away with me, not my musical past).

Though off the record avowels of Islamic belief among rappers of Franco-Maghrebi ancestry appear to be growing, probably for marketing reasons, lyrical testimonies of faith remain rare. More typical are small clues to the Arab or Islamic ancestry of performers in the form of Arabic phrases inserted in songs, the use of Middle Eastern instruments, or snippets of melodies or beats with an obvious Middle Eastern origin. That is the most common way of displaying some recognition of or attachment to the homeland.

At least that was the case until the middle-late 1990s. Starting around then, a hand full of Franco-Maghrebi groups took it upon themselves to address more or less head on conditions back in Algeria.

Gnawa Diffusion is one of the most "Maghreb-centric" of such French music groups. They got started in 1992 in the Grenoble region, coming out of the university student milieu there. They initially played only in small clubs, but can now fill halls in the 8-10,000 seat range. They have even toured outside Europe.

The members of Gnawa Diffusion were perhaps the first to address directly what was happening in Algeria. They put out a CD by the name, "Algèrie " in 1997. They left the words untranslated into French in the liner notes, they said, because," The conditions in Algeria cannot be translated and cannot be brushed off in a song, or an album. The songs in the album Algeria form part of a large, discrete family of Algerian alternatives," they claim. The group is extremely outspoken by immigrant standards in France, which speaks to their university origins. They have none of the hesitation to criticize Algeria in the face of the older generation, and little of the knee-jerk national pride which causes some of the immigrant suburban rappers to pause.

An interesting Gnawa Diffusion protest song about Algeria is, "Ouvrez les stores" (Bab le Oued/ Kingston. 1999. 7 Colors Music). The song opens in a ragga-Jamaican style, with its rapid pattering rhymes and its reggae beats. Even the vocal quality of the lead singer pays amusing homage to the great Jamaican ragga singer, Shabba Ranks, and his hoarse, grizzly voice. The song then shifts to Arabic instruments, particularly a zither-like synthesizer and lute. It also shifts back and forth between Algerian Arabic and French, and then ends with the sound of a muezzin giving the call to prayer.

The title, "Ouvrez les stores," refers to the way all shop owners in much of North Africa close their shops with pull-down, metal grate shutters at the end of the day or whenever there's trouble in the form of a demonstration, riot, or other potential violence. They are literally shutting up shop to avoid what's happening in the streets. The song plays metaphorically with this image as a reference to the way the whole country turns a blind eye to the corruption and killing carried out by the government and those struggling with it for power.

In 1999 another important reference to events in Algeria surfaced in French popular music in the song by the rapper Freeman called, "Bladi," from the CD L'Palais de Justice (Delabel). The song went gold in 1999 (sold over 100,000 copies in France). It also received airtime and an enthusiastic response in Algeria. We know Freeman, who went solo in 1998, in his first incarnation as Malek Sultan, the dancer and backup vocalist for Marseille's IAM (and the author of the song about Khaled mentioned previously). He was born in Marseille but was taken back to Algeria at 3 years old. He lived in and around the city of Algiers until he was 11, when he was moved back to France, where he had to relearn French.

Freeman's "Bladi" ("my country") opens with Algerian mega-star, Khaled, who plaintively sings in Arabic over what sounds like a sample of Hollywood strings movie music. The combination evokes a maximum, almost melodramatic, emotional response, which sets up the subject of the song. Khaled makes a couple of other musical interventions during the refrain where he repeats his longing for "my country," i.e., "bladi". Freeman is quoted as saying that he invited Khaled to perform on the single because his voice is the voice of Algeria for most people; he wanted people to take the song seriously. He figured that without Khaled, the song would just be tossed off, as he puts it, "as just another story about Arabs, it's the shits, and there you have it" (Forgues 1999: 21). Khaled, according to Freeman, gives it a serious Algerian imprimatur.

Freeman claims he wrote the song in part because he was angry over how little he understood of the crisis in Algeria. Today, he says, he feels he's both Algerian and Marseillais, and he always goes down to the boats coming into port from Algeria and asks passengers for news of the homeland. He claims it's his duty to inform his younger brothers. He wants to expose them to his particular analysis of the situation (Mezouane 1999b: 34) It is worth mentioning that the CD cover art uses the Islamic crescent and star as a dominant decorative motif, establishing visually Freeman's connection with his Arabo-Islamic roots.

Another 1999 rap hit also took up the Algerian crisis as its subject matter, only in a contrastive way. The group, 113, had a widely viewed music video to accompany their hit, "Tonton du Bled" ("Country Uncle") on the CD, Les Princes de la ville (Alariana/ Double H. SMA 496286). The group 113 come from Vitry (their name is the neighborhood address of one of the group), a southern suburb of Paris. They were made infamous in 1998 by a song that got a lot of publicity because of its scandalous line, "They gotta re-establish the death penalty for transexuals." Characterized as practicing a "brutal rap"; they are usually labeled as "ghetto rappers." One member is Algerian, one from Martinique, one from Mali (Williams 1999: 47).

"Tonton du Bled" by the Algerian member, Karim Brahmi, captures perfectly the highway-clogging, sweaty, tiring, month-long, annual summer return of North African immigrants to their homelands. Movies have been made about it; books written about it; jokes told about it; it is a traditional moment of intergenerational struggle between parental desire to return to the nostalgic romanticized homeland and youthful resistance to leaving the neighborhood.

The instrumental background of the song is all Arab inspired: Arabic orchestra, hand drum (derbouka), and ululation. The lyrics are all in French, but Arabic words are scattered throughout the text. Another feature worth remarking upon is that the song is so humorous. Brahmi's point would seem to be to portray Algeria with affection and a certain post-adolescent nostalgia. The song embraces those back in the old country as well as measures the distance between them and those now living in the immigrant suburbs in France. Only one direct mention of the war in Algeria surfaces, and that is in the form of the song's dedication in the last verse.

It is telling that Brahmi, in the liner notes dedication accompanying the CD Les Princes de la ville, uses the space to underline his Islamic heritage by declaring, "Allah U Akbar, merci de m'avoir permis d'aller au bout de ce projet et de veiller sur la famille Brahmi" (God is Great, thanks for having allowed me to go through with this project and for looking after the Brahmi family). In another interview, Brahmi states that, "I believe in God but I prefer not to talk about it" (Williams 1999:47).

Popular musical references to North African origins and events also continued into the new millenium. In 2000 the group, Seba (actually a family of six brothers named "Seba" from the suburbs of Paris with Algerian parents from the border region of northwestern Algeria), put out a, for the most part, light-hearted CD. The group plays affectionately with the stereotypical image of the simple North African green grocer (Èpicier) in France who only lives to please his customers. The image belies the sophisticated production values and slick worldbeat-inspired blend of acoustic North African instruments and rock, reggae, hip hop and other pop influences. The song, "Loukane" ("Liberty") stands out because of its mournful protest against the sacrifice of Algeria's youth, as exemplified by the bloody suppression of the Algerian riots of 1988.

Algerian French rap developed during the 1990s as a music of opposition critical of dominant society using language, lyrical references, and other cultural markers to identify themselves with their minority heritage. The bloody war in Algeria has caused Franco-Maghrebi rappers of Algerian descent to identify perhaps even more strongly with their ancestral land.

Most importantly, the very need to mark a distinction within dominant society suggests already that the second and third generations' point of reference is now solidly within metropolitan national culture. They now identify more as an ethnic subculture than as a branch of a community based overseas. Musically, this development is paralleled by the periodic inclusion of snippets of melody, or sampling of beats recognizable as belonging to traditional homeland genres. Such insertions are enough to signify an association with the homeland and thus an identity distinct from that of the dominant culture.

Finding no support for Muslim institutions, Muslim immigrants are moving in the direction of forming something along the lines of a transnational state within the European Union. People from many different countries, speaking many different languages are beginning to feel a similar sense of exclusion and unite under an Islamic identity, even if for many young people, as we have seen, "Islam" is more of a cultural heritage than a religion (Kastoryano 1999). Just as English language imperialism helped create a greater sense of community among Spanish speakers, so does the strident secularism of European states open the door to greater transnational links between Muslim populations in the diaspora. The transnational character of an identity erected upon an Islamic base, however construed, coupled with host state assaults on Islamic minorities is leading to ever greater identification with fellow Muslims who are also its victims. The subcultural world of Franco-Maghrebi popular music would appear to be both reflecting the trend towards greater identification as an Islamic diaspora as well as helping to lay its foundation.

Videos Accompanying

Remember, the actual video lectures can be accessed at the following url: http://oregonstate.edu/media/classes/index.php?className=anth210

Scroll down under the "Classes on Demand" heading and select "ANTH210: Comparative Cultures."

Video 12

This video starts with the following overheads:
Outline of lecture:

1. History of popular music in Algeria

2. History of Algerian popular music in France

3. Examples of culturally hybrid pop music in France

4. Reasons for studying Franco-Maghrebi popular music

Some Definitions

1. Rai: Algerian pop music from city of Oran

2. Franco-Maghrebi Diaspora: refers to the immigrant, exile, expatriate communities of North Africans living in France

3. Maghreb: Arabic/French word for French colonial North Africa (excluding Egypt, Libya)

We then showed a map of Algeria and pointed out the city of Oran (Wahran in Arabic) which is a port city on the northwest coast of Algeria.

We then showed a photo of Oran in the 1940s. We talked about its prosperity, its cosmopolitanism, its bars, and its economic and cultural importance to the region.

We talked about how the music called rai dates to the 1920s. It was the music of country peasants who moved into the cities of the coast. It was played in bars, bordellos, weddings, and at women's parties.

We talked about its characteristics: often a short, introductory passage; sung in the Wahranic dialect; drums are important; very rhythmic; lots of vocal ornamentation; subject matter tended to be either romantic or risqué; later, it became more a dance music

We then showed a slide with various instruments used by rai musicians: bendir (skin drum), ghaita (oboe-like instrument), qaraqeb (hand symbols), rebab (two-string violin), oud (Middle Eastern lute), gasba/nay (end-blown flute), derbuka (hand drums), tabl (bigger drums)

We next heard a song by Cheikha Remitti called "Ghir el baroud." She is known as the "Queen of Rai." She dates back to the early years of rai. We used the song to illustrate what early rai sounded like, with its completely acoustic accompaniment (before any electronic instruments or speakers were used). She sang in both Arabic and French, illustrating the fact that Oran was a French colonial city and she was probably used to singing to both French and Arabic speaking audiences. Notice too how low her voice is.

The topics that formed the subject of rai lyrics were sometimes drawn from local events during the colonial period. After independence in 1962 the Algerian govt. cracked down on forms of entertainment like rai. Female performers in particular suffered and gave way to male stars. Also during the 1960s, horn sections were added, oud was added, accordion, electronic devices entered the music, etc. We played a song (we didn't give the title) by Messaoud Bellemou to illustrate the way horns came to dominate rai music during the 1960s.

In the 1970s, with the rise of the cassette industry, rai took off. Even more electrification happened during this period as well (particularly with addition of keyboards). The music also got more risqué. The state again began to crack down. They banned the sale of rai cassettes, closed down recording studios, but to no avail. They couldn't stop the music. Worse, by banning it they were turning rai into oppositonal music. So the govt. turned around and decided to promote rai and try to control it that way. They put it on television, on the radio, in music festivals, and so forth. The fidelity of the music improved immensely during this time as the recording studios developed. We played a song (we didn't give the title) by Chaba Zahouania to illustrate the music of this period. She is one of the most popular of the female rai stars to have emerged over the last 20 or 30 years. Her dark alto voice is her signature.

We then played a song by Cheb Mami (didn't give the title) which was used to illustrate the mature form of the music during the 1970-1980s. He's known as the Prince of Rai. This song is interesting because of the violin and the lack of a bass beat. Mami's star continues to rise in France. Sting used him on his album entitled, Brand New Day. We played a bit of their duet from the album (title not given).

Speaking about the middle 1980s, this was also the time that rai was gaining a hold amongst the diasporic community there. The immigrants saw it as a marker of their origins and identity. French listeners also reached out and began to think of rai as a politically progressive music that represented a way to bring the two communities together. From the 1980s on, we said, rai could be bought around the country; it could be heard at many different venues as well.

As we said in the chapter, rai appealed more to the first generation of immigrants, people above the age of 20. It was also used during anti-racism demonstrations as a way of showing solidarity with the large, immigrant, North African population.

We then shifted to talk about the many kinds of music in France which have been influenced by North African musics. New kinds of musical hybrids have developed from the cross-fertilization of French and North African Arabic music.

The first illustration of this hybrid music was by the group, Fabulous Troubadours (no title given), playing a ragamuffin variety from Toulouse. Musicians from the city use Arabic and Occitan, the original language of the area, to try and suggest the medieval mix of cultures that once dominated the area. We next played a more experimental song by Sapho (no title given). The next song came from Rachid Taha and the group, Carte de Sejour, who identified very strongly as an immigrant band. We played a cover (didn't mention the title) they did of an old French popular song from World War II. The song was very nostalgic, very romantic. So to have an immigrant group pick it up gave the song a new meaning. We then talked about Rachid Taha's revelation while watching an American movie. He heard the soundtrack and immediately recognized it as Arabic in inspiration. He put out his own cover of the song, which we played. It turned out that he was listening to Dick Dale and the Del-Tones. Dale was really of Lebanese descent. He does acknowledge the inspiration of Arabic music behind what came to be considered the quintessential surf guitar sound that he pioneered in southern California. Talk about styles appropriating from each other and hybrid styles being born out of each other . . . . The whole incident is a wonderful testimony to the creative cultural force that immigrants bring with them. We then shifted to the heavy metal genre and played an illustration (song not named) of this by the mixed Moroccan-French group called Dazibao. We then went back in French popular musical history to talk about the artist Dalida, a woman absolutely central to pop music. Born in Cairo to Italian parents, she spoke Arabic, Italian, and French. She moved to France while in her early teens and became a famous diva. She doesn't normally sing in Arabic, but she did put out a huge hit in Arabic the late 1970s which we played (didn't give the name). We then talked about the hybrid music of the Algerian immigrant, Jimmy Oihid. We mentioned that he has incorporated several Western styles of music into his own. To illustrate this we played one of his songs (title not given), which borrowed heavily from James Brown. Amina was our next singer. Tunisian born but popular in France, particularly these days in the gay club scene. She is multilingual and she enjoys a multi-national audience. We played a club remix of hers (unnamed) to illustrate her hybrid style.

Last but not least we turned to discuss the "King of Rai," the most famous performer to cross the Mediterranean from Algeria to France, Khaled. He has sold millions worldwide and has had several big hits. He lives permanently in France and more than anyone made rai popular among the French. We played a clip of his MTV-style video for his first hit song, "Didi." It illustrates perfectly the hybrid, syncretic cultural styles that are behind the mixing going on among immigrant and French musics right now. We talked about how the video is loaded with various signifiers of both Western and North African origin. To comprehend them all one has to be of both cultures, one should, ideally, be an immigrant to completely appreciate the mix.

We then closed with the following overhead:

Why study Franco-Maghrebi Culture?

1. To explode the idea that "True France" is uniquely, exclusively white France; to show that immigrants are an integral part of French society

2. To demonstrate that French culture is hybrid; it cannot be divided into what is authentically "French" and what is "Third World." It's created from many sources; it's transnational

3. To undercut the growing influence of anti-immigrant, right-wing groups seeking to silence, marginalize, expunge, and expel immigrants from Europe

In general these points make the claim that France and French culture are mixtures, bastard creations, multiethnic at the roots, and that immigrants are absolutely central to them.

Video 13

We began by recapping the last video on the rise of rai, its spread throughout Algeria and then to France. We were also talking about how Arab musical influences have spread to all genres of French popular music.

We mentioned that in the reading, it stated that the mix of the two cultures was not so much syncretic as heterogeneous. What's the difference? In this case, the North African Arab influences are constantly being replenished so that new influences, new infusions are always flowing into

France as new things develop, in a way that African influences don't continue to feed into Brazil, for instance. The cultures exist almost side by side in a constant give and take in the immigrant diasporic case of North Africans in France.

We then talked about how the new Europe, the post-Soviet Europe, now finds itself in part defining itself against the Arabo-Islamic world. This forms the new Other. But in this case, the Other has already penetrated Europe, causing anxiety amongst particularly white Europeans who fear a loss of their culture. We saw a short video clip on touristic France to illustrate how white France portrays itself. We saw that the multicultural side of France was completely whitewashed out of the video. No mention was ever made of the large immigrant population.

We then saw a video that illustrated the living quarters and conditions of immigrants in France, quite the reverse of the tourist video. It showed, in contrast, the multiethnic banlieue, that is the tenement high rises of the suburbs, as well as the battles with police, and the creative popular cultural life of the suburbs.

We then put up the following overhead:

POP QUIZ! Match the country with the % of its population that is foreign born

United States	7%
Canada	16%
Australia	20%
France	11%

So what's the right answer(s)?:
They are lined up correctly in the chart!

We then put up the following overhead to give some sense of who makes up France's North African immigrant population:
North African Migrants and France (pop. figures are low, rough estimates)

1. 700,000 Algerian legal residents

2. 575,000 Moroccan legal residents

3. 230,000 Tunisian legal residents

Tens of thousands of illegal residents

1. 1,000,000 French citizens of North African origin (2nd and 3rd generation children, called "Beurs" in French)

2. 300,000 North African Jews who are French citizens

So, given this large immigrant population, we asked the question, "why does France deny its immigrant heritage while the United States embraces it?" We put up the following overhead to help explain the similarities and differences:

Comparison of French and American Immigration

1. Both have been populated by immigrants

2. In both few immigrant descendants still speak their language of origin after 3 generations

So why does France deny its immigrant heritage while the U.S. celebrates it?

1. Immigrants arrived after nation founded in France; they were the founders of the U.S.

2. In France, occupation identifies you; in U.S., race, ethnicity, religion are key

We turned after this to overhead photos of the appalling housing conditions of the immigrant banlieues (the French word for suburbs). We also discussed the economic vulnerability of the immigrants, as testified to by an overhead photo of a Renault car plant.

We next showed photos of an infamous police attack on immigrants during a demonstration on October 17, 1961, where hundreds of immigrants were killed. The purpose was to illustrate the political weakness and vulnerability of immigrants.

We then turned to the ways immigrants were imaged in France, particularly from the 1980s on when immigrants really began to assert themselves politically. They became a presence to be reckoned with. Two different responses flowed from that, as the following overhead explains:

Two responses to growing presence of North African immigrants in France:

1. Exploit them as a market niche; create a version of the immigrant as entertainer; develop "soft rap" groups
   (we used a song by the group Alliance Ethnik, called "Simple and Funky" to illustrate this first response)

2. Marginalize them; criminalize them; accentuate their cultural differences; construct them as a problem and a danger
   (We also showed several overheads that illustrated this way in which the immigrant youth were scapegoated for all of society's ills. They were banned from clubs, followed in stores, blamed for crime, accused of being Muslim fanatics and potential terrorists, all the while their suburbs were accused by the media of being the breeding grounds for most social problems in France.)

We then talked about the musical responses developed by the minority communities in France to the media and police assaults on them, as elaborated upon in the following overhead:

Two French rap responses to chronic clashes between suburban ghetto youth and the police:

1. Development of aggressive, boastful, defiant "hard rap"
   (MINISTERE AMER's song, "Sacrifice de poulets")

2. Calls for a truce, for an end to the violence, for a musical "attack" instead
   (Faouzi Tarkhani)

There was another element impinging on the consciousness of North African immigrant communities in France during the 1980s and 1990s; namely, the events back in Algeria. We put up the following overhead to illustrate the developments back in Algeria:

The undeclared Civil War in Algeria

1. 1965-88 single-party, military rule, command economy, govt./elite grow wealthy, food costs rising, housing shortages, scarcity of goods, lack of good jobs

2. 1988 October, demonstrations and riots led by youth; police/military respond savagely: massacre in Bab el Oued quarter of Algiers

3. 1991 December, FIS (militant Islamists) on the verge of winning Algerian elections; military annuls elections

4. 1992 June, Boudiaf (popular president installed by the military) is assassinated

5. 1992-2000 over 100,000 Algerians killed

We then talked about the ways these horrific events back in Algeria began to affect popular music back in France. The following overhead laid out the three responses we discussed:

Franco-Maghrebi musical responses to the undeclared Algerian Civil War

1. Ignore it; make very few references to French colonial history or current events in Algeria; down play connections between immigrants in France and the Algerian homeland
   (We didn't play a musical example of this.)

2. Market it; develop a pop music acceptable to Islamist conservatives in Algeria & France
   (We played the song by Cheb Anouar called "Bir Zem Zem" to illustrate this point.)

3. Establish solidarity between Algeria and its immigrants abroad; treat relations between the two as central to identity of both; treat migration as binding them together
   (First, we played a song [not mentioned] by the Algerian group MBS as an example of the way in which rap developed in Algeria itself as the music of the youngest generation. The lyrics had to be curtailed because of both govt. and Islamist surveillance. Nonetheless they rap about the connections with France and make their French cousins more aware of their North African origins.

The second example we played, Gnawa Diffusion's song, Ouvrez les stores," was a song by immigrants back in France. It takes so for granted the multilingualism of its Franco-Maghrebi audience that it shifts between the two languages with ease, even as the lyrics criticize corruption and venality back in Algeria.

The final example we played the song "tonton du bled" by the hardcore rap group, 113, which is a good example of the way the connections between the two countries figure into the lives of the immigrants who return home en masse every summer to visit the homeland.)

We finally ended with an overhead on the following three points about the importance of the study of Franco-Maghrebi music:

What the study of Franco-Maghrebi raï & rap teaches us:

1. Music is a crucial cultural form of expression through which North Africans struggle to assert and sustain their identities in France

2. Franco-Maghrebi expressive culture is a model of a heterogeneous culture with multiple affiliations

3. Franco-Maghrebis & their expressive culture form an integral part of French popular culture; they ethnicize it, decentralize it, de-homogenize it

NOTES

1. I want to thank Joan Gross and Ted Swedenburg who co-authored this chapter and who graciously gave their permission to have it reprinted here. The first part originally appeared in "Arab Noise and Ramadan Nights: Rai, Rap and Franco-Maghrebi Identity." (Co-authored equally by Gross, McMurray and Swedenburg) *Diaspora: A Journal of Transnational Studies* 3(1):3-39, Spring, 1994. The last section appeared in "[3]Visions of the Homeland in Puerto Rican and Franco-Maghrebi Diasporic Music.[2] (Co-authored with Joan Gross) In Alec Hargreaves (ed.) Minorités ethniques anglophones et francophones: etudes culturelles comparatives. Paris: L[1]Harmattan."

2. *Le Monde*, April 4, 1987, quoted in Stora 1992:217 (our translation).

3. The figure of 1 million Arabs killed is commonly cited; our figure for French casualties comes from Dupuy and Dupuy (1986).

4. Etienne Balibar contends that the two European ideological schemas of colonialism and anti-Semitism converge in the racism against minority populations of Arab-Islamic origin, "so that imagery of racial superiority and imagery of cultural and religious rivalry reinforce each other" (1991:12).

5. Koulberg (1991:34) shows that, amid the media onslaught, it was ignored that 48% of French Muslims actually opposed wearing the *hijab*.

6. One of the polls also found that 24% believe there are too many Jews in France. A March 1992 report by the National Consultative Commission on the Rights of Man found that nearly half the French expressed open antipathy toward North Africans, while 40% claimed to dislike North Africans born in France (*Minute-La France*, April 8-14, 1992, p.15).

7. For more background on French racism, see Balibar (1992), Ben Jelloun (1984), Lloyd and Waters (1991), Taguieff (1991) and Wieviorka (1992).

8. Muslims are required to abstain from sex as well as food from sunup to sundown during the month of Ramadan.

9. Virgin, 1988. Rachid Baba also produced *Pop Rai Rachid Style: Rai Rebels (Volume 2)* (Virgin, 1990), Chaba Fadela's *You Are Mine* (Mango 1988), and Chaba Fadela and Cheb Sahraoui's *Hana Hana* (Island 1989). The liner notes and song translations that accompany *Pop Rai Rachid Style*, for instance, emphasize the drinking and the risqué female behavior associated with rai.

10. This is how the 1990 WOMAD (World of Music and Dance) Festival program advertises Chaba Fadela and Cheb Sahraoui (WOMAD 1990). Our thanks to Rosemary Coombe for providing this source.

11. Estimates of "illegals" (Arab and others) in France range all the way from 300,000 to 1 million (*al-Hayat*, April 30, 1993, p. 9). When the new Socialist government proclaimed amnesty for undocumented residents in 1981, 131,000 came forward to claim citizenship (Lanier 1991:14).

12. This sketch is based on Balibar (1992), Naïr (1992) and Wieviorka (1992), though the term derives from the work of the French Regulation School (critiqued in Brenner and Glick 1991).

13. For an introduction to "flexible specialization" or post-Fordism, see Harvey (1991) and Hall (1991b).

14. A type of French slang that originated in criminal circles and is now used extensively by banlieusard youth (see Sherzer 1976).

15. Some so-called Beurs are French citizens, some are foreign residents, and others binationals. When we were in France, Algerians born in France after January 1, 1963, automatically received French citizenship, while those born before this date remained Algerian citizens. Children of Tunisian and Moroccan immigrants must decide whether they wish to opt for French citizenship at age 21 (Begag 1990:4). With the right-wing swing of the recent elections, these regulations have become more restrictive.

16. Sociologist Adil Jazouli's typology (1982) of Franco-Maghrebi cultural orientations was useful in constructing this spectrum of hybridity.

17. Adapted from Queer Nation's slogan: "We're here, we're queer, get used to it!" Our discussions with members of La Rose des Sables, a Franco-Maghrebi theater group from Valence, helped us understand this orientation.

18. The "I" in this section is Gross since McMurray and Swedenburg didn't attend this event.

19. A local musician, not the Cheb Kader heard on US rai releases (*From Oran to Paris*, Shanachie 1990).

20. We realize that this does not tally with the opinions expressed about mixed marriages by the radio listeners Bariki interviewed in 1984. This leads us to believe that he mainly interviewed young men who voiced opinions about their own marriages rather than parents who expressed their views on the marriage of their children.

21. Moroccan feminist Fatima Mernissi, for instance, regards the independent, companionate heterosexual marriage unit based on romantic love, in which partners are equal and share love for each other, as a real threat to the "Muslim system" (1987:8).

22. Island 1990.

23. *Maman Cherie*, Contact Music 1991.

24. See Bizot (1987) for an early account of the Parisian World Music scene.

25. Barclay 1992.

26. See Dominique Guillerm's review of "Didi" in *Max* (May 1992), p.21. The album was recorded in Los Angeles by noted producers Don Was (of Was Not Was) and Michael Brooks of 4AD Records.

27. The late Umm Kalthum, the most popular of all Egyptian singers, was probably the most canonical of those with a classical orientation. Among her lyrics: "come and we will finish our love in one night." Muhammad 'Abd al-Wahhab, one of few Egyptian singers who ranks with Umm Kalthum in terms of popularity and classicist orientation, sang "life is a cigarette and a cup [of wine and liquor]." Yet neither singer has a reputation for being "vulgar" (Armbrust 1992:534).

28. From ... *De la planète mars*, Labelle Noir/Virgin 1991.

29. Majid's gang in Mehdi Charef's *Tea in the Harem* (1989) is a fictional rendering of this tendency. So-called delinquent youth seem to provide the media with ready suspects whenever violence erupts in the *banlieues*. See, for instance, Tourancheau (1991) on the March 1991 Sartrouville riots and Moreira (1990) on the November 1990 Vaulx-en-Velin riots, as well as the sensationalist media treatment of the "*Bandes de Zoulous*" (Vivier 1991c).

30. *Minute-La France* 1565 (April 8, 1992), p. 19.

31. See Aïchoune (1991) to get a flavor of the everyday speech of banlieusard posses.

32. For useful discussions of French rap, see Lapassade (1991), Leibowitz (1992), Mézouane (1990), and Vivier (1991a; 1991b; 1991c; 1991d).

33. Our analysis is based primarily on the releases of Supreme NTM (*Authentik*, Epic 1991) and I AM (... *De la planete Mars*)—two of France's most well-known rap groups—as well as two important anthologies (*Rapattitude*, Labelle Noir, 1990, and *Rapattitude 2*, Labelle Noir, 1992) and a recording by Franco-Maghrebi rappeuse Saliha (*Unique*, Virgin 1991).

34. As evidenced, for instance, by the angry reactions when Bill Clinton equated black nationalist rapper Sister Souljah with neo-Nazi David Duke.

35. One interesting exception is Siria Khan's "La Main de Fatma," *Rapattitude 2*.

36. With the exception of Prophètes du Vacarme's very ambivalent "Kameleon," *Rapattitude 2*.

37. Many prominent US rappers are avowed Muslims (Brand Nubian, Ice Cube, Poor Righteous Teachers, Rakim of Eric B and Rakim, Professor Griff and the New Asiatic Disciples, Big Daddy Kane), but their rhymes almost never deal with specifically *Arab* subjects—with the exception of the occasional mention of Palestine.

38. Other liberal "intellos" also seem unable to undertake an analysis of rap without first establishing its pedigree, usually by citing other canonical examples of verbal artistic performances. Mézouane (1990:5) compares rap to the West African *griots*, the *meddah* (itinerant Berber poet), the *berrah* (traditional rai announcer), and even the reciters of *la chanson de geste* of the European Middle Ages. Georges Lapassade, the ethnographer of hip-hop who teaches at Paris VIII, likens rap performance to a Moroccan call-and-response ritual (*aît* and *daqa*) and the rapper to an Arab *majdoub* (a tranced-out religious ecstatic) (Loupias 1990:44). Another commentator claims that, "the importance of rap today for the Black community perhaps approaches that of the story tellers of the nineteenth century in our [sic] society" (Bouillier 1990:2).

39. One of their jokes: "What is the difference between 'migration' and 'immigration'?" Answer: "La migration c'est les oiseaux qui volent; l'immigration c'est les Arabes qui volent." ("Migration is birds that fly; immigration is Arabs who steal.")

40. The opening of one of Smaïn's stand-up routines: "Okay, all French people in the audience, put your hands in the air. Now, all North Africans in the audience, take your hands out of their pockets."

41. Sayad *et al* (1991) gives a breakdown on immigration to Marseille by arrondissement.

42. On *Salam Alikoum*, Musidisc, 1992.

43. The band was formed in Lyon during the first big Maghrebi youth upsurge of the early 80s (Azoulay 1991:17). Its former lead vocalist, Rachid Taha, now performs as a solo act; his latest release is *Barbès* (Barclay 1991).

44. Amina played the prostitute in Bertolucci's *The Sheltering Sky*, a film she subsequently condemned as orientalist. She was the only Arab artist to participate in the remake of "Give Peace a Chance," an all-star recording organized by Julian Lennon to mobilize opinion against the Gulf War which went virtually unremarked in the US. Her single US release is "Yalil" (Mango 1989).

45. On the 1961 massacre, see Aïchoune (1991), Ben Jelloun (1984), Cockburn (1991), Einaudi (1991), and Hargreaves (1989); on racist violence in the 80s, see Aïchoune (1991) and Jazouli (1992).

46. Although the Muslim population in France includes a growing number of Turks, as well as some Pakistanis and black Africans, in this context "Muslim" means Arab.

47. Our thanks to the late Philip Shehadeh for this information.

48. *Foreign Broadcast Information Service*, Near East and South Asia Daily Reports, March 27, 1991, p. 5; *Libération*, March 28, 1991, p. 33. An Algerian engineer we know in Seattle who loves rai and despises FIS visited Algiers in March 1991 and claimed that several people were killed in one FIS attack on a music audience and that one performance hall was burned down. We have been unable to confirm this

story. An Algerian graduate student at a US university and a critic of the FLN offered a quite different account, in which the state was the aggressor. He asserted that the Algerian government actively encouraged music performances during Ramadan in order to harass and provoke the Islamists. The government often issued permits for concerts to be held during Ramadan prayer time, he claimed, and specifically promoted the holding of concerts at venues next to mosques.

49. FIS's program would permit only widowed or divorced women, particularly with children to support, to hold paid employment. In late December 1991, Muhammad Said, a top FIS leader, told a huge crowd that it was time for Algerian women in the big cities to start wearing scarves to cover their hair and to stop looking like "cheap merchandise that is bought and sold" (Ibrahim 1991).

50. The spiritual power said to inhere in *sharifs*, the descendants of the prophet Muhammad.

51. Adapted from Steve Arra's translation on the liner notes to Cheb Khaled's release *Fuir mais où?*

52. Yúdice draws this definition from the work of Cuban theorist Fernando Ortiz and Uruguayan theorist Angel Rama.

53. Goldman's article (1993) is unique in the music industry coverage of Cheb Khaled for its mention of anti-Arab racism in France.

54. This segment of the chapter is adapted from McMurray, Gross (2004). See the bibliography for the full citation.

MUSIC, MIGRATION AND THE NADOR, MOROCCO DIASPORA

Nador was awash in music when we were living there. Over every telephone wire dangled the thin, brown, ribbon-like remains of a music cassette tape. Little kids played soccer in the streets using the tape bunched up to form a ball. Arabo-Andalusian music played every night on the television during the month of Ramadan. Record stores fronted for cassette copy shops where young and old queued up to make pirate copies of their favorite cassettes for their friends and family. The music stalls lining the street to the bus station blared out a cacophony of competing songs from their low fidelity sound systems. My neighbors adored Sweden's Abba (remember, this was in 1986-1987). The kids in the hanout (corner grocery) where I exchanged my spent butagaz bottles yelled at me "Get up! Stand Up!" every time I appeared in remembrance of a night spent together translating Jamaican Bob Marley's lyrics. Milkbar Muhammad across the street played only Qur'anic recitation tapes. The butcher kept his picture on the wall and swore that the famous Middle Eastern star, Farid al-Atrash, was the greatest composer and singer of all time. Sound saturated Nador.

The century and a half experience of mass labor migration from the Moroccan Rif has left a profound impression on this musical landscape in the Nador region. Many Rifis belong to families that have been sending emigrants abroad for 3, 4 or more generations. Thus the way the community imagined itself, the expressive cultural forms, such as music, that it used to represent itself, were deeply affected by the migratory process. And this had never been more the case than in the 1980s when for perhaps the first time a large diaspora existed in dynamic linkage with the homeland in such a way so as to begin seriously to influence the expressive cultural representations of the migratory process that bound them.[1]

In the case of Rifi popular music, I am thinking of how various popular narrative techniques or strategies had developed, been discarded, then revitalized or superseded as ways of thinking about global forces locally. Let me mention two of these: the first involved representing the consequences of massive labor migration in terms of its highly personal, emotional impact. Over the last several decades this had usually meant focusing on the effects of migration on male-female relations and, to a lesser extent, on intergenerational relations. The second but related popular narrative technique entailed taking a position within the song text as to the personal benefits or liabilities of migration. Over time, this had usually taken the form of celebrating the fortunes to be made by migrating or the freedom from social constraint migration offered as opposed, conversely, to emphasizing the loss and separation it necessarily entailed.

I want to illustrate in this chapter the variety of expressions of migration's effects on the Rifi homeland as they worked their way through popular music from the 1950s to the late 1980s. I also want to discuss the specific conditions in the European diaspora which caused popular cultural expression to be organized differently there as opposed to back in the Rifi homeland.

AY-ARALLA-BUYA AND THE GOLDEN '50S

The bedrock of Rifi popular music is the predominately women's genre known by its refrain, *ay-aralla-buya* (Oh my lady [mother], oh my father).[2] The refrain sandwiches in rhymed couplets (*izran*) which are, ideally, improvised female commentaries on the joys and sorrows of life and love. The music in 1980s-Nador was often associated with rural life and was confined to women's gatherings.[3] Furthermore, recorded versions no longer figured as part of the Nador soundscape, whereas in the 1950s they dominated the Rifi Berber hour on Moroccan national radio (Hart 1976:169).

Collections of these lyrics from the 1950s (and 1960s) reveal that the massive out-migration of men from the impoverished Rif was a particularly important topic for the women left at home. Some illustrative couplets commented as follows:

Oh Valenciana (name of the Spanish Protectorate bus line),
Oh my soul,
Please send a boatload of regrets to my sweetheart (working in Algeria).

or

The main road to Tangier stops there,
there my sweetheart works and in summer he will return to marry me.

or

Oh Lord (God), I want to telephone to the Mulwiya
So that I can speak personally to my sweetheart (who is working in Algeria).[4]

The topicality of these lyrics was in keeping with the character of *ay-aralla-buya* and spoke, at least on the surface, to the impact postwar migration from the Rif was having on male-female relations. Again on the surface, the dominant theme was one of lament for the absence of loved ones. What is intriguing is the question of whether the insertion of references to lovers abroad was not just a lament for the forced mobility of Rifi men and the enforced immobility of Rifi women, but was also a moment in a new form of competition between women over whether or not prestige accrued to women who sought out adventurous, migratory men.[5] Just as interesting, the songs suggested that one of the important struggles of the day was how the whole process of long-term male migration from the region was to be understood, that is, as a lucrative means of getting ahead ("in summer he will return to marry me") or as another form of deprivation, another kind of burden women had to bear ("please send a boatload of regrets to my sweetheart working in Algeria")?

THE 45 RPM DECADES

The incredible explosion of Rifi migration to Europe begun in the 1960s insinuated itself into most every form of popular expression. The 45 rpm records put out by regional musical personalities in the 60s and early 70s reveal that the struggle continued over the meaning and import of migration.[6] A good example of the celebration of migration was a duet from the period by Cheikh Mahand and Cheikha Manate.

He said to me: I will do for you what your father wouldn't do,
I will get you a passport to go with me to Germany.

Interestingly enough, only the female singer (*cheikha*) sang this couplet on the theme of migration, going so far as to suggest that she, the female lover, could go along. This represented an intriguing innovation in that it posited female migration as a new way of imagining defiance of parental authority, as opposed to the more usual lyrical representation of defiance via elopement.

The next female couplet in the song backed away from the promises of the first, choosing instead merely to remind the departing lover of her expectations of him while abroad.

> If you go to Germany, keep me in your thoughts.
> Bring me back a present, fill up your pockets (with money).[7]

The next excerpt suggests that the depiction of male migration as a socially/emotionally upsetting development surfaced just as often on the 45s of the 1960s and 1970s as it had in the earlier decade of the 1950s:

> I don't have an enemy, except the boat from Melilla.
> It has taken my lover, it has left me an orphan.[8]

Migration also provided the backdrop for competitive male posturing. as represented in the lyric of a Farid Enadori song of the period which goes as follows:

> The passport you've got, throw it in the water,
> Go fall down the well; don't cross to Germany.[9]

Locals glossed this song for us as being an insult. The singer suggests to his rival that he does not have what it takes to be a successful migrant; that he would be better off spending his time jumping down a well than trying to make a go of it in Germany.

Perhaps even worse, from the point of view of the female Rifis, was the fact that, not only did Germany the country attract their men, but German women began to appear on the horizon as competition for the emigrants' affections back in the homeland:

> What is it (with) your lover who has come back upset.
> He has brought back a German girl. He wants to get divorced.[10]

In reality there seemed to be few European wives in the Rif, far fewer than you would have thought judging by the widespread titillation stirred up when the subject was broached. Most likely the image of available German women and the theme of intermarriage expressed and personalized the anxieties felt by women about male abandonment and escape from commitment which were intensified by the rise of mass labor migration to Europe.

The fear of abandonment and the problem of women's immobility came up in the popular music of the time, not just in relation to migration to Europe, but also as an expression, I would like to think anyway, of the anxieties caused by the massive out migration from the countryside to the city so characteristic of Morocco in the postwar decades. The tremendous growth in the urban population took place in a more demographically egalitarian fashion than migration abroad. Nonetheless, women lagged behind men in the move to the city. Moreover, as the cities of the region developed, only the men of the families who remained in the country could move freely between rural and urban domains. The city, somewhat like Europe, appeared in the imagery of women's song lyrics as a rival for the affections of country men, as suggested in the following Cheikha Mimount song:

> You're going down to Nador.
> You've left me for another.
> You've exchanged me for a new lover.[11]

THE ERA OF FOLK-PROTEST MUSIC

The 1970s-80s, the period of the cassette boom, brought about a massive increase in the consumption of commercially produced music. In the eastern Rif, the era was most profoundly marked musically by the influence of folk-protest filtered through the Moroccan groups, Nass al-Ghiwane and Jil Jilala,[12] but embodied locally by the so-called Bob Dylan of the Rif: Walid Mimoun.[13]

As would be expected of someone patterning himself after Dylan, Walid Mimoun played acoustic guitar and harmonica backed by flute and derbouka. That innovation was only one source of his popularity, however. Local Nador fans equally appreciated the progressive Berber nationalist origins of his music. People of all ages recognized him as a cultural icon. They talked about him as the original Berber artist who spurned commercial viability to remain true to his Nador regional fans.

His reputation also rested on the seriousness of his lyrical subject matter. Corruption in and co-optation of local society provided him with his targets. For example, he lamented the plight of child labor in the informal economy in *Yaythma Imezianen* (My Little Brothers). In *Wa Y'ajaj Ghanaj* (Thunder Sing!), he attacked inequities of wealth and power, as in the lines: "Build your palaces/ On our backs/ With our tears/ With our sweat." He even purified the language as a kind of protest against its degradation at the hands of careless local users.[14]

In response to his popularity, the state seized his passport and restricted his appearances. He turned to drinking, stopped performing and became the subject of whispered, reverential gossip. All the while his tapes circulated furiously as barely audible fifth or sixth generation copies.

Let me back track for a moment and try to provide some sense of just how popular Walid Mimoun was in Nador.

While we were there, the none too popular government controlled television service (RTM, a branch of the Interior Ministry, naturally) decided to produce a weekly song contest focusing on the singing talent of the country's different provinces.[15] Nadoris waited expectantly for their turn. It never came. The powers that be decided to lump Al Hoceima Province in with Fez and Nador Province in with Oujda. They erased the Berber north.

The governor of the Province seemed to be trying to compensate for the over sight when he organized a Chamber of Commerce kind of extravaganza called "Nador Week." An exhibit area was set up on the dilapidated grounds of the Hotel Rif where each of the area industries was expected to self promote. At night, so rumor had it, there would be a big concert by Nador's favorite son, Walid Mimoun.

That first night we all crowded onto the bleachers set up around the hotel's abandoned swimming pool to view Walid Mimoun's show. Nothing happened. The next night everyone was convinced Walid Mimoun would perform and it would be a night to remember. Excitement was running high. Surprisingly, even higher status women showed up to take in the spectacle. What we got instead were line dancers from the Atlas Mountains. They were the ubiquitous men and women in white who shuffled through their dance routine and performed all over the country for most any occasion. There may have been only one; there may have been a hundred line dance troops, they all melted together. For all I knew, Moroccans in other parts of the country appreciated their presence at functions, though I think their major attraction was for tourists more than locals. That night they got booed, or the Nador equivalent: they got hissed–right off the stage. Initially people waited, expecting them to be an opening act. But when it became clear that they were the whole show, the audience let go. I was surprised that the fact that they were fellow Berbers meant nothing. The audience was as uncharacteristically rude as I ever witnessed in Morocco.[16]

After the line dance debacle, interest in Nador Week nightly entertainment cooled off. No one seemed to know if Walid Mimoun would ever perform, much less where or when. The last night of the week was apparently open. At least nothing was happening at the Hotel Rif. I remember going to bed about 10:00 p.m. I woke up about midnight to the unmistakable roar of a crowd. I scampered up to our roof and sure enough, something was happening in the soccer stadium by the lagoon. The cheering sounded louder than the regular soccer matches.

Down in the street I heard the news: Walid Mimoun had finally performed. The government tried to control the affair by changing the venue from the hotel to the stadium, charging 20 dirhams admission and "selling" as many of the tickets as they could to merchants and bureaucrats. They still could not control the audience's enthusiasm. When Walid Mimoun mounted the stage, the Nadori crowd went wild. They sang his lyrics by heart along with him and generated thunderous applause after each number. The government officials in charge became so shaken by the out pouring of excitement that they pulled the plug on Walid after only three songs. They claimed there had been a power failure.

The street was abuzz for weeks with talk about that night. Those lucky enough to have been on the inside recounted endlessly the details to the rest of us until we all felt as if we had been in the audience. It proved to be the cultural event of the year in Nador.

What is most interesting here for my purposes is that Walid Mimoun, a male, for the first time turned a critical eye on the phenomenon of migration. One of the three songs he sang that night was (*ad dwared amynu* [Return Oh My Son]) in which he decried the excesses of men abroad, men who lost themselves in the clubs and bars of Europe and forgot where they'd come from. Walid Mimoun's portrayal in this song was an interesting testimony to the psychic costs of the emigrant experience at a time when emigrants were utterly transforming the countryside with their new found wealth. Then as now, I imagine, few were willing to go public about their failures, preferring instead to represent their migration experience as an achievement, or as a successful conquest. This mournful ballad was structured as a simple dialogue between a mother and her separated son (though sung entirely by Walid Mimoun). The mother opened the song lamenting:

> Return oh my son.
> (to which the son replies)
> I stay here, Mother, in the land of the Europeans,
> My home, I see it as a cemetery,
> I'm staying here in Germany
> Drinking whiskey in the bars,
> I have a European wife and children from her.
> (The mother again responds)
> Return oh my son.

It is worth highlighting here the way Walid Mimoun portrayed emigrants in the song for what I believe to be the first time as something like reluctant recruits in the global reserve army of labor.

The son replied to his mother by claiming he had no choice in the matter, he was trapped in a European limbo, longing but unable either to adjust to Europe or to return home, all due to the inevitability of migration–understood by the son to be his only option in life.

The emotional personalization in popular song of the effects of mass labor migration continued to play just as important a role in Walid Mimoun's songs as in previous artists', as witnessed to by the fact that the emigrant's affections and responsibilities were portrayed as irreparably split between a mother on one side of the sea and wife and children on the other. Furthermore, the pressures of this dual life had led the emigrant to drink. But what was remarkable was that a kind of political economy explanation for this sorry state of affairs got inserted as the emigrant lamented that he was caught between work abroad or unemployment at home (My home, I see it as a cemetery).

The last of the three songs Walid Mimoun sang that night, called, *Dchar Innou*, (My Hamlet), took up in an oblique fashion the theme of rural to urban migration. Unlike Cheikha Mimount's earlier treatment of the process as threatening to women's claims on men's affections, Walid Mimoun instead evoked a wistful yearning for the old country hamlet of origin now in the process of being abandoned. The significance of the song, in my opinion, was that it represented the first time a nostalgic mode was used in discussing the effects of migration. The technique of personalizing the discussion was being discarded. In its stead, a kind of distance from any premigration experience was presumed, so much so that it could now be romantically mythologized.[17] The song slowly strung together a series of images of country life (for example: The prickly pear leaf and the spider web of my *dchar*; The sun setting over my *dchar*) and pledges of loyalty to the natal hamlet (ex..: I can't forget my *dchar*; I will remain forever faithful to my *dchar*) while repeating continuously the refrain:

> Alas for those who've forgotten their *dchar*.
> The wind and the dust in my *dchar*,
> Destroy the walls of my *dchar*.

Many of the young people of Nador who embraced *Dchar Inou* at the time of its release had only visited the countryside and villages of their parents, they had never actually lived there themselves. Their shared nostalgic vision of the country life was based, presumably, on not much more than such lyrical representations as Walid Mimoun provided. The song became very popular among the young of Nador who used to repeat its sad refrain over and over. I liked to think that the song represented a kind of memorial to a life left behind in the country. A life the urban youth had hardly known was being mourned as passing away, slowly destroyed by migration to the city and abroad. Even the music associated with rural life, the *ay-aralla bouya*, was invoked in the song at one point in a whispery, slow, and languid repetition of its refrain which robbed it of its festive vitality and, instead, had the effect of embalming it as a specimen of this earlier existence.

Ironically, the whole time Walid Mimoun's star was rising he was desperately trying himself to emigrate from Morocco, when he was not spending his time getting drunk and high. He was finally allowed out in the early 90s and immediately went to Amsterdam, the Mecca for dissident North Moroccans. He reportedly traveled around performing for the enclaves of Nadoris residing all over Germany and Holland before being sent back to Morocco in the mid 1990s.

THE DIASPORA COMES OF AGE

Walid Mimoun's flight to Amsterdam embodied precisely the old view in the Rif of migration as a form of escape, as we have seen. His ability to find work there as a performer, however, was dependent on a more recent development, namely, the growth to maturity of the Rifi diaspora in Europe.

Until recently, emigrants abroad figured musically back in the homeland mainly as the object of popular cultural scrutiny. Of course they have long been important for the socioeconomic prosperity and chaos they created in their wake, but they have done little creatively to contribute to Rifi popular musical production. They have traditionally been much more important as promoters or consumers abroad of popular music originating in the Rif. Now all of that was beginning to change. The diaspora had begun, for the first time I am aware of, to produce a popular music of interest to those back at home. This consisted for the most part of bootleg cassettes of Berber protest music soirées circulating back in Morocco among lycée and university students of Rifi origin. A group of Nador university students in Rabat played one of these tapes for me which they claimed was a recording of a 1992 festival in Amsterdam dedicated to the celebration of Berberness. They turned the tape on and out poured an a cappella, hand clap-accompanied ay-aralla-bouya, which went roughly as follows:

> The Berber is like a bird flying in the sky,
> Whose nest is between his wings.
>
> He can't come to rest anywhere,
> Wherever he puts his nest, they try to kill him.

I like to think of this music as an illustration that the migratory circuit between the diaspora and the homeland was now two-way; that the conditions in the diaspora were now leaving their mark on Rifi popular cultural expression. From the admittedly small sample I have provided, it seems clear that the most remarkable feature of the circuit was the overtly political reading of migration the diaspora contributed to Rifi popular music. First, there was the appropriation of the *ay-aralla bouya*. Unlike Walid Mimoun, the diaspora militants respected the form of the genre by sandwiching in rhymed couplets between repetitions of the traditional refrain. Apart from the large number of male voices participating and the rather fast tempo, the only difference between these examples and those to be found back home was in the subject matter of the couplets. Yet what set the diasporic example apart as much as new lyrical content was that it was revitalizing and legitimizing a somewhat passé, restricted genre. That move, I would argue, was a politically motivated attempt to establish the *ay-aralla bouya* as The Tradition, and to privilege as well the originary, pure country life associated nostalgically with it.

Secondly, the diasporic performers more overtly politicized Rifi popular music by shifting the narrative subject. No longer was it an individual lover or mother or son who suffered, but the whole community now, personified lyrically as the homeless Berber condemned to wander the globe. Gone, in the diasporic reading, were the tensions between men and women or between the generations which figured so prominently in the lyrics generated back in the homeland.[18] A critique of the age of migration was thus both implied musically in the choice of a genre associated with an earlier, country life, while also of course being made explicit in the lyrical portrayal of Berbers as a people chased from place to place by those intent on destroying them.

MUSIC AND IDENTITY IN THE DIASPORA

I want to argue for the priority of two particular factors at work in the diaspora which best explain the turn there to a politicized construction of a persecuted, pure, moral community as lyrical subject, as well as to the identification of the older *ay-aralla-bouya* genre as a privileged musical signifier of Rifi ethnicity.[19] The first of these factors was the fact that attempts at community mobilization in Europe, like most any other form of political or cultural organization or protest movement, entailed few costs when compared to similar activities back in the homeland. The relative freedom to protest outright in Europe was thus an important influence on popular cultural production in the diaspora.[20] These conditions were not as favorable in the homeland. There, instead, something like an apolitical cultural activism had been fairly successfully promoted.[21]

The second important political factor was that when compared to those at home, Rifi Berbers, as members of the North African immigrant mass in Europe, were becoming more marginalized and ghettoized, in short, racialized. That is, they were more and more identified and forced to self-identify in an essentialist way. Living under the weight of that kind of stigma takes its toll. Berbers were thus becoming, on a day to day basis, more conscious in Europe of themselves as a minority ethnic group, and thus more disposed to appeal to a sense of a pure, original community founded on differences that distinguish them–unfortunately, not just from dominant European culture (for those were distinctions forced upon them), but from the immigrant mass in Europe, as well as from the dominant Arab population back home.[22]

These two factors: 1. greater racialization or ethnicization of immigrants and 2. relative freedom to protest combined to create conditions favorable to the development of an essentialist, traditionalist protest music in Europe. These, I would argue, were the specific conditions most implicated in the diasporic turn towards an overtly political use of Rifi popular music as a marker of Berber identity and community.

Finally, I want to reiterate that the homeland reception of the diasporic move to politicize Rifi music has been enthusiastic but thin so far because the conditions outlined above do not pertain in the homeland.[23] Thus, whether the development of a new musical direction in the diaspora leads to cross-fertilization with the Rif or rather to a more permanent divergence between the two communities remains to be seen. I do know–by way of illustration of where this might all be heading–that one young, local Rifi poet wrote a song in 1993 for the Al Hoceima group, *Tifridjass* (swallow), which was inspired by the political direction taken in diasporic music. The lyric states:

> Some say Germany,
> Some say the Arabian Peninsula,
> But I say that Berbers come from here,
> Their roots are North African.

The song reflects diasporic influences in that it obviously addresses the highly contentious topic of Berber origins while also focusing on the community at large as subject. At the same time, though, I would like to read its evocation of pan-North African origins as a gentle reminder to the diasporic community of the pride of place still enjoyed by the community of origin, a community that is safer, larger, and more inclusive than the one sometimes imagined in the popular songs of migrants living abroad.[24]

VIDEOS ACCOMPANYING

Remember, the actual video lectures can be accessed at the following url: http://oregonstate.edu/media/classes/index.php?className=anth210

Scroll down under the "Classes on Demand" heading and select "ANTH210: Comparative Cultures."

Video 14

(The video opens with a reference to the book called, *In and Out of Morocco*. We are reading only a chapter from this book which is chapter 6 in this text and is entitled, "Music, Migration and the Nador, Morocco Diaspora."

We began the first session by watching a video clip that introduced Moroccan history and culture, and then spotlighted several of the country's largest cities. The video explained how the indigenous Moroccan Berbers had been conquered by a variety of civilizations, including the Phoenicians, Carthaginians, Romans, Vandals, Arabs, French and Spanish. The most important of these, the movie stated, was the Arab invasion that began in 682 AD and ended with the submission of the Berbers in 701. The spread into Morocco of the Islamic religion and the Arabic language slowly pulled the country into the mighty Arabo-Islamic civilization. In 711, a largely Berber army crossed the Strait of Gibraltar and spread the same civilization across Spain and Portugal and southern France. Arabo-Islamic culture flowered in the Iberian Peninsula (i.e., Portugal and Spain where it became known as Andalusian culture) to the point where it became the most cosmopolitan and enlightened culture of the Medieval period. But it was not to last. The Christian reconquest of the Iberian Peninsula began in the tenth century and ended in 1492 with the fall of Grenada, the last Adalusian city-state. By 1502, all Muslims and Jews had been expelled from Spain. The French conquest of the region began in Algeria in 1830 and culminated in the invasion of Morocco in 1912. Morocco finally won independence in 1956.

Point

According to the video, as a consequence of these invasions, Morocco today is an amalgam of three influences:

1. the pure, primitive vision of the Berbers with its color, energy, and boldness

2. the order, authority, and command of visual space brought by the Arabs

3. the habits and designs of everyday, urban living brought by the French.

Counterpoint

This list and the video in general need some contextualizing. I would go so far as to say that the list tells us nothing about the musical scene in Morocco today. It even smacks of lazy, Western stereotypes of indigenous Berber "primitives" and French contemporary "cosmopolitans." What I want to pursue here is a different list, one which emphasizes the following three intertwining influences on Moroccan music:

1. **Berber tribal influences.** These continue to have an impact on the language (Berber), as well as on the performance setting, musical style, and instruments used in much local music in Morocco.

2. **Arabo-Islamic cultural influences.** The use of the Arabic language in Morocco in sacred musical genres owes a debt here. Think of the Sufi tradition, the Gnawa genre, as well as Andalusian forms of music played throughout Morocco. Equally important are the profane musical genres in Arabic that connect Morocco to the rest of the contemporary Arabic world music scene and make Moroccans great consumers as well as producers of popular Arabic language music.

3. **Colonial and post-colonial context.** The use of the French language is fairly restricted in Moroccan music, but modern commercial production values, international distribution circuits, worldbeat influences, electronic instrumentation, stadium performance settings, rock music influences, etc., can all be linked more or less to the opening up of Morocco by the French colonizers, the migration of Moroccan workers to Europe, the spread of tourism, etc.—all stemming from Morocco's collision with the West.

Let's take these three intertwining sources for Morocco's rich musical heritage and analyze them in a little more depth. We will then return to talk about the kinds of music that have arisen from their mixing.

Berber, Tribal Influences

For the last 3,000 years, Morocco, like most of North Africa, had a predominately Berber population that was organized along tribal lines. This meant that at the lowest level there were extended families who worked and lived closely together. They were tied to their close neighbors by common descent from a common ancestor three to five generations removed. These commonly descended extended families thought of each other as cousins, and formed what we call lineages (or sometimes clans). Various lineages also recognized each other as related by virtue of their being descended from one original (sometimes mythical) ancestor. The lineages that recognized each other as commonly descended formed what we call a tribe. Relations between these various units of a tribe, as well as relations between one tribe and another were handled by mediators or abitrators. The people who held these traditional offices were some of the most important in the region. They determined how conflicts should be resolved and they presided over all negotiations. They were often not from the local tribes so that their in-between status would be recognized by all. Or they were the eldest men who were thought to be the wisest. Sometimes they were women. They even held their councils in special places set apart where combat was not allowed. Over time the office of arbiter became hereditary and whole hereditary lineages evolved to monopolize the office. The position of arbiter also evolved into a quasi mystical role, with certain magical or priestly powers associated with it.

Arabo-Islamic Cultural Influences

The Berbers rapidly accepted the Islamic religion because the local arbiter/holy men found under Islam that their power and authority dramatically increased. Their traditional, oral cultural authority was enhanced by the quick monopoly they established over the new written religion. They alone among the illiterate Berbers could determine what the holy law said and how it was to be applied. The holy lineages further increased their prestige by concocting over time family connections with the Prophet Muhammad. They were thus "sharifs" which meant that they were descendants of the Prophet himself. Thanks to the spread of Islam, the local Moroccan social structure developed a hierarchy in which the ultimate leader became an intermediary between the Divine and the human worlds. He was understood to be the head arbiter and community leader.

> He was to be the successor of the Prophet and imitate his example. He was the imam (leader of community prayers) and as religious leader was the head of an increasingly complex institution involving mufti-s (legal advisors), qadhi-s (religious judges) and 'ulema (teachers). He also had responsibilities with respect to the

general welfare and order of society. This involved a civil administration the chief function of which was collecting Quranic dues to be spent for the good of the community.... He moreover had to increase the capacity for self-defense of the dar al-Islam (land in which Islam is established) in a non-Muslim environment. This made the sultan (which signifies 'the one who has power') not only the head of a religious and civil administration, often referred to as 'the men of the pen,' but also of a military force, the 'men of the sword.' (Morsy 1984:24)

This congenial adaptation of Islamic society to Berber social structure caused the rapid conversion and mobilization of the Berbers. By the tenth century, Islam had spread throughout the nomadic Berber populations of the Sahara. In the eleventh century a Berber tribal confederacy surged up out of the Sahara all the way into Spain and founded an Islamic empire (Almoravid) based in their new capital, Marrakech. A similar Berber confederacy (Almohad) did the same thing in the middle of the twelfth century. By this time the empire stretched south all the way down to include much of recently converted West and Central Africa. North-south trade across the Sahara was thus established and continued to dominate the Moroccan economy into the modern period. Caravans returned with ivory, gold, and slaves and provided much of the wealth that allowed for the development of the burgeoning merchant class culture of the trade route and cities of North Africa (especially Fez and Marrakesh). Another invasion in the sixteenth century strengthened anew the cultural and economic ties between West and Central Africa and Morocco to the north.

The Sufi Connection

Another important feature of North African life ignored by our video clip was the influence of Sufism. Sufism itself is the mystical branch of Islam. Its followers seek to achieve a mystical union with God. Almost since the beginning of Islam shaykh-s (in this case meaning 'spiritual guides') have been teaching disciples how to achieve heightened spiritual awareness. They do so by providing their disciples with a tariqa ('way'), i.e., a series of steps or a program to achieve greater spiritual consciousness (besides a long period of apprenticeship and study, they often included prayers or phrases repeated in a chant-like manner, special ceremonies, trance-inducing activities, and so forth).

On a societal level the disciples are organized into zawiya-s (lodges) which owe absolute allegiance to their shaykh. This provided them with a strong sense of unity and continuity. The movement as it developed in North Africa also developed a strong interest in community service (such as public education), even becoming the center of community life in some localities. This attracted a popular following for the Sufi fraternities and caused many people to give gifts of support to the local zawiyas. As can be imagined, the potential power of the Sufi fraternities made them a potential threat to central authority. Where possible state leaders would belong to fraternities or use other methods to try and co-opt them.

The Sufi fraternities began to spread throughout North Africa for two important reasons.

1. One was due to the spread of capitalist trade networks throughout the region. The fraternities with their scattered lodges provided a ready-made network for traders which cut across national, ethnic, and, to a lesser extent, class boundaries, thus creating an excellent means of fostering long-distance trade.

2. Secondly, the Sufi fraternities became one of the major means of organizing the defense of the western reaches of the Islamic world as the European expansion began to target the African coasts in the fifteenth century. The Portuguese and Spanish (and later the French and British) coastal assaults often overwhelmed individual states in the region. Sometimes, only the far flung Sufi networks provided any real resistance to European encroachment.

Colonial and Post-Colonial Context

A final note needs to be added on colonial influences, particularly French colonial ones in North Africa. As already mentioned, the Portuguese and Spanish began bypassing North African trade routes in the fifteenth century by setting up trading entrepots along the African coasts. The European powers competed to wrestle trade away from the north-south routes and redirect it towards the coast by penetrating up the rivers of West Africa and enticing locals to trade directly with them. Earlier the Muslim North African empires had sent their locally made goods south in exchange for interior African goods heading north. With the rise of European manufacturing and their dominance of the world market, locally produced items were slowly pushed out of the transSaharan trade mix, to be replaced by European imports. By the end of the seventeenth century, Morocco's control and influence in Central and Western Africa had become limited and more indirect. Even while the French were beginning to redirect trade to their new colonial outpost of St. Louis at the mouth of the Senegal River, Saharan tribal notables continued to send their children to southern Moroccan zawiyas. The Moroccan Sultan's prestige and influence over holy men throughout the Sahara also provided a loose kind of unity in the face of French expansion along the Senegal.

North African states were also losing the competition at sea. By the eighteenth century European navies had managed to monopolize the major sea-routes, leaving Muslim navies to turn to piracy. The Barbary pirate period should thus be seen as a kind of last resistance on the part of North African navies to the spread of European naval power. By 1820, Morocco had only one ship left in its fleet. The whole of North Africa was forced from that time forward to be an unequal partner in trade with European nations. From Egypt to Morocco, none had the military might necessary to enforce treaty rights or to insure the protection of their economic interests. The Europeans were relentless in pressing their advantage. Finally, the French, being rebuffed after invading Egypt in 1798, began the colonial conquest of Algeria in 1830. By the 1880s, Egypt had become a British satellite and Tunisia a French Protectorate. Morocco began to fall to the invading French in 1912, with a small northern section of the country becoming a Spanish Protectorate by the end of the 1920s.

The French Protectorate over Morocco was led during its formative early years by a French officer named Lyautey. He held the position of resident-general and was the real power in the kingdom. He kept the Moroccan Sultan and administration in place, but he and his French advisors made all of the decisions and appointments. He sought to leave the mountainous, mainly Berber regions of the country alone and to concentrate instead on gaining control over what he called "useful Morocco," i.e. the region of fertile plains and mineral resources that stretched along the Atlantic coast and then cut back east inland to Fez and on to Oujda on the Algerian border. This had the effect of isolating the Berber speaking from the Arab speaking populations, and maintained a kind of forced traditionalism in the mountains as opposed to colonial economic development in the plains. The French used these divisions as a way to divide and conquer Morocco. They often appointed Berber chiefs to act as their local overlords and seemed to favor the use of Berber troops to enforce their rule in Arab areas. Moreover, the Islamic law courts of the Sultan's Morocco no longer had jurisdiction over the mountainous Berbers, whose own traditional legal system was made legitimate by the French.

The size of the French colonial community in Morocco swelled to over 300,000 by the 1950s (out of a total of about 10,000,000), earning a living from all manner of activities. The richest several thousand became large landowners, or acquired wealth through natural resource exportation. Abun-Nasr has this to say about the Spanish Protectorate in the north of Morocco:

> In contrast to the French zone, the Spanish zone did not undergo any radical
> economic transformation. Having an area of 22,000 square km, it was about one-
> twentieth the size of the French zone. Its population, including Spaniards and
> other foreigners, was about one million in 1955, or nearly ten percent of the total
> population of the country. Its economic resources were meagre .... Thus
> agriculture, particularly the cultivation of cereals, remained the basis of the

economy. The industries remained few and were geared to local
consumption...Colonization by Spanish farmers was not encouraged...Only
about 1,000 km of roads had been paved by 1956, only half of these were surfaced,
and the Spanish efforts to improve and maintain ports were half-hearted.
Economically the northern zone was thus a liability rather than an asset to Spain,
and was retained mainly for the sake of prestige (Abun-Nasr 1987:376-377).

The Spaniards, like their French counterparts in the rest of Morocco, governed jointly with Moroccan officials while actually holding all of the reins of power.

In sum, the colonial legacy of the French (to a lesser extent the Spanish) included a division between the countryside and the city into a traditional, precolonial and a modern, colonial region. This carried over into the cities themselves so that even today there exist traditional and modern quarters of most big cities. The legal system tended to be patterned after the French model; large, state bureuacracies were created with centralized planning and control; the French language became the language of government and commerce, education and the press (less so as time goes on); a powerful, centralized surveillence system was set up with its headquarters in the Interior Department, as in the French system; Agro-capitalism spread throughout the country and brought a great disparity in landholdings and massive rural to urban migration in its wake; little value-added manufacturing developed; rather, Morocco became reliant on imported goods; mass emigration to Western Europe became one of the best sources of employment.

Examples of Cultural Influences on Moroccan Music

Now that we have some sense of the historical context, let's go back now and pick up again on the three cultural influences on Moroccan music. Here's the list we presented earlier:

1. **Berber tribal influences**. These continue to have an impact on the language (Berber), as well as on the performance setting, musical style, and instruments used in much local music in Morocco.

2. **Arabo-Islamic cultural influences**. The use of the Arabic language in Morocco in sacred musical genres owes a debt here. Think of the Sufi tradition, the Gnawa genre, as well as Andalusian forms of music played throughout Morocco. Equally important are the profane musical genres in Arabic that connect Morocco to the rest of the contemporary Arabic world music scene and make Moroccans great consumers as well as producers of popular Arabic language music.

3. **Colonial and post-colonial context**. The use of the French language is fairly restricted in Moroccan music, but modern commercial production values, international distribution circuits, worldbeat influences, electronic instrumentation, stadium performance settings, rock music influences, etc., can all be linked more or less to the opening up of Morocco by the French colonizers, the migration of Moroccan workers to Europe, the spread of tourism, etc.—all stemming from Morocco's collision with the West.

Musical examples of traditional Berber tribal influences: We first showed some slides of the various acoustic instruments used in North Africa and then played several selections from around the country (the Souss in the south, Najaat Aatabou from the Middle Atlas, the Jibala in the northwest) (titles not given). The musical excerpts were meant to illustrate the styles of Berber and tribal/ traditional music played in Morocco, as well as the everyday settings in which the music is heard (taxis, weddings, at saints shrines, festivals, etc.). We mentioned that they shared 2 features in particular; namely, they were acoustic, and they were very localized, that is, they used the local dialect, they used a local style of play, and they were performed in local settings.

Musical examples of traditional Arabo-Islamic Influences: We then played examples of more classical musical arrangements from North Africa (we didn't play, but we mentioned the commonly heard Andalusian-style music), such as more classically Middle Eastern-style "belly dance" music featuring the 'oud, or lute. We also played some examples of religious music, such as the music of the Sufis. The most significant example came from the Gnawa, a Sufi-like brotherhood of musicians who have become famous over the centuries for introducing Moroccans to SubSaharan rhythms. We mentioned that they play for tourists in the great square in Marrakesh, as well as at private ceremonies where they are often hired to make someone well or to break a streak of bad luck hanging over a household. They are thought to be able to create a kind of mystical, healing, trance-like state with their music. We then played an excerpt of a song by Abdelwahab Doukali, a famous Moroccan singer in the modern Arabic song style. His influences are Middle Eastern modern, particularly Egyptian and Lebanese, and he, too, is considered a popular musical star throughout the Arabic speaking world.

Examples of Moroccan music in the post-colonial contemporary context:

We went back first to play the cabaret clip of Najat Aatabou, the Berber diva in the nightclub in Casablanca. This clip illustrated the extent to which Berber music has been professionalized, commercialized and made palatable to a larger audience. We then played an example of the way Gnawa music has been popularized for the Worldbeat musical crowd, as illustrated by Hassan Hakmoun, a local Moroccan innovator of Gnawa music. We then played an excerpt of the local folk revivalist Gnawa music of the Moroccan group, Nass el Ghiwan. We next headed north to see the influence of Western tourism on Moroccan music in the 1960s and 1970s, and used as an illustration the tribute to the ex-Rolling Stone, Brian Jones, performed by the Jajouka musicians.

Sources for Video 14 Notes

Morsy, Magali. *North Africa 1800-1900: A survey from the Nile Valley to the Atlantic.* London: Longman. 1984.

Abun-Nasr, Jamil M. *A History of the Maghrib in the Islamic Period.* Cambridge: Cambridge University Press. 1987.

Laroui, Abdallah. *The History of the Maghreb: An Interpretive Essay.* Ralph Mannheim (trans.) Princeton: Princeton University Press. 1977.

Video 15

The next video took up directly the task of illustrating the book, *In and Out of Morocco.* Remember, we are reading only the chapter entitled "Music, Migration and the Nador, Morocco Diaspora." We began with a tour of the city of Nador and an introduction to the life of Haddou, the Nador migrant laborer. The first several slides provided some sense of what the city of Melilla is like. As you could see, it's an old port which has been guarded for centuries as an outpost of Spain on the African continent. The only contact with the motherland is by boat. In talking about Melilla, we mentioned that the reconquest of the Iberian Peninsula (Spain and Portugal) by the Christian Spaniards led by Ferdinand and Isabella was completed in 1492. All Moors (Iberian and North African Muslims) and Jews were exiled from Spain by 1502. Spanish fanatic militarism continued to press outward with the conquest in earnest of North Africa. Fortunately for North Africans, the New World was discovered and that drained Spanish energies off in a new direction. Only the ports of Ceuta (Sebta) and Melilla and the Spanish Sahara were left as mementos of the conquest. They remained Spanish outposts until 1912 when they were used to launch the Spanish invasion of what became the Spanish Protectorate over northern Morocco. Even today tension runs high between Moroccans who want the territory returned, and Spaniards who see it as an integral part of greater Spain. As we saw the slides of Melilla, it was mentioned that almost 50% of the population of the fortress city is now Moroccan. This is because the city is a duty-free Spanish port for Spaniards from the mainland, as well as a source of cheap goods for smugglers from Morocco.

The countryside in the eastern Rif and around Melilla, the area where Haddou grew up, was very rural even though it's densely populated. Out of the mountains, the main crops were barley intermixed with various vegetables and other products. The family photos were of the poor coal miner's family from chapter 3. I put them here because they lived in a traditional country house similar to the ones shown in the slides. A small percentage of the population around Nador are Bedouin nomads living in tents such as the one shown in the slide. The whole area been periodically ravaged by plagues caused by locusts, such as the one held up by the woman in the slide. We mentioned that peasant farmers around Nador suffer from the following problems:

1. drought

2. pests and plagues:

3. low crop prices

4. insufficient landholdings

5. mass rural to urban migration

I mentioned earlier that the rural area around Nador raised mainly barley and vegetable crops. The area also raises lots of citrus products east of town on large irrigated fields. West of town as you head up into the mountains, you start seeing the crop shown in this slide. Haddou and his family never cultivated it. Its spread is really pretty recent. Any idea what it is? Right: marijuana. Made into hash, smuggled through border towns like Nador and then to Europe.

Thanks to the smuggling traffic and the tens of thousands of migrants away working in Europe, Nador has become a pretty prosperous little burg. As you can see from the photos, the city is bustling. Smugglers, merchants, and migrants are pouring their wealth into building all sorts of dwellings. Many of them stand vacant, as in Haddou's neighborhood, because the migrants are still abroad.

We showed several slides of smugglers preparing to cross the border at Melilla and then we read a passage from the book about what it was like to have to smuggle in the region. This was accompanied by photos of a woman all wrapped up with her smuggled wares waiting for a taxi to take her to someplace else in Morocco.

We next talked about how difficult borders can be for migrants too, returning in the summer by the tens of thousands and having to worry about being shaken down at the border, having some of their goods or cash confiscated, being harassed—perhaps even beaten. This occurs when migrants head back to Europe as well. We read the section on the Brussels airport chaplain to illustrate what awaits some migrants returning to Europe.

We next saw a photo of Haddou on the construction site where he worked in the early 1960s in France. We read the book section about his "dream house." We then saw several slides showing the various kinds of migrant mansions built back in the countryside by migrants using the wages they'd saved from working in Europe. We discussed how whole new villages and suburbs crop up due to the men's desire to live in the countryside. This causes tensions with the rest of the family, however, for they all prefer life in the city. We read a short excerpt from the book which illustrated this tension.

We then showed slides of new housing going up all over Nador. How the building boom goes on almost unchecked by any regulation. We showed slides of the smugglers' shops and the suq (market) as well as read a short excerpt on the itinerant street vendors and their constant cat-and-mouse game they play with the police.

I then showed you some of the people you've been reading about. We saw earlier a picture of Haddou when he was a younger man working in Europe. Then we saw a picture of him taken in the early 1990s as he is aging. The next picture was of one of his sons, Hassan, arguing with their maid in their house (we read a small excerpt on the tension between Hassan and Haddou over household expenses). That's followed by a slide of his daughter, Malika and his wife, Thraithmes, holding our new-born son, Charles Anwal. There was another one of Anwal a bit older. My wife, Joan Gross, who also teaches in the Anthropology Dept. was pictured next with her hands hennaed in preparation for Anwal's birth.

The next slides showed some of the neighborhood women dancing at the infamous issm, or naming feast we had for Anwal, mentioned in chapter 4 of the book. You can tell by their elegant robes that they do not come from poor families. Aicha, one of the women who used to visit us in order to smoke, is pouring tea in this slide. We then saw a series of slides of the house interior and of various people, highlighting my getting Milkbar Muhammad in trouble with the police.

I mentioned our issm, or naming feast a second ago which runs throughout chapter 4 of the book. I showed a picture of the maid from downstairs who did all of the cooking, and a photo of the men from the neighborhood who came to it and then got in a fight over whether or not it should be videotaped. The intellos who objected were ranged along the very back of the room under the window. Finally I closed the "who's who" illustrations with the one from the book which showed the local neighborhood kids, or "drari" who lived down in the street. The last one was of three preteen girls who were still allowed to play in the street but were too old to hang out with the young boys.

We then turned to the music of the Nador area. We talked about the original ay-arralla-bouya style of music played during the 1950s and 1960s (and read an excerpt from chapter 5 on the subject, but didn't play any examples of it). We then shifted to the 45-rpm decades and played a song by Cheikh Mahand and Cheikha Manate mentioned in the book. It was used to illustrate the way tensions between males and females over mass migration played themselves out in the music of the era.

We finally shifted to a discussion of Walid Mimoun and the protest music of the 1980s and 1990s. We read a section of chapter 5 pertaining to Walid Mimoun, and then played an excerpt of his protest song that cried out against the deleterious effects of migration. The song was called "Ad Dwared Amynu." It was about an emigrant son torn between his old life back in Nador and his new life in Europe. Neither satisfies him or sustains him. He drinks to forget. We then finished with a more communal, solidarity-building song by Walid Mimoun called "Dchar Innou." Here Mimoun gives voice to a common, romantic and nostalgic longing for the old country hamlet of birth. It's a sad and intimate vision of a place now long gone, destroyed and then forgotten by the mass migration from the country to the city, and then overseas. But at the same time, it appealed to a whole generation of youth who had known only city life and the boom times of migration. They had never really grown up in rural areas. They only looked upon country life as a vital part of their roots; an important part of who they were.

NOTES

1. As contemporary folklore research has taught us, such popular representations are not just contingent on constantly changing historical conditions, but also on who is in charge of projecting the representations in question. The community does not act as a homogeneous entity. Instead, it is certain musical performers/ consumers of a certain specific age, gender, educational background, etc., who are most integrally involved in the construction of popular understandings of historical phenomena such as mass labor migration. Equally importantly, a consensus does not necessarily develop around one construction versus another. Competing representations are just as common and just as often left in tension with each other in the popular cultural arena.
2. David Hart (1976) provides the most thorough discussion of the importance of this musical genre in the Rif–dating from the 1950s. Ursula Hart (1994) provides a very readable account of the music in the context of that same time period. Joseph and Joseph (1987) discuss examples they collected in the 1960s. Toufali (1980) also briefly describes the genre.
3. Such gatherings, because of the growth of urban middle class leisure time, can be held for most any reason, and not just reserved as in earlier decades for the traditional celebrations of weddings, circumcisions, and naming feasts. The older tradition of restricting the genre strictly to unmarried women has also been relaxed.
4. These examples are taken from Hart (1976: 479).
5. This interesting idea is suggested by Joseph & Joseph (1987: 104-105), who reprint on the same pages the lyrics cited in my text that were originally collected by David Hart in the middle 1950s. It is a tribute to Hart's exhaustive research on the Rif that we all continue to mull over his findings.

6. Cut in studios in Casablanca and consumed, presumably, in just the niche market of the Rifi north, this was the music the first big wave of emigrant men took with them to Europe. These were low fidelity love songs featuring the high nasal whine vocal technique of the region backed by various regional instruments and sometimes accompanied by hand clapping. The subjects of the verses changed rapidly and sometimes were repeated on more than one recording. I never located an ay-aralla-buya among them, though many performers tipped their hats to the older style by including refrains with the lament, "Oh my mother, Oh my parents."

7. *"Thaffaghd Minigib"* (side b) Cheikh Mahand & Cheikha Manate. Koutoubiaphone KTP no. 1499.

8. This recording is difficult to cite. The title transliterated into French is given as *"Dakraza Maminour"* while its transliteration into Arabic script is *"Ad Khazagh Maminu."* The singers are identified as Chikha Malika Mohamed and Fatima Nadori AKA Malika Nadoria and Cheikh Mohant Drawi! The cover of the record shows two women while the song is actually a male and female duet.
    Voix du Soleil no. 10031 (side a).

9. *"Atoukay Oukya"* (side b) Farid Enadori. Voix du Soleil no. VDS 1005.

10. This verse occurs later in the song cited in ftnt 7.

11. *"Maimi HidaHi nish"* Cheikha Mimount Nadori. Voix du Soleil No. 1009 side B.

12. See Derounay (1980), Jibril (1976), Joki (1983), Schuyler (1993) for sources on the folk revival of the period.

13. This was a local way of referring to Walid Mimoun, not my ethnocentric attempt to categorize him. He reportedly embraced the comparison at one time.

14. The Arabic word for freedom, *hurriya*, was used in *Thamazight* for the same semantic purpose. Walid Mimoun, however, (re)introduced the *Thamazight* word for freedom, *thirli*, in one of his songs and people have been talking about it ever since. In fact, he borrowed it supposedly from the famous Algerian Berber singer, Idir.

15. Morocco as of 1989 has cable television and thus a greater choice of programming. It is one of the first African nations to get wired. Reports make it sound as if the citizenry more or less demanded it: "One dramatic indication of public dissatisfaction with RTM during this period is the so-called 'revolt of the couscousiers.' (a couscousier is a cooking utensil in which Morocco's famous national dish is prepared.) A rumor circulated in the Moroccan capital of Rabat that attaching a couscousier to a television antenna would make it possible to pick up foreign signals, and the pots appeared on antennas all over Rabat. Even when the couscoussiers proved to be inadequate televisions receivers, they were left atop buildings as a sign of dissatisfaction with RTM. Eventually King Hassan II ordered them removed." (Poindexter 1991:29)

16. I shared the audience's impatience with the line dancers as I, too, wanted to see Nador's rock star on stage. I admit to judging them too hastily without any appreciation for the dance tradition they come from. Mea culpa. On the other hand, it is intriguing to think about the possibility that the Nador audience was also reacting against the way state-sanctioned folklore constantly equates ethnicity and regionalism with traditional cultural productions. Perhaps "modernity" is exactly what Walid Mimoun's folk protest represented to his appreciative fans? I am thinking here of Urla's (1993) discussion of the way young Basque listeners respond to local pirate radio stations and their mix of contemporary sounds with contemporary slang, providing a vital contrast to the more stilted, institutionalized forms of minority language propagated by intellectuals, for instance.

17. Walid Mimoun was the product of the new urban environment of the region. Though he criticizes so-called traditional cultural practices (such as the arrangement of youth marriages) and associates them with rural life, his music lacks that town bias against the rural 'hicks' found, for instance, in Juju music in Nigeria (Waterman 1990:14), and which is of growing importance throughout Nador social life.

18. This is the case in the diaspora only, romantic laments of lovers lost to migration still figure importantly in homeland lyrics.

19. Migrant family reunification in Europe has relieved much of the demographic imbalance which marked so clearly the earlier epochs. Rifi Berbers, like other North Africans, now live in multigenerational communities that reproduce themselves more through local high birth rates than through in-migration, so the tensions caused by mass male out-migration are no longer so acute in the Rifi diaspora in Europe. That, at least, is an important demographic development characterizing the diaspora and possibly

conditioning the turn to the community as subject in its music. I do not think it deserves causal priority, however.

20. This is the observation of Leveau (1989: 116-117). See also Tilmatine (1996/97) for a comparison of the minority language policies of various European countries as it affects the use of Berber.

21. As testified to by the following three examples: 1. the Moroccan state no longer seeks to interdict unauthorized forms of organization so much as its seeks to organize everyone into something. Every educated worker is urged to belong to some form of association or another, including things like Berber cultural associations–now open with the aid and blessing of the authorities.

    A second and related example is that musical protest as an effective, explicit form of cultural commentary has been officially co-opted. Police used to ring the concert sites of Nass al-Ghiwane thus heightening the antiestablishment tensions associated with their music. Today, dozens of groups knock off Nas al-Ghiwane songs without turning the heads of anyone (cf Schuyler 1993). 3. studies of the spontaneous sit-down strike of youth in a voc-tech school in Salé in 1991 revealed that none of them held to any political persuasion, party or association. Their only demand was for the right to work. They even marched around with pictures of the king at the head of their processions! (Bennani-Chraïbi, 1994).

22. Berbers will often self-identify as of lighter skin than Arabs; as being smarter, harder workers, having ancestral links to northern Europeans, more independent than Arabs, better fighters, more religious–or less, depending on the context–sometimes claiming Christian origins when talking to Europeans, reminding them that Saint Augustine was a Berber (Gross & McMurray 1993). What is particularly interesting in the Anti-Arab climate in France is that they reciprocate in this tendency to select out the Berbers as more "civilized." See, for example, Auque (1995) on the Berber city of Boujaya, the only one in Algeria without a curfew in place. Another interesting article on the spillover of ethnic Arab-Berber tensions in France is Derderian's (1997) article on the demise of the famous North African radio station in Paris, Radio Beur.

23. Nador Berber students embrace the move because they are presently on the front lines in university struggles for power against the Islamist student groups. Obviously issues of ethnic identity are intensely important to them right now. On the other hand, the residents of the city of Nador are known for their relative piety (much more so than, say, those of the neighboring provincial capital city, Al Hoceima) and the Islamists have made large inroads in the city. Furthermore, many other Nador residents are dependent for jobs, licenses, favors, contracts, etc., on the Arab-dominant state bureaucracy and so are hesitant to involve themselves with overt manifestations of ethnic consciousness. To further complicate the picture, the Moroccan government has also been playing the Berber card of late, using it presumably to generate Berber ethnic resistance to the influence of Islamism in society at large. This is testified to by the fact that supplements devoted to Berber poetry, language, history, etc., have routinely appeared in the Moroccan national press in the 1990s. A Berber cultural center was opened by the government in Nador in 1992 even though the earlier, independently operated one had been closed by the government in 1983. Furthermore, in Algeria, where Kabylie resistance has led to the formation of anti-Islamist paramilitary squads, the government in 1995 began teaching Kabylie in the Schools and began running Berber language ads in the media–for the first time ever. So both regimes seem to be trying to establish a Berber bulwark against the Islamist movements.

24. The literature on the importance of diasporic spaces in popular cultural production is moving too quickly in the direction of the celebratory; the diaspora has too conveniently become that terrain of cultural studies where the emphasis rests exclusively on the new, the syncretic, the anti-hegemonic, the strategic fusion, the reappropriation of elements of the master code, the space of cultural heterogeneity, etc., all this has come to characterize diasporic culture (I'm parodying my own contribution to this rush to celebrate. See Gross, McMurray, Swedenburg 1994). This kind of emphasis can be useful, but we need to remember that it is paralleled by the downside of diasporic existence, that is, the criminalization of immigration and its racialization. The experience of minority marginalization and criminalization led, as often as not, to the development of cultural nationalist essentialism. These more ominous developments, though too often neglected, need to be treated seriously as diasporic cultural practices in their own right which also find their way back through the passages linking the homeland to the various segments of the diaspora. And speaking of homeland linkages, there is another characteristic of some diasporic studies that needs pointing out, namely, the tendency to privilege the dynamism of the diaspora at the expense of the homeland leaving, in effect, an image of homeland cultural production as peripheral, static, homogeneous, and tradition-bound by comparison to its dynamic, synergistic offspring.

CONCLUSION

During our investigations into the politics of popular music around the world, we have mentioned in passing some of the structural features of the music we studied. The primacy of rhythm in Afro-Brazilian music or the accent on the second and fourth beats in Jamaican music are two examples of such structural features. However, we spent most of our energies on the various socio-historical aspects unique to each of the case-study cultures we examined—much more so than on the formal, structural features differentiating them. That means we have begun to build an understanding of how Jamaican, Brazilian, Franco-Maghrebi, Moroccan, Cambodian, Hawaiian—even punk—musics function politically in their respective domains. Now it is time to go back and briefly take stock of some of the similarities and generalizations we can make across our case studies, something we could only do at the end, after we have gotten some sense of the specificities of each individual case. What is mentioned below does not of course exhaust the possible ways to think about popular music, but it does push us in the direction of thinking about the things we have in common as well as the things that separate us.

We mentioned way back in the introduction that popular music has at least two important political functions. The first, we said, is as social protest and social criticism, as a kind of resistance, usually via the oppositional character of the lyrics (though not always), which recognize and condemn injustice and inequality and provide a morally outraged attack on them. Music operates to provide inhabitants struggling for survival with a way to fight against forces that would deny them a future as legitimate citizens of their own land and nation.

We have now come across numerous examples of this political aspect of music. Think, for instance, of the way Hawaiian music and dance became important forms of protest against American encroachment during the nineteenth century. Or in reference to Jamaica, we saw that the worldwide popularity of reggae suggests that the specific issues of class and racial oppression addressed in the music can be transposed so that they resonate in other settings. The specific conditions present in Jamaica that created the music in the first place seem to be universally accessible, at least the oppositional traditions and symbols present in the music seem to strike a sympathetic chord around the world. As another example, think of the way rap has been used by Franco-Maghrebi musicians to struggle against French racist attempts to impose rigid boundaries around French national culture. Think of how Franco-Maghrebi rap operates to give voice to the concerns of multiethnic French minorities by linking the Algerian homeland with the diasporic communities of the French metropole. Or take the example of shell-shocked Cambodian immigrants trapped in ghetto-like communities in the U.S. who are learning to use music to come to grips with the weight of their past and to speak about it across the generational divide. Not least is the case of the people of Nador and the way music has historically been used by women to protest against some of the onerous aspects of mass migration. Lastly, remember that punk music continues to provide youth with a way to express their opposition to the dominant culture as well as their resistance to mainstream, business-as-usual political and economic arrangements.

And yet a no less important role of music, we suggested, is as an affirmation of our individual and collective humanity and thus as a foundation of our identity. One of the most effective ways of fighting against demoralization and social disintegration is by using musical forms to express and create attachments to particular spaces and places associated with freedom from oppression and alienation. Music creates in us the recognition that we are not in this alone. Just as importantly, the music constructs for us a sense of ourselves, a way to present ourselves to the world, a way to experience collective identity.

As an example of this, think of the ways in which music, dance and the Hawaiian language became the foundation of the Hawaiian renaissance after 1970, and were used to express a resurgent pride in a newly recovered native Hawaiian identity and community. The case of the older generation of rai music fans in the Franco-Maghrebi diaspora puts us in mind of another marginalized minority population that attaches great significance to the music which arises out of its community. The music instills in them a feeling of belonging to a larger collective, it provides them with a sense of solidarity and attachment to a homeland and its culture. The Nador diasporic community in Europe chose to make use of the traditional ay aralla buya genre of music to mark its attachment to the Nador homeland. Likewise, punk bands and their audiences and independent record labels and "zine" publishers and squatters and punk anarchists, etc., used the expressive music and performance settings of punk to foster a sense of subcultural community solidarity with one another. Take another example: The discussion of slavery reminds us once again of the foundational role played by the slave experience for African communities in the New World. We have seen that slavery, that greatest of all human outrages, has left Brazilians, Jamaicans, and African Americans with an enduring sense of community founded on the constant struggle against social injustice as well as on a determination not to just survive as a people, but to thrive. Music, perhaps more than any other expressive cultural form, has been the means used by descendants of Africans in the New World to both escape those conditions and to make those conditions known. It has also been a powerful means of creating solidarity and a sense of belonging to a community of the oppressed that stretches across the New World and back to the African cultures of origin.

Two other comparative generalities arise out of our investigations of the politics of music. First, we can now appreciate—because we have seen it so often before— the extraordinary musical creativity and expressiveness of the poor and the downtrodden wherever they may be around the world. We have witnessed time and again the extent to which powerless people outstrip their oppressors when it comes to being in the world and understanding the world in musical terms.

Second, we need to remind ourselves that the various popular musics we have been studying are the products of cultural hybridity. By that I mean that we need to underline the fact that music never develops in isolation from the rest of the world, but in a symbiotic relationship to it. For instance, the currents that created Rastafarianism and reggae perhaps developed in a unique way in Jamaica, but they were not unique to the island. The use of rap by Franco-Maghrebi youth to make sense of their Algerian heritage, the use of rap to express the outrage of youth in Sao Paolo, Brazil, these are both illustrations of the important role that musical influences emanating from elsewhere have had on local musical expression. Thanks, perhaps, to the hybrid nature of popular music, the cultural icons and images associated with the de-colonization struggles of people of color in the nations of the South are capable of appealing to white youth in the nations of the North set adrift by de-industrialization and rampant consumer capitalism. The creative solidarity developed during centuries of black anti-colonialism in Brazil and Jamaica, and in the more recent struggles of Hawaiians in their islands and North African immigrants in France—all give hope to alienated northern youth longing to belong to some sort of meaningful community. So though we must not forget that Algerian immigrant rai/rap, Jamaican reggae, Brazilian samba, Cambodian immigrant rap, and Hawaiian chants remain important products of specific cultural histories, we must also understand that they provide messages of liberation and dignity and self-affirmation attractive to youthful audiences the world over.

VIDEOS ACCOMPANYING

Remember, the actual video lectures can be accessed at the following url: http://oregonstate.edu/media/classes/index.php?className=anth210

Scroll down under the "Classes on Demand" heading and select "ANTH210: Comparative Cultures."

Video 18

There are no notes accompanying video #18, which is an interview with a local blues musician about the history and nature of blues music in the United States, then followed by a presentation of the conclusion.

Bibliography

Abrahams, Peter. 1957. *Jamaica: An Island Mosaic.* London: Her Majesty's Stationery Office.

Adu Boahen, A., ed. 1985. *The UNESCO General History of Africa: Africa under Colonial Domination, 1880-1935*, volume vii. Berkeley, CA: Heinemann.

Aïchoune, Farid. 1991. *Nés en banlieue.* Paris: Editions Ramsay.

Aïchoune, Farid. 1992. "Une mouvance en question." *Qantara* (3, April-June):14-15.

Alcalay, Ammiel. 1993. *After Jews and Arabs: Remaking Levantine Culture.* Minneapolis: University of Minnesota Press.

Armbrust, Walter. 1992. "The National Vernacular: Folklore and Egyptian Popular Culture." *Michigan Quarterly Review* 31(4):525-542.

Attaf, Rabha. 1991. "Ecoutez: comment ferons-nous la paix?" *Actuel* (February):49-57.

Auque, Roger. 1995. "Algerie: J'ai visité Bougie, la seule ville qui a vaincu la terreur du GIA." VSD. 19-25 October. no. 947: 54-57.

Azerrad. Michael. *Our Band Could Be Your Life: Scenes from the American Indie Underground 1981-1991.* Boston: Little, Brown and Company. 2001.

Azoulay, Eliane. 1991. "La déchirure: Rachid Taha." *Télérama* (February 13):17.

Bakan, Michael. B. 2007. *World Music: Traditions and Transformations.* New York: McGraw Hill.

Balibar, Etienne. 1991. *"Es Gibt Keinen Staat in Europa*: Racism and Politics in Europe Today." *New Left Review* 186:5-19.

Balibar, Etienne. 1992. *Les frontières de la démocratie.* Paris: La Découverte.

Barber, Karin (1987). "Popular Arts in Africa." *African Studies Review* 30(3):1-78.

Bariki, Salah Eddine. 1986. "Identité religieuse, identité culturelle en situation immigrée," in *Nouveaux enjeux culturels au maghreb*, Jean-Robert Henry et al., pp.427-45. Paris: Editions du CNRS.

Barrett, Leonard E. 1976. *The Sun and the Drum: African Roots in Jamaican Folk Tradition.* London: Heinemann.

Barrett, Leonard E. 1988. *The Rastafarians: Sound of Cultural Dissonance.* Boston: Beacon Press.

Barrow, Steve and Peter Dalton. 1997. *Reggae: The Rough Guide.* London: The Rough Guides.

Begag, Azouz. 1990. "'The Beurs,' Children of North-African Immigrants in France: The Issue of Integration." *Journal of Ethnic Studies* 18(1):1-14.

Bekkar, Rabia. 1992. "Taking Up Space in Tlemcen: The Islamist Occupation of Urban Algeria." Interviewed by Hannah Davis. *Middle East Report* 22(6):11-15.

Ben Jelloun, Tahar. 1984. *Hospitalité française. Racisme et immigration maghrébine.* Paris: Editions de Seuil.

Ben Jelloun, Tahar. 1991. "I Am an Arab, I Am Suspect." *Nation* (April 15):482-484.

Bender, Wolfgang. *Rastafarian Art.* Kingston, Jamaica: Ian Randle Publishers. 2005.

Benkheira, Mohamed Hocine. 1986. "De la musique avant toute chose: Remarques sur le raï." *Peuples méditerranéens/Mediterranean Peoples* 35-36:173-177.

Bennani-Chraïbi, Mounia. 1994. "Le Makhzen pris au piège: Le mouvement de Salé, été-automne 1991." In Gilles Kepel (ed.) *Exils et royaumes: Les appartenances au monde arabo-musulman aujourd'hui.* Paris: Presses de la Fondation Nationale des Sciences Politiques.

Bennett, Andy & Richard A. Peterson (eds.). 2004. *Music Scenes: Local, Translocal, and Virtual.* Vanderbilt University Press.

Bennett, Andy. 2002. *Cultures of Popular Music.* Maidenhead, UK: Open University Press.

Benson, Todd. 2007. "Rising Protestant Tide Sweeps Catholic Brazil." Reuters. May 3. http://news.yahoo.com/s/nm/20070503/lf_nm/brazil_pope_religion_dc

Bernard, Philippe. 1991. "Les beurs, entre la fierté et la crainte." *Le Monde* (January 17):5.

Billard, François. 1987. "Rock, Sapho." *Jazz magazine* (359, March):24-25.

Bizot, Jean-François and Fadia Dimerdji. 1988. "Le blues de l'espoir." *Actuel* (March):92-99, 132-133.

Bizot, Jean-François. 1987. "Ces musiciens grandissent la France." *Actuel* (June):145-155.

Bizot, Jean-François. 1988. "Sex and Soul in the Maghreb." *The Face* 98:86-93.

Blaut, J.M. 1993. *The Colonizer's Model of the World.* New York: The Guilford Press.

Bouillier, Grégoire. 1990. "Urban Rap." *Dire* (12 , Fall):2-10.

Bradley, Lloyd. *Reggae: The Story of Jamaican Music.* London: BBC Worldwide Ltd. 2002.

Brenner, Robert, and Mark Glick. 1991 The Regulation Approach: Theory and History. *New Left Review* 188(July):45-119.

Brisebarre, Anne-Marie. 1989. "La célébration de l'Ayd El'Kebir en France: Les enjeux du sacrifice." *Archives des Sciences Sociales des Religions* 68(1, July-September):9-25.

Buck, Elizabeth. 1993. *Paradise Remade: The Politics of Culture and History in Hawai'i.* Philadelphia: Temple University Press.

Burns, E. Bradford. 1993. A *History of Brazil.* Third edition. New York: Columbia University Press.

Burton, Richard D.E. 1997. *Afro-Creole: Power, Opposition, and Play in the Caribbean.* Ithaca, NY: Cornell University Press.

Caldwell, Christopher (2000) "The Crescent and the Tricolor", *The Atlantic Monthly* (November): 20-34.

Cambio, Sam. 1991. "Marseille: verification d'une rumeur." *Actuel* (February):33-38.

Campbell, Horace. 1987. *Rasta And Resistance: From Marcus Garvey to Walter Rodney.* Trenton, NJ: African World Press.

Chan, Sucheng. *Survivors: Cambodian Refugees in the United States.* Urbana: University of Illinois press. 2004.

Chandler, David. *The Land and People of Cambodia.* New York: HarperCollins. 1991.

Chang, Jeff. 2005. *Can't Stop Won't Stop: A History of the Hip-Hop Generation.* NY: St. Martin's Press.

Charef, Mehdi. 1989. *Tea in the Harem.* Translator Ed Emery. London: Serpent's Tail.

Chernoff, John Miller. 1979. *African Rhythm and African Sensibility: Aesthetics and Social Action in African Musical Idioms.* Chicago: University of Chicago Press.

Chevannes, Barry. 1994. *Rastafari: Roots and Ideology.* Syracuse, NY: Syracuse University Press.

Cloonan, Martin and Bruce Johnson. 2002. "Killing Me Softly with His Song: An Initial Investigation into the Use of Popular music as a Tool of Oppression." *Popular Music.* 21 (1): 27-39.

Cockburn, Alexander. 1988. "Beat the Devil." *Nation* (October 10):300-301.

Cockburn, Alexander. 1991. "Beat the Devil." *Nation* (December 23):802-803.

Colegrave, Stephen and Chris Sullivan. *Punk: The Definitive Record of a Revolution.* New York: Thunder's Mouth Press. 2001.

Cooper, Carolyn. 1995. *Noises in the Blood: Orality, Gender, and the "Vulgar" Body of Jamaican Popular Culture.* Durham, NC: Duke University Press.

Corn, Charles. 1998. *The Scents of Eden: A History of the Spice Trade.* New York: Kodansha International.

Cox, Paul Alan. 1991. "Polynesian Herbal Medicine," in *Islands, Plants, and Polynesians: An Introduction to Polynesian Ethnobotany.* Paul A. Cox and Sandra A. Banack, eds. Portland, OR: Dioscorides Press.

Crook, Larry and Randal Johnson, eds. 1999. *Black Brazil: Culture, Identity, and Social Mobilization.* Los Angeles: UCLA Latin American Center Publications.

Curtin, Philip D. 1995. *Why People Move: Migration in African History.* (The Sixteenth Charles Edmundson Historical Lectures, Baylor University, March 7 & 8, 1994.) Waco, TX: Markham Press Fund.

De Neys, Anne. 1993. "Rai Rocks Egyptian Pop." *Al-Ahram Weekly* (May 13-19):9.

Deleuze, Gilles and Felix Guattari. 1983. "Rhizome." Translated by John Johnston. In *On the Line*, pp.1-65. New York: Semiotext(e).

Derderian, Richard. 1997. "Broadcasting from the Margins: Minority Ethnic Radio in Contemporary France." In Alec G. Hargreaves and Mark McKinney. *Post-Colonial Cultures in France.* New York: Routledge.

Derounay, Mohamed and Boujmâa Zoulef. 1980. "Naissance d'un chant protestataire: Le groupe marocain Nass el Ghiwane," *Peuples Méditerranéens/ Mediterranean Peoples.* 12: 3-31.

Diamond, Jared. 1997. *Guns, Germs, and Steel: The Fates of Human Societies.* New York: W.W. Norton.

Diawara, Manthia. 1993. "A Symposium on Popular Culture and Political Correctness." *Social Text.* no. 36.

Dickey, Christopher and Beatrix de Koster. 1993. "Rai Rocks the Mosques." *Newsweek* (April 26):53.

Drewal, John Henry. 1999. "Art History, Agency, and Identity: Yorùbá Transcultural Currents in the Making of Black Brazil," in *Black Brazil: Culture, Identity, and Social Mobilization*, Larry Crook and Randal Johnson, eds. Los Angeles: UCLA Latin American Center Publications.

Drozdiak, William. 1991. "French at Odds Over Immigrants." *Washington Post* (July 12):A24.

Dupuy, R. Ernest and Trevor N. Dupuy. 1986. *The Encyclopedia of Military History.* New York: Harper & Row.

Ebihara, May. "Interrelations between Buddhism and Social Systems in Cambodian Peasant Culture." In Manning Nash (ed.) *Anthropological Approaches to Theravada Buddhism.* Yale University Cultural Report Series no. 13. 1996.

Echols, Alice. 2002. *Shaky Ground: The Sixties and Its Aftershocks.* NY: Columbia University Press.

Efird, Robert. 2001. "Rock in a Hard Place: Music and the Market in Nineties Beijing." in *China Urban: Ethnographies of Contemporary Culture.* Nancy N Chen, et al. (eds.) Durham: Duke University Press.

Einaudi, Jean-Luc. 1991. *La bataille de Paris, 17 Octobre 1961.* Paris: Editions du Seuil.

Erlewine, Michael, et al., eds. 1997. *All Music Guide.* New York: Miller Freeman Books.

Espírito Santo França, Maria José. 1999. "Candomblé and Community," in *Black Brazil: Culture, Identity, and Social Mobilization*, Larry Crook and Randal Johnson, eds. Los Angeles: UCLA Latin American Center Publications.

Etienne, Bruno. 1991. *La France et l'islam.* Paris: Hachette.

Eyre, Banning. 1991. "A King in Exile: The Royal Rai of Cheb Khaled." *Option* 39:42-45.

Eyre, Banning. 1992. "Rai: North African Punk." *Option* 42:19-20.

Ferguson, Isaac. 1997. "So Much Things to Say: The Journey of Bob Marley," in *Reggae, Rasta, Revolution: Jamaica Music from Ska to Dub*, Chris Potash, ed. New York: Schirmer Books.

Finnegan, Ruth. 1992. *Oral Traditions and the Verbal Arts: A Guide to Research Practices.* Routledge.

Fonarow, W. 2006. *Empire of Dirt: The Aesthetics and Rituals of British Indie Music.* Wesleyan University Press.

Fourgues, Y. (1999) "Freeman: Le Bon, le brut, et l'Arabe", *Syndikat.* no. 3, December 4-20, pp. 21-23.

Freedman, Maurice. "The Chinese in Southeast Asia: A Longer View." In Robert O. Tilman (ed.). *Man, State and Society in Contemporary Southeast Asia.* Praeger, New York. 1969.

Frith, Simon and John Street. 1992. "Rock Against Racism and Red Wedge: From Music to Politics, from Politics to Music," in Rebe Garofalo, ed. *Rockin' the Boat: Mass Music and Mass Movements.* Boston: South End Press.

Frith, Simon. 1996. *Performing Rites: On the Value of Popular Music.* Oxford: Oxford University Press.

Fryer, Peter. 2000. *Rhythms of Resistance: African Musical Heritage in Brazil.* Hanover, NH: Wesleyan University Press.

Gardner, W.J. 1909. *A History of Jamaica from Its Discovery by Christopher Columbus to the Year 1872.* New York: Appleton & Company.

Garofalo, Reebee. (ed.). 1992. *Rockin' the Boat: Mass Music and Mass Movements.* Boston: South End Press.

Gibbs, Alvin. *Destroy: The Definitive History of Punk.* Great Britain: Britannia Press Publishing. 1996.

Gilroy, Paul. 1987. *"There Ain't No Black in the Union Jack": The Cultural Politics of "Race" and Nation.* London: Hutchinson.

Gilroy, Paul. 1990. "One Nation Under a Groove. The Cultural Politics of 'Race' and Racism in Britain," in *Anatomy of Racism*, David Theo Goldberg, ed., pp.263-82. Minneapolis: University of Minnesota Press.

Gilroy, Paul. 1992. "Cultural Studies and Ethnic Absolutism," in *Cultural Studies*, Lawrence Grossberg et al., pp.187-198. New York: Routledge.

Gilroy, Paul. 1993. *The Black Atlantic: Modernity and Double Consciousness.* Cambridge, MA: Harvard University Press.

Gilson, Dave. "1992-2002: Moving Ahead, Looking Back." From Chronicle of Survival (Frontline world special titled, "Cambodia: Pol Pot's Shadow." By Amanda Pike. Oct., 2002 http://www.pbs.org/frontlineworld/stories/cambodia/tl05.html.

Goldman, Antony. 1993. "The Man from Oran." *Focus on Africa* (April):81.

Gooden, Lou. *Reggae Heritage.* Bloomington, IN: First Books. 2003.

Gorce, Paul-Marie de la. 1991. "Chirac joue du tam-tam." *Jeune Afrique* (July 3-9):30-31.

Gordon, David M. "Capitalist Development and the History of American Cities." In William K. Tabb & Larry Sawers (eds.). *Marxism and the Metropolis.* New York: Oxford University Press. 1978.

Goytisolo, Juan. 1987a (1982). *Landscapes After the Battle.* Trans. Helen Lane. New York: Seaver Books.

Goytisolo, Juan. 1987b. *Space in Motion.* Translator Helen Lane. New York: Lumen Books.

Gross, Joan E. and David A. McMurray. 1993. "Berber Origins and the Politics of Ethnicity in Colonial North African Discourse." *PoLAR: Political and Legal Anthropology Review.* 16(2): 39-57.

Gross, Joan E., David A. McMurray, Ted Swedenburg. 1994. "Arab Noise and Ramadan Nights: Rai, Rap, and Franco-Maghrebi Identity. *Diaspora.* 3(1): 3-39.

Hall, Stuart & Tony Jefferson (eds.). 1975. *Resistance through Rituals: Youth Subcultures in Post-War Britain.* London: Routledge.

Hall, Stuart. 1989. "Cultural Identity and Cinematic Representation." *Framework* 36:68-81.

Hall, Stuart. 1991a. "Brave New World." *Socialist Review* 21(1):57-64.

Hall, Stuart. 1991b. "Europe's Other Self." *Marxism Today* 35(8):18-19.

Hargreaves, Alec G.. 1989. "Resistance and Identity in Beur Narratives." *Modern Fiction Studies* 35(1):87-102.

Hargreaves, Alec G.. 1991. "La famille Ramdan: un sit-com 'pur beur'?" *Hommes et migrations* 1147 (October):60-66.

Hart, David M. 1976. *The Aith Waryaghar of the Moroccan Rif: An Ethnography and History.* Tucson: University of Arizona Press for the Wenner-Gren Foundation, Viking Fund Publications in Anthropology.

Hart, Ursula K. 1994. *Behind the Courtyard Door: The Daily Life of Tribeswomen in Northern Morocco.* Ipswich, Mass.: The Ipswich Press.

Harvey, David. 1991. "Flexibility: Threat or Opportunity?" *Socialist Review* 21(1):65-77.

Hebdige, Dick. 1979. *Subculture: The Meaning of Style.* London: Routledge.

Hebdige, Dick. 1987. *Cut 'N' Mix: Culture, Identity and Caribbean Music.* London: Routledge.

Herzberg, Nathaniel and Cécile Prieur (2001) "Danger of Islamist Proselytism inside Jails Ignored", *Guardian Weekly* November 15-21, p. 34.

Heylin, Clinton. *From the Velvets to the Voidoids: The Birth of American Punk Rock.* Chicago: A Cappella Books. 2005 (1993).

Hinton, Alexander Laban. *Why Did They Kill?: Cambodia in the Shadow of Genocide.* Berkeley: University of California Press. 2005.

Holt, Thomas C. *The Problem of Freedom: Race, Labor, and Politics in Jamaica and Britain, 1832-1938.* Baltimore: The Johns Hopkins University Press. 1992.

Home, Stewart. *Cranked Up Really High: Genre Theory and Punk Rock.* Hove, UK: CodeX. 1995.

Howe, John. 1992. "The Crisis of Algerian Nationalism and the Rise of Islamic Integralism." *New Left Review* 196:85-100.

Huang, Hao. 2001. "Yaogun Yinyue: Rethinking Mainland Chinese Rock 'n Roll. *Popular Music* 20(1): 1-11.

Ibrahim, Youssef M.. 1991. "In Algeria, Clear Plans to Lay Down Islamic Law." *New York Times* (December 31):A4.

infoplease.com. 2007. Gap between Rich and Poor: World Income Inequality. http://www.infoplease.com/ipa/A0908770.html

Ireland, Doug. 1992. "Press Clips." *Village Voice* (January 14):8.

James, Barry. 1991. "French Rap and the Art of Vandalism," *International Herald Tribune* (July 4):6.

James, C.L.R.. 1963. *The Black Jacobins: Toussaint L'Ouverture and the San Domingo Revolution.* New York: Vintage Books.

Jazouli, Adil. 1982. *La nouvelle génération de l'immigration maghrébine, Essai d'analyse sociologique.* Paris: Centre d'Information et d'Etudes sur les Migrations.

Jazouli, Adil. 1992. *Les années banlieues.* Paris: Editions du Seuil.

Jibril, Mohamed. 1976. "Nass Al Ghiwane-Jil Jilala: Les limites d'une expérience." *Lamalif* 81: 12-18.

Joki, Kathleen Louise. 1983. A Discussion of the Emergence of Nas Al-Ghiwan, Its Musical Model, and Its Relationship to Four Music Traditions in Morocco. Master's Thesis, University of Texas at Austin.

Jones, Andrew F. 1992. *Like a Knife: Ideology and Genre in Contemporary Chinese Popular Music.* Ithaca, NY: Cornell East Asia Series.

Joseph, Roger and Terri Brint Joseph. 1987. *The Rose and the Thorn: Semiotic Structures in Morocco.* Tucson: University of Arizona Press.

Kalab, M. *Monastic Education, Social Mobility, and Village Structure in Cambodia.* The Hague: Mouton. 1976.

Kamakau, Samuel Manaiakalani. 1991. *Tales and Traditions of the People of Old: Na Mo'olelo a ka Po'e Kahiko.* Translator Mary Kawena Pukui. Honolulu: Bishop Museum Press.

Kanahele, George S. 1986. *Ku Kanaka Stand Tall: A Search for Hawaiian Values.* Honolulu: University of Hawai'i Press.

Kapil, Arun. 1990. "Algeria's Elections Show Islamist Strength." *Middle East Report* 20(5):31-36.

Kastoryano, Riva (1999) "Muslim Diaspora(s) in Western Europe", In *Diaspora and Immigration*, a special issue of *The South Atlantic Quarterly* 98(1/2) Winter/Spring, pp. 191-202.

Keyes, Charles F. *The Golden Peninsula.* New York: Macmillan. 1977.

Kiernan, Ben. "The 1970 Peasant Uprising in Kampuchea." *Journal of Contemporary Asia* 9(3): 310-324. 1979.

Kiernan, Ben. *The Pol Pot Regime: Race, Power, and Genocide in Cambodia under the Khmer Rouge, 1975-1979.* (2nd ed.). New Haven: Yale University Press. 2002.

King, Stephen. *Reggae, Rastafari, and the Rhetoric of Social Control.* Jackson, MI: University of Mississippi Press. 2002.

Kingston, Maxine Hong. 1989 (1977). *China Men.* New York: Vintage International.

Koulberg, André. 1991. *L'Affaire du voile islamique: Comment perdre une bataille symbolique.* Marseille: Fenêtre Sur Cour.

Labi, Philippe, Marc Daum, and Crazy J.-M.. 1990. "Jack Lang: Je crois à la culture rap." *VSD* (October 31):40-41.

Lacoste-Dujardin, Camille. 1992. *Yasmina et les autres de Nanterre et d'ailleurs: Filles de parents maghrébins en France.* Paris: Editions la Découverte.

LaFranchi, Howard. 1991. "Immigrants Cool toward Saddam—and the Coalition." *Christian Science Monitor* (January 3):4.

Laing, Dave. 1992. "'Sadeness', Scorpions and Single Markets: National and Transnational Trends in European Popular Music." *Popular Music* 11(2):127-140.

Lanier, Pierre. 1991. *Les nouveaux visages de l'immigration.* Lyons: Chronique Sociale.

Lapassade, Georges. 1991. "Qu'est-ce que le hip-hop?" *Hommes et migrations* 1147 (October):31-34.

Lavie, Smadar, and Ted Swedenburg, eds. 1996. *Displacement, Diaspora and the Geographies of Identity.* Durham, NC: Duke University Press.

Leblanc, Lauraine. *Pretty in Punk: Girls' Gender Resistance in a Boys' Subculture.* New Brunswick, New Jersey. Rutgers University Press. 2005.

Leblond, Renaud. 1991. "Les folles rumeurs de Grasse." *L'Express* (January 24):61.

Leibowitz, Nicole. 1992. "Attali: 'Le rap remplace le bal.'" *Le Nouvel Observateur* (June 18):20.

Leveau, Rémy. 1989. "Immigrés, États et sociétés." *Revue Européénne des Migrations Internationales.* 5(1):113-126.

Lewis, George. 1985. "Beyond the Reef: Role Conflict and the Professional Musician in Hawai'i," in *Popular Music 5: Continuity and Change*, Richard Middleton and David Horn, eds. Cambridge: Cambridge University Press.

Lewis, George. 1992. "Don' Go Down Waikiki: Social Protest and Popular Music in Hawai'i," in *Rockin' the Boat: Mass Music and Mass Movements*, Reebee Garofalo, ed. Boston: South End Press.

Lewis, J. Lowel. 1992. *Ring of Liberation: Deceptive Discourse in Brazilian Capoeira.* Chicago: University of Chicago Press.

Lewis, William F. 1993. *Soul Rebels: The Rastafari.* Prospect Heights, IL: Waveland Press.

Lhomea, Jean-Yves. 1991. "Un entretien avec le président de SOS-Racisme." *Le Monde* (June 8):3.

Lindsey, Kamuela Kuali'i. Accessed 7/7/00. *The Kumulipo: Hawaiian Chant of Creation* (Kalakaua Version).

Lipsitz, George. 1994. *Dangerous Crossroads: Popular Music, Postmodernism and the Poetics of Place.* London: Verso.

Lloyd, Cathie and Hazel Waters. 1991. "France: One Culture, One People?" *Race & Class* 32(3):49-65.

Lomax, Alan. 1993. *The Land Where the Blues Began.* New York: Delta.

Loupias, Bernard. 1990. "Le rap français trouve ses mots." *Liberation* (October 20-21):44.

Mabbett, Ian & David Chandler. *The Khmers.* Oxford: Blackwell. 1995.

Magaldi, Cristina. 1999. "Adopting Imports: New Images and Alliances in Brazilian Popular Music of the 1990s." *Popular Music* 18(3):309-329.

Malkmus, Lizbeth and Roy Armes. 1991. *Arab and African Film Making.* London: Zed Press.

Malo, David. 1951. *Hawaiian Antiquities: Moolelo Hawai'i.* Translator N.B. Emerson. Honolulu: Bishop Museum Press.

Manuel, Peter L. 1995. *Caribbean Currents: Caribbean Music from Rumba to Reggae.* Philadelphia: Temple University Press.

Marcus, Greil. *Lipstick Traces: A Secret History of the Twentieth Century.* Cambridge, MA: Harvard University Press. 2003 (1989).

Martin, Marie Alexandrine. *Cambodia: A Shattered Society.* Mark W. McLeod (trans.) Berkeley: Univeristy of California Press. 1994.

McGowen, Chris and Ricardo Pessanha. 1991. *The Brazilian Sound: Samba, Bossa Nova, and the Popular Music of Brazil.* New York: Billiard Books.

McMurray, David A. The Cambodian Refugee Community of Austin, Texas. Unpublished M.A. thesis. Department of Anthropology. Univeristy of Texas at Austin. 1983.

McMurray, David and Joan Gross. 2004. "Visions of the Homeland in Puerto Rican and Franco-Maghrebi Diasporic Music." In Alec Hargreaves (ed.) *Minorités ethniques anglophones et francophones: etudes culturelles comparatives.* Paris: L'Harmattan.

McMurray, David and Ted Swedenburg. 1991. "Rai Tide Rising." *Middle East Report* 21(2):39-42.

Mentore, George. 1999. "Notting Hill in Carnival," Peter Marshall, photos. *Visual Anthropology Review* 15(1, Spring/Summer):45-69.

Menzies, Gavin. 2002. *1421: The year China Discovered America.* NY: Harper Collins.

Mercer, Kobena. 1987. "Black Hair/Style Politics." *New Formations* 3:33-54.

Mernissi, Fatima. 1987. *Beyond the Veil: Male-Female Dynamics in Modern Muslim Society.* Revised edition. Bloomington and Indianapolis: Indiana University Press.

Mezouane, Rabah (1999a) "Le rap sans rupture de Coran", *L'Affiche* No. 75, Dec., pp. 45-47.

Mezouane, Rabah (1999b) "Freeman: Justice pour tous", *L'Affiche.* No. 74. Nov., p. 34.

Mezouane, Rabah. (1999c) "MBS la rue algérienne retrouve la parole", *L'Affiche.* Nov., pp. 48-49.

Mézouane, Rabah. 1990. "Le rap, complainte des maudits." *Le Monde Diplomatique* (December):4-5.

Miller, Judith. 1991) "Strangers at the Gate." *New York Times Magazine* (September 15):33-37, 49, 80-81.

Moreira, Paul. 1990. "La mal-vie des jeunes." *Le Monde Diplomatique* (December):4-5.

Morin, Georges. 1991. "Le mosaïque des Français du Maghreb et des Maghrébins de France," in Camille and Yves Lacoste, eds., *L'Etat du Maghreb*, pp.533-537. Paris: Editions La Découverte.

Morley, David and Kevin Robins. 1990. "No Place Like *Heimat*: Images of Home(land) in European Culture." *New Formations* 12:1-21.

Morris, Brian. 2006. *Religion and Anthropology: A Critical Introduction.* Cambridge: Cambridge University Press.

Mudimbe, V. Y. and Sabine Engel. (1999) "Introduction", In *Diaspora and Immigration*, a special issue of *The South Atlantic Quarterly* 98(1/2) Winter/Spring, pp. 275-325.

Naïr, Sami. 1992. *Le regard des vainqueurs: Les enjeux français de l'immigration.* Paris: Bernard Grasset.

Nelson, Gersham A. 1994. "Rastafarians and Ethiopianism," in *Imagining Home: Class, Culture and Nationalism in the African Diaspora*, Sidney J. Lemelle and Robin D.G. Kelley, eds. London: Verso Books.

Nettl, Bruno, et al. 2004. *Excursions in World Music* (4th ed.). Upper Saddle River, NJ: Prentice Hall.

O'Hara, Craig. *The Philosophy of Punk: More Than Noise!* London: AK Press. 1999.

Obeyesekere, Gananath. 1992. *The Apotheosis of Captain Cook: European Mythmaking in the Pacific.* Princeton: Princeton University Press.

Ong, Aihwa. *Buddha Is Hiding: Refugees, Citizenship, The New America.* Berkeley: Univeristy of California Press. 2003.

Pawson, Michael and David Buisseret. 1975. *Port Royal, Jamaica.* Oxford: Clarendon Press.

Poindexter, Mark. 1991. "Subscription Television in the Third World: The Moroccan Experience." *Journal of Communication.* 41(3): 26-39.

Potash, Chris, ed. 1997. *Reggae, Rasta, Revolution: Jamaican Music from Ska to Dub.* New York: Shirmer Books.

Poverty Net. 2007. Brazil-Poverty Assessment. The World Bank http://poverty2.forumone.com/library/view/8638/

Raha, Maria. *Cinderella's Big Score: Women of the Punk and Indie Underground.* Emoryville CA: Seal Press. 2005.

Reynolds, Simon. *Rip It Up and Start Again: Postpunk 1978-1984.* London: Penguin Books. 2005.

Riding, Alan. 1990. "A Surge of Racism in France Brings a Search for Answers." *New York Times* (May 27):I1, I16.

Riding, Alan. 1991. "Europe's Growing Debate Over Whom to Let Inside." *New York Times* (December 1):E2.

Riding, Alan. 1992. "Parisians on Graffiti: Is it Vandalism or Art?" *New York Times* (February 6):A6.

Roberts, John Storm. 1972. *Black Music of Two Worlds.* Tivoli, NY: Original Music.

Rombes, Nicholas. *Ramones 331/3.* New York: Continuum. 2006.

Rosen, Miriam. 1990. "On Rai." *Artforum* (September):22-23.

Safran, William. 1986. "Islamization in Western Europe: Political Consequences and Historical Parallels." *Annals of the American Academy of Political and Social Science* 485:98-112. Beverly Hills: Sage Publications.

Sahlins, Marshall. 1985a. "Hierarchy and Humanity in Polynesia," in *Transformations of Polynesian Culture*, Antony Hooper and Judith Huntsman, eds. Auckland, NZ: The Polynesian Society.

Sahlins, Marshall. 1985b. *Islands of History.* Chicago: University of Chicago Press.

Sahlins, Marshall. 1992. "Anahulu: The Anthropology of History in the Kingdom of Hawai'I, volume 1: Historical Ethnography," in *Anahulu: The Anthropology of History in the Kingdom of Hawai'I*, Patrick V. Kirch and Marshall Sahlins. Chicago: University of Chicago Press.

Sayad, Abdelmalek, et al. 1991. *Migrance, Histoire des migrations à Marseille.* Aix-en-Provence: Edisud.

Schreiner, Claus. 1993. *Música Brasileira: A History of Popular Music and the People of Brazil.* Translator Mark Weinstein. New York: Marion Boyars.

Schuyler, Philip D. 1993. "A Folk Revival in Morocco," in Donna Lee Bowen and Evelyn A. Early (eds.) *Everyday Life in the Muslim Middle East.* Bloomington: Indiana University Press.

Scott, James C. & Benedict J. Kerkvliet. *How Traditional Rural Patrons Lose Legitimacy.* Madison: Land Tenure Center, University of Wisconsin Press. 1975.

Segal, Robert A. 1999. *Theorizing about Myth.* Amherst: University of Massachusetts Press.

Shaw, Lisa. 1999. *The Social History of the Brazilian Samba.* Brookfield, VT: Ashgate Publishing Co.

Shawcross, William. *Sideshow: Kissinger, Nixon and the Destruction of Cambodia.* New York: Simon and Schuster. 1981.

Sherzer, Joel. 1976. "Play Languages: Implications for (Socio) Linguistics," in Barbara Kirshenblatt-Gimblett, ed., *Speech Play*, pp.19-36. Philadelphia: University of Pennsylvania Press.

Shore, Brad. 1989. "*Mana* and Tapu," in *Developments in Polynesian Ethnology*, Alan Howard and Robert Borofsky, eds. Honolulu: University of Hawai'i Press.

Silverstein, Paul. (2000) "Islam, Soccer, and the French Nation-State", *Social Text 65*, 18:4, Winter, pp. 25-53.

Singer, Daniel. 1988. "In the Heart of Le Pen Country." *Nation* (June 18):845, 861-864.

Singer, Daniel. 1991. "Le Pen's Pals—Blood and Soil." *Nation* (December 23):814-816.

Stephens, Gregory. 1999. *On Racial Frontiers: The New Culture of Frederick Douglass, Ralph Ellison, and Bob Marley.* Cambridge: Cambridge University Press.

Stewart, Frank and Sharon May (eds.). *In the Shadow of Angkor: Contemporary Writing from Cambodia.* Manoa 16(1). Honolulu: University of Hawaii Press. 2004.

Stolzoff, Norman C. 2000. *Wake the Town and Tell the People: Dancehall Culture in Jamaica.* Durham, NC: Duke University Press.

Stone, C.S. Scott and John E. McGowan. *Wrapped in the Wind's Shawl: Refugees of Southeast Asia and the Western World.* San Rafael, CA: Presidio Press. 1980.

Stora, Benjamin. 1992. "L'intégrisme islamique en France: entre fantasmes et réalité," in *Face au racisme*, Pierre-André Taguieff, ed., volume 2, pp.216-222. Paris: Editions la Découverte.

Surin, Kenneth. (1999) "Afterthoughts on 'Diaspora'", in *Diaspora and Immigration*, a special issue of *The South Atlantic Quarterly* 98(1/2) Winter/Spring, pp. 275-325.

Swedenburg, Ted. (2001) "Islamic Hip-Hop vs. Islamophobia: Aki Nawaz, Natacha Atlas, Akhenaton", in Tony Mitchell (ed.), *Global Noise: Rap and Hip-Hop Outside the USA.* Middletown, CT: Wesleyan University Press.

Taguieff, Pierre-André, ed. 1991. *Face au racisme*, volume 1. Paris: Editions la Découverte.

Talha, Larbi. 1991. "La main-d'oeuvre émigrée en mutation," in *L'Etat du Maghreb*, Camille and Yves Lacoste, eds., pp.497-500. Paris: Editions la Découverte.

Tauch, Sokhom. "Cambodians in Portland, Oregon." In Sucheng Chan (ed.) *Not Just Victims: Conversations with Cambodian Community Leaders in the United States.* Urbana: University of Illinois press. 2003.

Thomas, Deborah A. *Modern Blackness: Nationalism, Globalization, and the Politics of Culture in Jamaica.* Durham: Duke University Press. 2004.

Tilmatine, Mohand. 1996/97. "La Lengua Berérber en Europea: elementos de aproximación." *El Vigía de Tierra* (Melilla). No. 2/3: 205-222.

Titon, Jeff Todd (ed.) 2002. *Worlds of Music: An Introduction to the Music of the World's Peoples* (4th ed.). Belmont, CA: Wadsworth Group/ Thomson Learning.

Toufali, Mohammed. 1980. "Min al-Adab al-Shâabi al-Rifi: al-Musiki," *Al-Zaman Al-Maghribi.* no. 3-4: 59-71.

Tourancheau, Patricia. 1991. "'Assistance sécurité': épinglée par police." *Libération* (March 30-31):19.

Trask, Haunani-Kay. 1997. "Feminism and Indigenous Hawaiian Nationalism," in *Feminist Nationalism*, Lois A. West, ed. New York: Routledge.

Treece, David. 1997. "Guns and Roses: Bossa Nova and Brazil's Music of Popular Protest, 1958-1968." *Popular Music* 16(1): 1-29.

Turner, Terisa E. 1994. "Rastafari and the New Society: Caribbean and East African Feminist Roots of a Popular Movement to Reclaim the Earthly Commons," in *Arise Ye Mighty People!: Gender, Class and Race in Popular Struggles*, Terisa E. Turner and Bryan J. Ferguson, eds. Trenton, NJ: Africa World Press.

Urla, Jacqueline. 1990. "Contesting Modernities: Theorizing Resistance and Domination in Ethnic Minority Cultural Politics." American Anthropological Association, New Orleans, November 28-December 2.

Urla, Jacqueline. 1993. "Contesting Modernities: Language Standardization and the Production of an Ancient/ Modern Basque Culture." *Critique of Anthropology.* 13 (2): 101-118.

Valeri, Valerio. 1985. "The Conqueror becomes King: A Political Analysis of the Hawaiian Legend of 'Umi," in *Transformations of Polynesian Culture*, Antony Hooper and Judith Huntsman, eds. Auckland, NZ: The Polynesian Society.

Videau, André. 1991. "À la recherche de la culture immigrée." *Hommes et migrations* 1144 (June):35-39.

Virolle-Souibès, Marie. 1988a. "Le ray, côté femmes: Entre alchimie de la douleur et spleen sans idéal, quelques fragments de discours hédonique." *Peuples méditerranéens* 44-45:193-220.

Virolle-Souibès, Marie. 1988b. "Ce que chanter erray veut dire: Prelude à d'autres couplets." *Cahiers de littérature orale* 23:177-208.

Virolle-Souibès, Marie. 1989. "Le raï entre résistances et récupération." *Revue d'études du monde musulman et méditerranéen* 51:47-62.

Vivier, Jean-Pierre. 1991a. "Culture hip-hop et politique de la ville." *Hommes et migrations* (1147, October):35-44.

Vivier, Jean-Pierre. 1991b. *Culture hip-hop et politique de la ville.* Paris: Centre d'études et d'actions sociales de Paris.

Vivier, Jean-Pierre. 1991c. *"Bandes de zoulous" et culture hip-hop: Revue de presse (Mai 1990-Mars 1991).* Paris: Centre d'études et d'actions sociales de Paris.

Vivier, Jean-Pierre. 1991d. *"Malaises" des jeunes et politique de la ville: Revue de presse (Octobre 1990-Août 1991).* Paris: Centre d'études et d'actions sociales de Paris.

Wald, Elijah. 2004. *Escaping the Delta: Robert Johnson and the Invention of the Blues.* NY: Harper-Collins.

Walser, Robert. 1993. *Running with the Devil: Power, Gender, and Madness in Heavy Metal Music.* Hanover, NH: Wesleyan University Press

Walser, Robert. Running with the Devil: Power, Gender, and Madness in Heavy Metal Music. Hanover, NH: Wesleyan University Press. 1993.

Ward, Brian. 1998. *Just My Soul Responding: Rhythm and Blues, Black Consciousness, and Race Relations.* Berkeley: University of California Press.

Waterman, Christopher. 1990. *Jùjú: A Social History and Ethnography of an African Popular Music.* Chicago: University of Chicago Press.

Werner, Craig. 1998. *A Change is Gonna Come: Music, Race and the Soul of America.* NY: Plume/ Penguin/ Putnam.

Wieviorka, Michel. 1992. *La France raciste.* Paris: Editions du Seuil.

Williams, Patrick (1999) "113 faux durs vrai rap", *L'Événement du jeudi.* 16-22 Dec., pp. 46-47.

Willis, Paul E.. 1978. *Profane Culture.* Boston: Routledge & Kegan Paul.

Willmott, William E. *The Chinese in Cambodia.* Vancouver, B.C.: University of British Columbia Press. 1967.

Winders, James A. 1997. "From Reggae, Rastafarians and Revolution: Rock Music in the Third World," in *Reggae, Rasta, Revolution: Jamaican Music from Ska to Dub*, Chris Potash, ed. New York: Shirmer Books.

WOMAD (World of Music and Dance). 1990. Festival program, August. Toronto.

Yawney, Carole D. 1994a. "Moving with the Dawtas of Rastafari: From Myth to Reality," in *Arise Ye Mighty People!: Gender, Class and Race in Popular Struggles.* Terisa E. Turner and Bryan J. Ferguson, eds. Trenton, NJ: Africa World Press.

Yawney, Carole D. 1994b. "Rasta Mek a Trod: Symbolic Ambiguity in a Globalizing Religion," in *Arise Ye Mighty People!: Gender, Class and Race in Popular Struggles*, Terisa E. Turner and Bryan J. Ferguson, eds. Trenton, NJ: Africa World Press.

Yúdice, George. 1992. "We Are Not the World." *Social Text* 31/32:202-216.